Daniela Peterhoff

Human Resource Due Diligence

WIRTSCHAFTSWISSENSCHAFT

ebs Forschung

Schriftenreihe der
EUROPEAN BUSINESS SCHOOL
International University Schloß Reichartshausen

Herausgegeben von
Univ.-Prof. Dr. Utz Schäffer

Band 52

Die EUROPEAN BUSINESS SCHOOL (ebs) – gegründet im Jahr 1971 – ist Deutschlands älteste private Wissenschaftliche Hochschule für Betriebswirtschaftslehre im Universitätsrang. Dieser Vorreiterrolle fühlen sich ihre Professoren und Doktoranden in Forschung und Lehre verpflichtet. Mit der Schriftenreihe präsentiert die EUROPEAN BUSINESS SCHOOL (ebs) ausgewählte Ergebnisse ihrer betriebs- und volkswirtschaftlichen Forschung.

Daniela Peterhoff

Human Resource Due Diligence

A Concept for Evaluating Employee Competences in Mergers & Acquisitions

With a foreword by Prof. Dr. Jean-Paul Thommen

Springer Fachmedien Wiesbaden GmbH

Bibliografische Information Der Deutschen Bibliothek
Die Deutsche Bibliothek verzeichnet diese Publikation in der Deutschen Nationalbibliografie; detaillierte bibliografische Daten sind im Internet über <http://dnb.ddb.de> abrufbar.

Dissertation European Business School Oestrich-Winkel, 2005

1. Auflage September 2005

Lektorat: Ute Wrasmann / Britta Göhrisch-Radmacher

Der Deutsche Universitäts-Verlag ist ein Unternehmen von Springer Science+Business Media.
www.duv.de

Umschlaggestaltung: Regine Zimmer, Dipl.-Designerin, Frankfurt/Main

Gedruckt auf säurefreiem und chlorfrei gebleichtem Papier

ISBN 978-3-8350-0125-1 ISBN 978-3-322-82144-7 (eBook)
DOI 10.1007/978-3-322-82144-7

Foreword

Mergers & Acquisitions (M&A) has almost become an emotive phrase in academic research and business practice in recent years, especially due to the large number of studies that report on their failure. One of the most prominent reasons for the low success rate of M&A transactions is the insufficient involvement of employees in such transactions. Although in recent years human resource issues have increasingly been addressed in M&A due diligence, the specific employee competence requirements that ensue from M&A transactions have to date hardly been investigated in academic research and business practice.

Daniela Peterhoff develops a concept for Human Resource Due Diligence (HRDD) in M&A that addresses the context-specific employee competence requirements resulting from such transactions. In developing her concept, the author presents a three step HRDD process. In step one she develops focus areas for HRDD based on the objectives underlying an M&A transaction. The second step shows how the HRDD information identified as relevant in step one can be generated. The author develops indicators to break down employee competences, and identifies valuation tools through which these indicators can be assessed. In the third and final step, she compiles the HRDD information generated in step two based on controlling ratios and human resource portfolios.

An expert survey carried out with both company representatives and consultants in the context of this thesis shows that practical HRDD still seems to be very much focused on past and present human resource information. Competence assessments have so far rarely been included in HRDD, but according to the majority of the practitioners interviewed, they should be in the future, in order to determine M&A specific human resource requirements. Two case studies at the end of the thesis show how the HRDD concept developed in this study can be applied to business practice. These case studies underline the fact that the specific human resource requirements of an M&A transaction determine the focus areas for HRDD and, as a consequence, the choice of indicators, tools, controlling ratios as well as the design of human resource portfolios.

This thesis presents a major contribution to ongoing research on human resource issues within the context of M&A transactions. It provides professionals intending to conduct a future-oriented HRDD in the course of an M&A transaction with a valuable concept. Still, whilst being of use for business practice, the concept is general enough to be adapted to the specific M&A context in which it is applied.

Prof. Dr. Jean-Paul Thommen

Acknowledgements

During the course of my work on this thesis, many people have supported me with their helpful comments, corrections, and suggestions. I would particularly like to thank Dr. Matthias Baur, Dr. Anja Karlshaus, Dr. Sandra Niewiem, Christopher Rock, Daniel Svensson and Christina von Weymarn for their patience and spare time invested. Also, I acknowledge Philipe Gerlach's assistance in transcribing the interviews conducted in the empirical part of this study, as well as Anne Dilk's help in proofreading the bibliography.

Prof. Dr. Ronald Gleich kindly served as co-evaluator of this study.

I am especially grateful to Prof. Dr. Jean-Paul Thommen for supervising my research by asking questions rather than providing answers and by enabling me to see new realities throughout the entire process.

Without the support and enthusiasm of the people closest to me, finalising this project would not have been possible.

Daniela Peterhoff

Table of Contents

Table of Figures

Table of Tables

Table of Abbreviations

AG	Aktiengesellschaft (PLC – Public Limited Company)
cf.	compare (confere (Latin))
ditto	same as above
Ed.	Editor
Eds.	Editors
e. g.	exempli gratia (Latin) (for example (English))
et al.	et alii (Latin) (and other(s)) (English))
f.	following (one page following)
ff.	following (several pages following)
HRDD	Human Resource Due Diligence
HRM	Human Resource Management
M&A	Mergers & Acquisitions
p.	page
pp.	pages
Vol.	Volume
w. p.	without page

1 Introduction

1.1 Problem Definition and Purpose of Study

In the context of many Mergers & Acquisitions (M&A), detailed analyses – due diligence investigations – of one or all firms involved in a transaction are carried out. Financial, tax and legal aspects have traditionally been subject to such due diligence investigations.[1] Human resource aspects have long been neglected in M&A due diligence, but have been considered increasingly important in business practice in recent years.[2] Especially during the past five to ten years, the question of how to design a Human Resource Due Diligence (HRDD) has been addressed repeatedly in academic literature.

A review of thirty-five HRDD-related contributions in the M&A literature revealed that most previous studies elaborated on historical and present-day information about employees that should be collected in an M&A context.[3] However, in the majority of the previous studies reviewed, one important problem has so far been neglected. M&A transactions impose specific requirements on employees, which result from the objectives underlying them.[4] These requirements must be well understood to be able to proactively enhance their fulfilment. If the human resource requirements of M&A transactions are unknown to management, high integration costs, brain drain and a disruption of relationships with customers can be the consequence.[5] The expected future human resource requirements, deriving from M&A transactions, should be addressed in HRDD to find out whether employees are prepared for them.[6] Further M&A management measures can then be taken based on the generated human

---

1 Cf. Marten, Kai-Uwe/Köhler, Annette G. (1999), pp. 337f.

2 As preliminary interviews with five consultants illustrated, firms increasingly require their M&A consultants to offer HRDD. Also cf. Berens, Wolfgang/Strauch, Joachim (2002), p. 62.

3 Cf. Aldering, Christoph/Hutten, Christina Freiin von. In: Berens, Wolfgang/Brauner, Hans U./Strauch, Joachim (Eds.) (2002), pp. 410ff. Berens, Wolfgang/Brauner, Hans U./Strauch, Joachim (Eds.) (2002), pp. 615f. Bing, Gordon (1996), pp. 87, 130ff. Burke, Joe (2000), p. 38. Burrows, Donald M. (2000), p. 39. Clemente, Mark N./Greenspan, David S. (1999), p. 127. Corporate Leadership Council (1999), pp. 2, 19ff. Daniel, Teresa A. (1999), pp. 34ff. De Voge, Sylvia/Spreier, Scott (1999), p. 30. Dickmann, Michael (2002), p. 67. Dielmann, Klaus (1997), p. 471. Felder, Rupert (2001), pp. 157f. Gerpott, Torsten J. (1993), pp. 33 – 347. Goldberg, Andrew J. (1999), p. 21. Gut-Villa, Cornelia (1997), p. 166. Haspeslagh, Philippe C./Jemison, David B. (1991), pp. 352f. Hunt, John W./Lees, Stan/Grumbar, John J./Vivian, Philip D. (1987), p. 27. Jaeger, Michael (2001), pp. 45 – 47. Jansen, Stephan A./Pohlmann, Niko (2000), p. 36. Kerr, Christine (1995), p. 8. Mayerhofer, Helene (2002), pp. 68 – 71. Picot, Gerhard. In: Picot, Gerhard (Ed.) (2002), pp. 24f. Lajoux, Alexandra Reed/Elson, Charles M. (2000), pp. 105, 108. Rockholtz, Carsten (1998), pp. 110f. Schmeisser, Wilhelm (1999), pp. 55f. Schmitz, Winfried F. (1996), pp. 9 – 13. Schweiger, David M./Weber, Yaakov (1989), pp. 71ff. Shields, Karen (2000), p. S2. Unterköfler, Herbert. In: Kranebitter, Gottwald (Ed.) (2002), pp. 128ff. Van Fleet, Lisa (1996), p. 883. Whalley, Michael/Semler, Franz-Jörg (1996), pp. 409f. Wood, Judy (1992), pp. 54 – 56. Wucknitz, Uwe D. (2001), pp. 675ff. Wucknitz, Uwe D. (2002a), pp. 145 – 148. Wucknitz, Uwe D. (2002b), pp. 36 – 38. Zingheim, Patricia K./Schuster, Jay R. (2001), p. 38.

4 M&A-specific human resource requirements are an important reason for the relevance of a HRDD, according to a large number of the 22 company representatives and 8 consultants included in an expert enquiry about practical HRDD.

5 Cf. Burrows, David (2000), p. 36.

6 This view was shared by the majority of the 30 experts included in the enquiry mentioned in footnote 4. Cf. chapters 5.2.1.1 and 5.2.1.2.

resource information. The human resource requirements of M&A transactions may vary significantly from one M&A context to another.[7] This fact has yet hardly been accounted for in previous studies, but should be considered in future HRDD.[8] If knowing about M&A-specific human resource requirements, management can concentrate its further activities on addressing these requirements, thereby coping with the complexity of M&A transactions.[9]

The purpose of this thesis results from the academic and practical relevance of the research gap, as described above.

The purpose of this thesis is to develop a concept[10] for Human Resource Due Diligence in Mergers & Acquisitions that addresses the context-specific human resource requirements deriving from such transactions.

1.2 Philosophical Positioning of Study

The perspective from which scientific insights[11] are generated in this thesis is elaborated on in order to philosophically position this study.[12] According to Ulrich, two different perspectives can be taken to arrive at insights in socio-managerial research: a non-systemic or a systemic perspective.[13] Both these perspectives differ amongst other according to their

(1) underlying way of thinking,

(2) modelling of social systems and

(3) problem-solving approach.

First, the non-systemic perspective is based on an analytical way of thinking. Linear cause-effect relationships are assumed to exist between the elements of social systems. These cause-effect relationships are referred to in an isolated way, without accounting for the social

---

7 As Bing puts it, there is no "canned due diligence". Bing, Gordon (1996), p. 1. Cf. also Müller-Stewens, Günter/ Frankenberger, Sebastian (2004), p. 34f.

8 This fact has hardly been addressed yet in business practice, either, but was considered as increasingly important by the enquired experts.

9 Cf. Ulrich, Hans (2001), p. 118ff.

10 "A concept is an idea or a [...] principle." Sinclair, John (1995), p. 332. Concepts facilitate managerial problem-solving. Cf. Ulrich, Hans (2001), pp. 87ff.

11 According to Chalmers, insights are scientific when they are new and based on thorough background knowledge. Cf. Chalmers, Alan F. (2001), p. 58.

12 The philosophy of science deals amongst other things with the process of arriving at scientific insights and the nature of these (translation by the author, original: "wissenschaftliche Methode" und "Struktur wissenschaftlicher Erklärungen"). Cf. Carrier, Martin. In: Mittelstraß, Jürgen (Ed.) (1996), pp. 739f.

13 Cf. Ulrich, Hans (2001), p. 319. The reason for referring to Ulrich's distinction is that it is considered suitable to express the specifics of the perspective taken in this study. Apart from Ulrich's distinction, also, the distinctions by Burrell/Morgan, Kirsch and Astley/Van de Ven could have been referred to. Cf. Burrell, Gibson/Morgan, Gareth (1979), p. 22. Kirsch, Werner (1997), p. 534. Astley, Graham W./Van de Ven, Andrew H. (1983), p. 247.

systems in which they are embedded. The systemic perspective is based on a holistic way of thinking. Circular relationships are assumed to exist between the elements of social systems. These relationships are thought to depend on the social systems in which they exist, and are therefore analysed in an integrative way. Second, from a non-systemic perspective, social systems can be modelled by use of analytically determined input-output-relationships. From a systemic perspective, social systems are synthetically determined, meaning that they can produce differing outputs based on the same input, at different points in time. Third, taking a non-systemic perspective, optimum solutions to specific problems are possible determining by use of algorithmic methods. From a systemic perspective, a heuristic problem-solving approach should be taken, meaning that different solutions for specific problems should be allowed for.[14] This thesis follows the systemic perspective of arriving at scientific insights. The problem addressed in this thesis is elaborated on based on a holistic, circular and integrative way of thinking, synthetically determined input-output-relationships and a heuristic problem-solving approach.

This thesis follows the systemic perspective of arriving at scientific insights.

1.3 Research Method

The research method describes the way of arriving at the purpose of a study. It can be broken down into five main questions (see figure 1.1):[15]

- What is the underlying research object?
- What is the research goal?
- What research strategy is employed?
- What research phase can the study be allocated to?
- What research results are aimed at?

The research object refers to what is being researched in terms of academic study. The research goal describes what the research results related to the research object are supposed to be used for. The research strategy encompasses the major steps undertaken in order to arrive at the research goal. The allocation of a study to a research phase is useful for understanding its significance for the work of a research community. The determination of research results demonstrates the nature of the insights generated related to the research object. All five questions are closely intertwined with each other, as well as with the philosophical positioning of this study from chapter 1.2.

---

[14] Cf. Ulrich, Hans (2001), p. 318ff

[15] Cf. Thommen, Jean-Paul (1983), p. 29. The first three questions are taken from this source. Cf. also Thommen, Jean-Paul (2004), p. 442. The first three and the fifth questions are taken from this source.

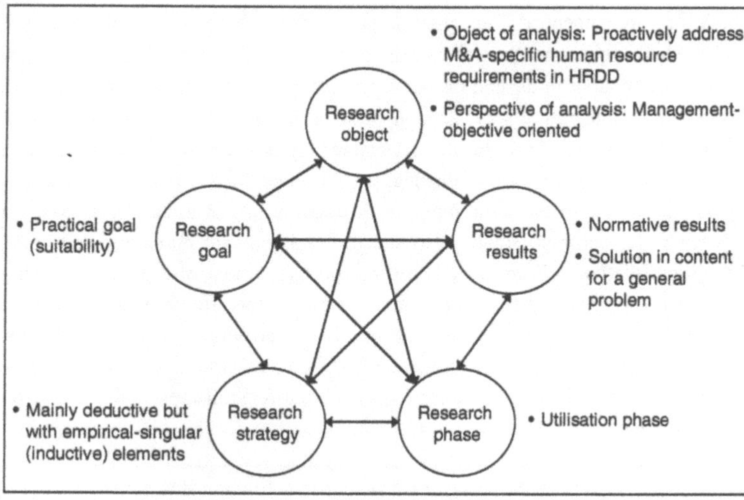

Figure 1.1: Research Method

1.3.1 Research Object

The benefit of determining a research object is twofold. First, it helps the researcher to focus his work. Second, it helps to clarify the perspective from which this work is conducted. When determining the research object, a distinction is often made between the object of analysis and the perspective of analysis of a study.[16]

(1) In its classical interpretation, the object of analysis refers to the part of reality, namely the type of institutions that is being analysed. In the past 100 years, the object of analysis in business administration research has been extended from an initial focus on firms in specific industries to a broader focus on firms in all industries, public institutions and pro-bono institutions.[17] In its modern interpretation, the object of analysis refers to the problem that is at the core of academic study. In this thesis, the modern interpretation of the object of analysis is employed. The problem which is at the core of this study is to proactively address M&A-specific human resource requirements in Human Resource Due Diligence.

---

[16] Translation by the author, original for object of analysis: "Erfahrungsobjekt" and for perspective of analysis: "Erkenntnisobjekt". Thommen, Jean-Paul (1983), p. 32. The distinction between object of analysis and perspective of analysis can be traced back to Amonn, Alfred (1911) and is often made use of in German speaking countries.

[17] Cf. Thommen, Jean-Paul (2002), p. 122. The choice of the research object is a value judgement (translation by the author, original: "Werturteil") referring to the value base (translation by the author, original "Wertbasis").

The object of analysis of this thesis is to proactively address M&A-specific human resource requirements in Human Resource Due Diligence.

(2) The perspective of analysis is the part of the object of analysis or the point of view from which the object of analysis is investigated (see figure 1.2).[18] It is defined by the researcher by means of selection criteria.[19] The perspective of analysis cannot be deduced logically – it is a highly subjective mental object. Business administration research was long focused on the single selection criterion of profitability. However, real business problems are seldom one-dimensional, which is why, according to Ulrich, a multidimensional (problem-oriented) or multi-theoretical approach should be used.[20] In this study, a problem-oriented approach is employed to arrive at the perspective of analysis.[21] The object of analysis is elaborated on from a management objective-oriented perspective. The human resource requirements of M&A transactions are assumed to result from objectives pursued by management.[22] These objectives serve as a basis for proactively addressing M&A-specific human resource requirements in Human Resource Due Diligence. Thus, the perspective of analysis for this thesis is defined as follows:

The perspective of analysis for this study is the proactive address of M&A-specific human resource requirements in Human Resource Due Diligence, in line with management's objectives.

---

[18] Cf. Sachs, Sybille/Hauser, Andrea (2002), p. 32. Wöhe, Günter (2002), p. 23. Thommen, Jean-Paul (2002), p. 122.

[19] Translation by the author, original: "Abgrenzungskriterien", "Auswahlprinzipien" or "Identitätsprinzipien". Thommen, Jean-Paul (1983), p. 31.

[20] Especially when aiming to influence business practice. Cf. Ulrich, Hans (2001), p. 194.

[21] The selection criterion for this study is based on the insights from previous studies. Apart from taking a problem-oriented – non-theoretical – perspective, one might also have argued according to a certain theoretical perspective. However, this would not have been adequate to grasp the research gap.

[22] M&A-specific human resource requirements may also result from other factors, such as the new firm's ecological, technological, economic and social environment. Cf. Ulrich, Hans (2001), p. 48. However, this thesis focuses on management objectives, since this is in line with its systemic philosophical positioning.

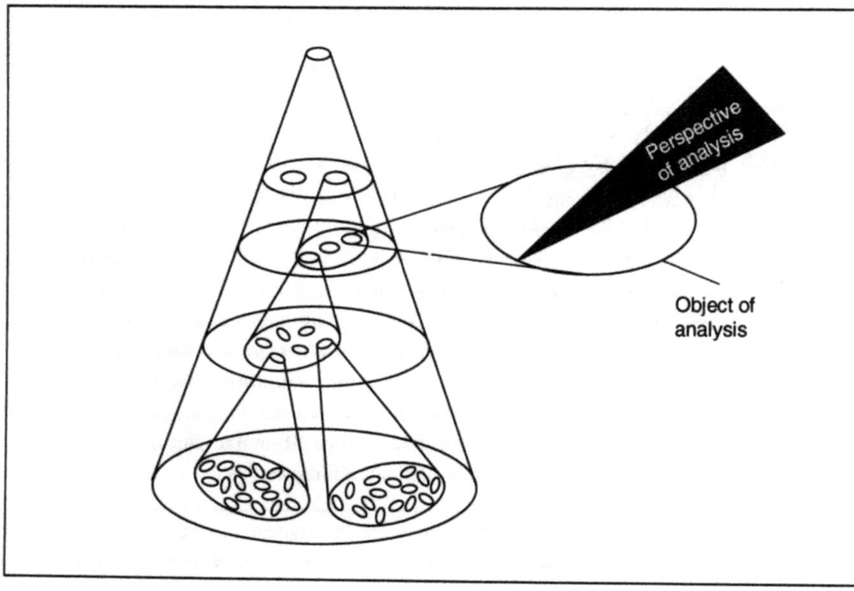

Figure 1.2: Research Object

Source: Ulrich, Hans (2001), p. 245.

1.3.2 Research Goal

The formulation of a research goal is necessary in order to define what the research results related to the research object can be used for.[23] The research goals of business administration research can be divided into theoretical goals and practical goals. Theoretical goals are aimed at solving a research problem derived from theory in a descriptive, non-normative manner. Practical goals aim to directly or indirectly influence business practice, presuming that the research problem is of practical relevance.[24] One type of business administration research that serves to influence business practice is applied business administration research.[25] The research goal of this thesis is of a practical nature – to develop a concept to be used in business practice. The reason for this practical research goal is the practical relevance of Human Resource Due Diligence as described in chapter 1.1. The concept which is to be developed for HRDD is intended to serve as a tool for M&A management. The research goal of this study will be achieved, if the research results are suitable for business practice. The

---

23 Cf. Thommen, Jean-Paul (1983), p. 41.

24 Theoretical and practical goals are hard to separate from each other. E. g. applicable theory can provide the basis for problem solving in practical studies. Cf. Thommen, Jean-Paul (2002), p. 125.

25 Cf. Ulrich, Hans/Krieg, Walter/Malik, Fredmund. In: Ulrich, Hans (1976), pp. 135f. Thommen, Jean-Paul (1983), p. 41.

suitability of the research results for business practice can be seen from not only the number of steps to be taken by professionals, in addition to applying the concept for HRDD as suggested in this thesis, but also from the number of cases in which the concept is applicable.

The research goal of this thesis is to develop a concept to influence business practice. Hence this study can be classified as applied business administration research.

1.3.3 Research Strategy

The research strategy describes the process through which the research goal of a study is reached. Two general options for generating scientific insights are to work either empirically or theoretically.[26] Empirical (inductive) studies arrive at insights based on observed reality.[27] Empirical studies can be subdivided into empirical studies in a narrower sense and in a wider sense. Empirical studies in a wider sense aim at explaining reality by supporting or refuting certain hypotheses (empirical-general research) related to the object of analysis. Empirical research in the narrower sense aims at collecting and classifying insights about observed (singular) reality (empirical-singular research).[28] Theoretical (deductive) studies arrive at insights by developing notional connections and assumptions related to the object of analysis. The application of a deductive research strategy can often be explained by the fact that the assumptions made by the researcher cannot be proved empirically.[29] This explanation also holds for this thesis, since it aims at developing a concept, which is assumed to be generic to business practice. Insights are arrived at by means of logic (deductive-statistical research).[30]

This thesis is mainly based on a deductive research strategy. However, it contains empirical elements which serve to supplement (and not to test) the theoretical ones. Theoretical insights are generated, then complemented with empirical-singular insights, and finally, their application to business practice is illustrated. The following steps are taken to attain the research goal of this study[31]:

(1) Definition of the research goal. (chapter 1.3.2)

(2) Generation, analysis and classification of problem-related insights from business administration research which are relevant for the perspective of analysis. The main insights are

---

26 Other options are action research or a hermeneutical approach. Cf. Kromrey, Helmut (1998), p. 61.

27 Cf. Eichhorn, Wolfgang. In: Raffée, Hans/Abel, Bodo (Eds.) (1979), pp. 76ff.

28 Cf. Thommen, Jean-Paul (2002), pp. 125ff.

29 Cf. Müller, Böling, Detlef/Klandt, Heinz (1996), p. 96. Chapters 2 to 4 will illustrate that the HRDD Concept cannot be proved empirically.

30 Cf. Chmielewicz, Klaus (1994), p. 82. Sachs, Sybille/Hauser, Andrea (2002), p. 41. In contrast, deductive-nomological research is based on the covering-law-model of explanation. Cf. Kromrey, Helmut (1998), p. 61.

31 Cf. Ulrich, Hans (2001), p. 195. Albert, Hans. In: Topitsch, Ernst (1993), p. 129.

acquired from recent management literature[32], performance measurement literature[33], M&A literature, psychological literature, and controlling literature. (chapters 1 to 4)

(3) Construction of a concept for the perspective of analysis. (chapters 2 to 4)

(4) Complement of the concept with empirical insights[34]. (chapter 5)

(5) Illustration of the application of the concept developed to business practice. (chapter 6)[35]

(6) Consultation of business practice. (chapters 2 to 7)

In summary, the research strategy for this study can be described as follows:

This thesis mainly follows a deductive research strategy. A concept is constructed based on theoretical insights. This concept is complemented with empirical-singular insights. Finally, the application of the empirically complemented concept to business practice is illustrated.

1.3.4 Research Phase

The research method of this study can also be illustrated by allocating it to a research phase. Every research process can be divided into three phases – discovery, explanation and application phase.[36]

(1) Discovery refers to a phase where the definition of a problem, terminological foundations, and frames of reference concern the researcher most.

(2) In the explanation phase, the researcher aims to arrive at new insights that can be generalised.

(3) In the application phase, ways of applying theoretical insights to business practice are given attention to. Furthermore, the researcher is concerned with the positioning of scientific work with regard to business practice.

All three phases are of relevance in academic work. However, the weight each phase carries depends amongst other things on the research goal, which, again, depends on the state of

---

32 The Zurich Management Model represents recent management theory, in this study. Cf. Rühli, Edwin (1996), p. 45. For the literature review strategies, see chapter 2.

33 A review of four recent human resource related streams of literature illustrated, that the performance measurement literature is most suitable to support the subsequent argumentation, given the research gap and the research goal underlying this study.

34 The reason for generating empirical-singular insights is the aim of step four of the research strategy to complement the theoretical HRDD.

35 For the empirical research strategies, see chapter 5.1 for step four and chapter 6.1 for step five.

36 Translation by the author, original: "Entdeckungszusammenhang", „Begründungszusammenhang" and „Verwendungszusammenhang". Mittelstraß, Jürgen (Ed.) (1996), p. 549. Cf. Hanson, Norwood R. (1958). Reichenbach, Hans (1938), (1966), § 1: "context of discovery, context of explanation and context of usage".

research in a particular field.[37] This thesis aims at applying scientific insights to business practice. Thus the application phase is concentrated on, as will be illustrated in chapters 2 to 7. Nevertheless, in all three phases, the researcher must cope with certain problems. In the discovery phase, he must avoid constructing instead of discovering social reality. In this study, the danger of constructing social reality is tackled by basing its central assumptions on thorough reviews of literature.[38] Still, value judgements cannot be avoided. In the explanation phase, the researcher must avoid drawing subjective, general conclusions based on individual insights. To reduce the subjectivity of the selections made in this study, extensive and broad literature reviews have been carried out in order to arrive at the concept for HRDD.[39] In the empirical section, the findings of this study are consciously based on empirical-singular insights. In the application phase, the researcher must avoid taking the perspective of only one interest group (e.g. management) and neglecting the perspective of others. This thesis is consciously written from a management perspective. However, employees' perspective is also considered when it comes to recommendations for business practice.[40]

In the discovery and in the explanation phase, thorough literature reviews are carried out. Moreover, the empirical-singular insights are reviewed critically. In the application phase, the applicability of the concept developed to business practice is discussed, both from a managerial and from an employee perspective.

1.3.5 Research Results

The results of academic study can be of different kinds. Firstly, they can be descriptive and hence serve to illustrate the object of analysis. Secondly, they can be explicative, i.e. show interdependencies related to the object of analysis. Thirdly, research results can be guidelines for achieving certain practical goals – technical results. Fourthly, they can be of a normative nature.[41] Normative studies in business administration research aim at prescribing how things should be done in practice.[42] The results that it is intended to arrive at in this study are primarily of a normative nature. The way in which a study helps to solve practical problems depends on the problem being solved and on the type of results generated. Accordingly, Ulrich distinguishes four types of normative results (see figure 1.3):

(1) Concrete solutions to practical problems,

(2) Procedures for solving practical problems,

---

37 In previous M&A research, especially the discovery and the explanation phase have been contemplated. For details see chapter 2.1.2.

38 Cf. chapters 2 to 4.

39 Cf. chapters 2 to 4.

40 Cf. chapters 5 to 7. Cf. Ulrich, Peter/Hill, Wilhelm (1976), pp. 306f.

41 Cf. Raffée, Hans (1995), p. 15.

42 Cf. Sauermann, Sabine (2000), p. 4. Normative results are neither true nor false, but suitable or non suitable for problem-solving. Cf. Flor, Jan Riis. In: Hügli, Anton/Lübcke, Paul (Eds.) (1993), p. 76.

(3) Concepts for changing social reality and

(4) Rules for developing concepts for solving practical problems.[43]

Types 1 and 2 relate to individual problems, whereas types 3 and 4 allude to general problems. Types 1 and 3 bear on solutions in content, types 2 and 4 correspond to rules for the design of solutions in content.[44] This study concludes by producing a concept for changing social reality. It aims to develop a solution in content to a general practical problem.[45] Hence, this study produces results that can be allocated to type 3 of Ulrich's categorisation.

This thesis results in a normative[46] solution in content to the general problem addressed in the research object.

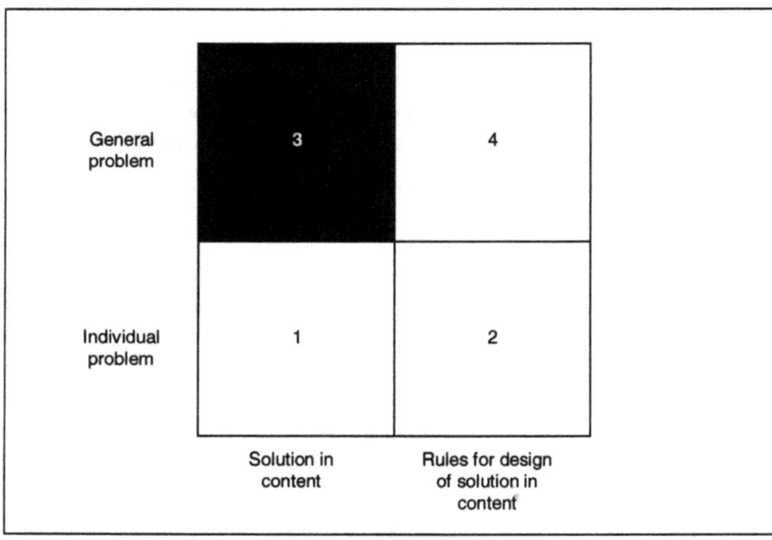

Figure 1.3: Research Results

Source: Pöck, Thomas (2002), p. 7.

---

[43] Cf. Ulrich, Hans (2001), p. 180.

[44] Cf. Pöck, Thomas (2002), p. 7.

[45] Solutions in content are recommendable in case of complex problems of general practical relevance. Cf. Ulrich, Hans (2001), pp. 87ff

[46] Three different types of results can be the outcomes of scientific work – orientation results (translation by the author, original: "Orientierungswissen"), disposition results (translation by the author, original: "Verfügungswissen") or tools (translation by the author, original: "Beeinflussung der Realität, Instrumente"). This thesis is supposed to produce a tool. Cf. Mittelstraß, Jürgen (2002), w.p.

1.4 Terminology of Study

The following chapter aims to ensure that the main terms used in this study can be generally understood. Therefore, the interpretations of the terms "Mergers & Acquisitions", "due diligence", "Human Resource Due Diligence", "human resource requirements" and "M&A management", as used in this study, are presented.

1.4.1 Mergers & Acquisitions

Mergers & Acquisitions are featured by two main characteristics. They represent long term transactions between at least two firms or parts of them. Moreover, they are accompanied by a loss of the economic independence of the firms involved. In academic literature, the term Mergers & Acquisitions is often subdivided into mergers and acquisitions.[47] Mergers are accompanied by a loss of the firms' legal and economic independence. In acquisitions, firms or parts of firms lose their economic independence, but they can keep their legal independence.[48] Spin-offs can be characterised as reverse acquisitions – firms become independent in a legal, but not necessarily in an economic sense.

In order to arrive at the purpose of this study, it is not necessary to define a difference between mergers and acquisitions. Most insights arrived at in this study are applicable to both types of transactions. However, some insights apply solely to acquisitions (mostly to spin-offs), solely. These particular insights are indicated as such in chapter 2.2 of this study.

The term Mergers & Acquisitions, as defined for this study, refers to transactions between at least two firms or parts of them, accompanied by a loss of their economic independence/a gain in their legal independence (in case of spin-offs).[49]

---

47 M&A in a narrower sense, cf. Achleitner, Ann-Kristin (2001), pp. 141f. Cf. also Vogel, Dieter H. (2002), p. 3. The above definition excludes strategic alliances and joint ventures. Transfer of ownership is a lengthy process, the result of which is harder to change than a co-operation. Cf. Clever, Holger (1993) (entire book). For different definitions of the terms acquisition, merger, strategic alliance and joint venture cf. Bamberger, Burkhard (1994), pp. 4 – 8.

48 There are two types of acquisitions – share and asset deals. In a share deal, the buyer takes over all assets, rights, contracts and liabilities of the other firm. In case of change-of-control clauses, employees have the right to leave the firm if a new owner comes in. In an asset deal, not all assets etc. are transmitted, but instead, all to-be-transferred items are identified individually. Cf. Achleitner, Ann-Kristin (2001), pp. 142ff. One of the few exemptions are employee contracts, which always need to be taken over by the new owner (§ 613a BGB). Cf. Felder, Rupert (2001), p. 156.

49 The terms M&A, Mergers & Acquisitions, M&A transactions and transactions are used interchangeably in this thesis.

1.4.2 Due Diligence

In its traditional interpretation, due diligence[50] means the auditing of the information memorandum of a firm in the event of a sale or public offering of shares, or in the event of a Going Public.[51] Due diligence in this traditional interpretation signifies that an investor evaluates the quality of a firm. Today, the term due diligence is used in many different contexts, ranging from financing decisions to credit requests and Mergers & Acquisitions.[52] In this study, due diligence in Mergers & Acquisitions is concentrated on.

Due diligence can be carried out as a result of a legal obligation[53] or for business reasons.[54] If carried out for legal reasons, due diligence means detecting liabilities, guarantees, indemnities and warranties for pre-contractual representations.[55] If conducted for business reasons, due diligence means providing M&A management with the information it requires. In this thesis, the business reason for performing due diligence is the focus of attention.

When elaborating on due diligence, three different aspects can be at the core – the due diligence process, tools for due diligence or the institutional grounding of due diligence. The due diligence process refers to the steps undertaken when performing due diligence. Tools for due diligence relate to the design of means for getting access to due diligence information. The institutional grounding of due diligence encompasses the person(s) in charge of due diligence.[56] In the subsequent argumentation, the due diligence process is at the centre of attention. As part of this process, general principles for developing tools for due diligence are referred to. However, no concrete tools are designed, since this would require insights about the M&A context in which they are supposed to be applied.

As far as the time frame for due diligence is concerned, Rockholtz distinguishes between a due diligence in a wider sense and due diligence in a narrower sense. Due diligence in a wider sense means analyses, which take place on several occasions before and upon completion[57] of an M&A transaction.[58] Due diligence in the narrower sense relates to analyses performed once

---

50 "Someone who is diligent works hard in a careful and conscientious way." Sinclair, John (1995), p. 459. "Due attention and consideration is the proper, reasonable, or deserved amount of it under the circumstances." Sinclair, John (1995), p. 514.

51 Cf. Jaensch, Günther (1992). In: Colbe, Walther Busse von/Coenenberg, Adolf G. (Eds.), p. 386. Berens, Wolfgang/Strauch, Joachim. In: Berens, Wolfgang/Brauner, Hans U./Strauch, Joachim (Eds.) (2002), pp. 5 – 13. Volkart, Rudolf (1999), p. 33.

52 Cf. Thommen, Jean-Paul (2004), p. 168.

53 Cf. Godefried, Christoph (2000), p. 46. Zhang, Charles (1998), p. 56. Angersbach, Carsten J. (2002) (entire book). Vorbrugg, Georg. In: Droste (Ed.) (1995), p. 115.

54 Cf. Scott, Cornelia (2001), pp. 14f.

55 Cf. Whalley, Michael/Semler, Franz-Jörg (1996), pp. 106f.

56 Cf. Rühli, Edwin (1995), p. 13.

57 An M&A transaction is assumed to be complemented, when contracts that close the transaction are signed.

58 For different classifications of due diligence, cf. Canepa, Ancillo (1998), pp. 8ff. Jemison, David B./Sitkin, Sim B. (1986), p. 148.

only, often before completing an M&A. In this study, due diligence is referred to in a wider sense.[59]

Due diligence, as defined for this thesis, refers to a process performed without legal obligation in the context of Mergers & Acquisitions, at different times, in order to generate information required by M&A management.

1.4.3 Human Resource Due Diligence

Human Resource Due Diligence comprises measures performed without legal obligation in the context of Mergers & Acquisitions, at different times for the sake of collecting information about the transaction parties' employees. Hence, in the context of this study, the term Human Resource Due Diligence is defined as follows:[60]

Human Resource Due Diligence is a special type of M&A Due Diligence where information about the transaction parties' employees is at the core.

1.4.4 Human Resource Requirements

Human resource requirements are assumed to be demands imposed on employees, calling for a specific kind of future behaviour. In the subsequent argumentation, the construct of competencies is used to describe the human resource requirements of M&A transactions.[61] Competences relate to a person's dispositions to act in a certain way in the future.[62] Five different competence groups are referred to describe the competence requirements of Mergers & Acquisitions – social, systems, methods, specialist and change competence (see figure 1.4).[63]

---

59 Cf. Rockholtz, Carsten (1998), p. 69.

60 Cf. Thommen, Jean-Paul (2004), p. 282.

61 Apart from this construct, also another future-related construct, namely the construct of motivations, could have been used. Cf. Frey, Bruno S./Osterloh, Margit (2002), p. 23. Rosenstiel, Lutz von (2001), p. 5. However, the construct of competences is considered to be more consistent with the assumed behavioural nature of human resource requirements, than the construct of motivations is, which is why it has been chosen. Moreover, using several constructs in one study may imply difficulties, if the results obtained for the different constructs contradict each other. Cf. Graf, Jürgen (2002), p. 111.

62 Cf. Erpenbeck, John/Rosenstiel, Lutz von. In: Erpenbeck, John/Rosenstiel, Lutz von (Eds.) (2003), p. XI. The understanding of competences used here relates to individual employees, and has been derived from psychological literature. Apart from psychology, the construct is also used in sociology, organisation theory and strategic management (core competences according to Hamel, Gary/Prahalad, Coimbatore K. (1990) p. 5.) For details cf. Behler, Steffen (2002), pp. 43ff. For different definitions of the term competences, cf. Schuler, Heinz. In: Rosenstiel, Lutz von/Lang-von Wins, Thomas (Eds.) (2000), p. 54. Holmes, Len (1995), p. 36.

63 Based on Backhausen, Wilhelm/Thommen, Jean-Paul (2004), p. 226f. Thommen, Jean-Paul. In: Thommen, Jean-Paul (Ed.) (1995), p. 17. Apart from the competence grid by Thommen, also other competence grids could have been used in the subsequent argumentation. Cf. Reetz, Lothar. In: Reetz, Lothar/Reitmann, Thomas (Eds.) (1990), pp. 22ff. Jetter, Wolfgang (1996), pp. 12 – 15. Gerig, Valentin (1998), p. 170. Katz, Robert L. (1974), pp. 92f. Hilb, Martin (2002), pp. 72ff. Wunderer, Rolf/Bruch, Heike (2000), p. 28. Kauffeld, Simon/Grote, Sven/Frieling, Ekkehart. In: Erpenbeck, John/von Rosenstiel, Lutz (2003), p. 261. Erpenbeck, John/Rosenstiel, Lutz von. In: Erpenbeck, John/Rosenstiel, Lutz von (Eds.) (2003), p. XVI.

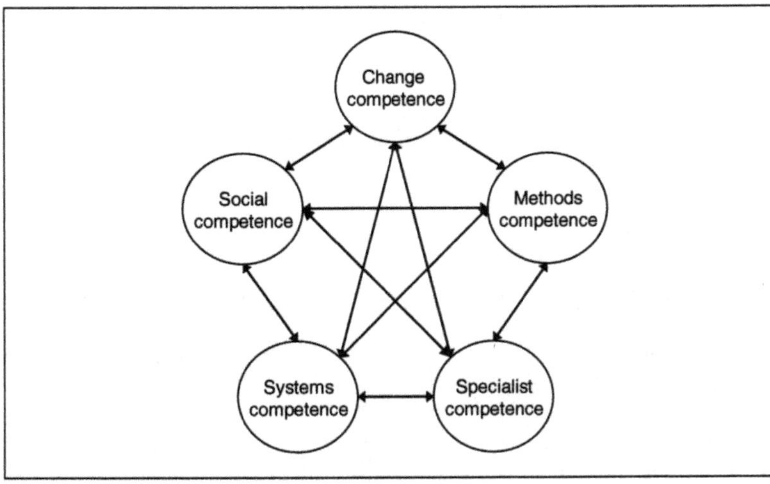

Figure 1.4: Competence Grid used in this Thesis

Source: based on Backhausen, Wilhelm/Thommen, Jean-Paul (2004), p. 226f.

Social competence encompasses those competences needed to successfully associate with other people, groups or society.[64] Social competence can be manifested on three different levels, namely an individual, an organisational and a societal level. The individual level relates to a person's behaviour towards himself; the organisational level focuses on behaviour towards other members of an organisation. The societal level is about how a person behaves towards society. In this thesis, only the organisational and the individual levels are referred to. The reason for this is that employee behaviour within firms is contemplated in this thesis, and not their behaviour towards society.[65] Before defining the term **systems competence**, the term system is briefly defined for this thesis. A system is a unit composed of different elements that are connected with each other by functional relations.[66] The relations between the elements of a system are non-linear and can take several states.[67] Each system is part of a larger system surrounding it.[68] Not all spheres of its environment are of the same importance to a system. The importance of the different spheres depends on the underlying problem a system is inten-

Staudt, Erich/Rehbein, Monika (1988), p. 12. The grid by Thommen has been chosen, since it covers a broad variety of competences and is therefore suited to reflect the complex requirements implied for employees in M&A transactions.

64 Cf. Backhausen, Wilhelm/Thommen, Jean-Paul (2004), p. 226. For a different definition of the term social competence cf. Kanning, Uwe Peter (2001). In: Wenninger, Gerd (Ed.), p. 197. Kanning, Uwe Peter. In: Kanning, Uwe Peter (Ed.) (2002), p. 155.

65 This is due to the systemic philosophical positioning of this thesis, which reflects second order cybernetics.

66 Cf. Girod, Bernd/Rabenstein, Rudolf/Stenger, Alexander (2003), p. 7. Thommen, Jean-Paul (2004), p. 599.

67 Cf. Berghaus, Margot (2003), p. 23. Girod, Bernd/Rabenstein, Rudolf/Stenger, Alexander (2003), p. 7.

68 Cf. Luhmann, Niklas (1984), pp. 35ff.

ded to solve.[69] Firms are complex social systems. Decision-making situations are complex if a large number of elements (variety) which are characterised by a variety of relations between them (connectivity) must be dealt with. There must be a time lag between these relations (functionality).[70] Given the above, systems competence means the competence to understand the firm as a system and its evolution over time, taking impulses from the firm's environment into account. Moreover, it refers to competence in making use of the systemic understanding for the benefit of a firm.[71] **Specialist competence** encompasses the competences used by a person for carrying through concrete tasks in an accurate and reliable manner.[72] Specialist competence both relates to someone's own and to superior and lateral tasks.[73] **Methods competence** encompasses the competence to successfully make use of business administration methods and tools in business practice.[74] **Change competence** refers to a person's competence to successfully and in a sustainable manner cope with dynamic (human resource) requirements.[75] To be able to cope with dynamic requirements, a person must reduce complexity to retain his ability to act. A reduction of complexity automatically implies an interpretation, and thereby a construction of reality. Employees must be aware of this construction of reality and constantly reflect on it, to be able to show change competence.[76]

Four of the five competence groups in figure 1.5 make up a person's management competence, according to Thommen.[77] For this thesis, the five competence groups are assumed to make up an employee's competence to fulfil the human resource requirements implied by an M&A transaction. The five competence groups do not intersect, meaning that attributes of social competence do not apply to systems competence or vice versa.[78] Competences show strong coherence with their underlying competence groups, which is why they are assigned to these in the subsequent argumentation. Within each competence group, there is no hierarchy between the competences. The five competence groups differ in their task relatedness. As can be seen from figure 1.5, specialist competence is very much task-related as is, even though somewhat less, methods competence. At the same time, social competence is related to types

69 Cf. Willke, Helmut (2000), p. 53.

70 Cf. Reither, Frank (1997), p. 12. Systems complexity is in place in case the number of potential incidences in a system is superior to the number of actual incidences. Cf. Krause, Detlef (2001), p. 7.

71 Cf. Backhausen, Wilhelm/Thommen, Jean-Paul (2004), p. 226. Katz, Robert L. (1974), pp. 92f. Pollack, Walter/Pirk, Dieter (2001), p. 41. Kriz, Willy Christian (2000), p. 14. Manteufel, Andreas/Schiepek, Günter (1993), p. 25.

72 Cf. Blaschke, Dieter (1987), p. 51. Backhausen, Wilhelm/Thommen, Jean-Paul (2004), p. 226. Thommen, Jean-Paul. In: Thommen, Jean-Paul (Ed.) (1995), p. 17.

73 Cf. Gerig, Valentin (1998), p. 137. Staudt, Erich/Rehbein, Monika (1988), p. 95.

74 Cf. Selzer, Helmut M. In: Schweizer, Gerd/Selzer, Helmut M. (Eds.) (2001), pp. 15f. Ueckert, Hans. In: Sarges, Werner (Ed.) (2000), p. 255. Backhausen, Wilhelm/Thommen, Jean-Paul (2004), p. 226. Thommen, Jean-Paul. In: Thommen, Jean-Paul (Ed.) (1995), p. 17.

75 Cf. Dr. Wieselhuber und Partner Unternehmensberatung (2003), p. 77. Große-Oetringhaus, Wigand F. (1993), p. 275. Krüger, Wilfried. In: Krüger, Wilfried (Ed.) (2000), p. 21. Mary, Michael/Nordholt, Henny (2004), pp. 60 – 67. The more thorough the changes that occur within a firm, the more grave the consequences for those hit by these changes. Cf. Vahs, Dietmar (2003), p. 2.

76 Cf. Backhausen, Wilhelm/Thommen, Jean-Paul (2004), p. 226.

77 Cf. Thommen, Jean-Paul. In: Thommen, Jean-Paul (Ed.) (1995), p. 17.

78 Cf. Behler, Steffen (2002), p. 50.

of interaction more than to tasks. Systems and change competence are related to types of problems/systems and cannot be associated with concrete tasks.[79]

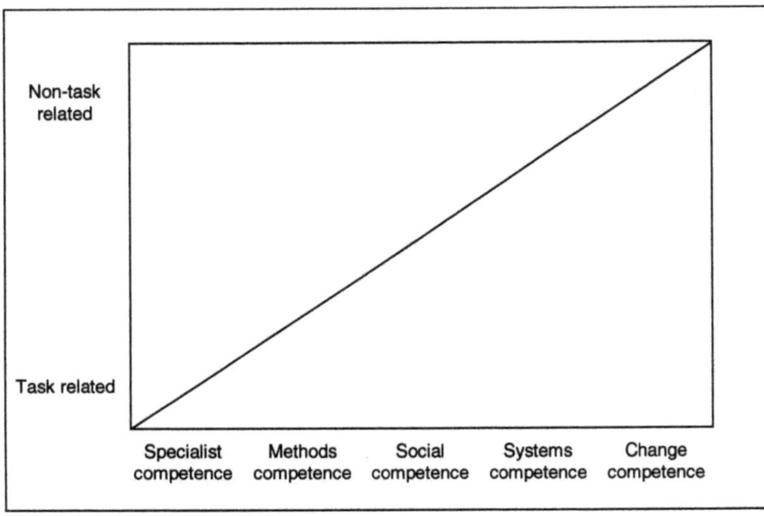

Figure 1.5: Task relatedness of the Competences of the Competence Grid

Source: based on Backhausen, Wilhelm/Thommen, Jean-Paul (2004b), p. 228.

The five competence groups can be found to a certain extent within every person. When assessing competences, the question is not whether a person possesses certain competences or not, but to what extent he possesses these competences. This extent, the parameter value of competences, is often expressed in relation to a desired and/or in relation to other people's competence level.[80] The importance of each competence group for an employee depends on the level of a firm's hierarchy he works at[81] as well as on the M&A management objectives aimed for.

79 Cf. Backhausen, Wilhelm/Thommen, Jean-Paul (2004), p. 228.
80 Cf. Wunderer, Rolf/Schlagenhaufer, Peter (1994), p. 77.
81 Cf. Katz, Robert L. (1974), pp. 95f.

1.4.5 Merger & Acquisition Management

M&A management is the shaping, steering[82] and development of two formerly independent social systems/of one formerly dependent social system (in case of a spin-off) in line with certain objectives.[83] M&A management can be considered as a temporary phenomenon, which is due to the time horizon of the objectives it addresses.[84]

M&A management takes place based on objectives in four different dimensions – strategy, structure, culture and human resource management.[85] Strategy refers to long term management decisions and deals with the contents-related, material substance of business activities.[86] Structure relates to organisational, rather technical aspects of management, and can be subdivided into organisational structures and processes.[87] Culture encompasses the norms and values predominant in an organisation.[88] For the human resource dimension, the definition by Hilb is taken as a point of departure, since it is consistent with the understanding of management, underlying the other three dimensions. Human resource management means all activities performed to steer the firm's human resources.[89]

---

82 This can be done by fostering certain states and preventing other states from appearing. Cf. Ulrich, Hans/ Krieg, Walter/Malik, Fredmund. In: Ulrich, Hans (1976), pp. 139f. „If you steer people towards a particular course of action or attitude, you try to lead them gently in that direction." Sinclair, John (1995), p. 1633.

83 Cf. Ulrich, Hans (2001), p. 103. Wirtz, Bernd W. (2003), p. 12.

84 Short and middle term objectives can be distinguished. Short term objectives are pursued prior to or directly upon completion of an M&A transaction. Middle term objectives are aimed for during the first two to three years upon completion of an M&A transaction.

85 The first three dimensions have been derived from the Zurich Management Model. Cf. Rühli, Edwin (1996), p. 44. The fourth dimension has been added to the three others by Tichy. Cf. Tichy, Noel M./Fombrun, Charles J./Devanna, Mary Anne (1982), pp. 47ff.

86 Cf. Rühli, Edwin (1996), p. 44. For alternative definitions of the term strategy, cf. Müller-Stewens, Günter/Lechner, Christoph (2003), p. 11. Leibold, Marius/Probst, Gilbert J. B./Gibbert, Michael (2002), pp. 196f.

87 Ditto. For another definition of the term structure cf. Schreyögg, Georg (2003), p. 4.

88 Ditto. For additional definitions of the term culture cf. Pümpin, Cuno. In: Allgemeine Treuhand AG (Ed.) (1984), pp. 11 – 26. Thommen, Jean-Paul (2002), p. 1161. Sackmann, Sonja A. (2002), p. 25.

89 Cf. Hilb, Martin (2002), pp. 12f. For other definitions of the term human resource management, cf. Baron, James N./Kreps, David M. (1999), p. 4. The term "human resources means the current and potential future capacities of a firm's employees. Cf. Casse, Pierre (1994), pp. 24ff. Karlins, Marvin (1981), p. 10. Thommen, Jean-Paul (2004), p. 282. For different understandings of the term "human resources" cf. Ridder, Hans-Gerd (1999), p. 98. Worrach, Cornelia (2001), p. 66.

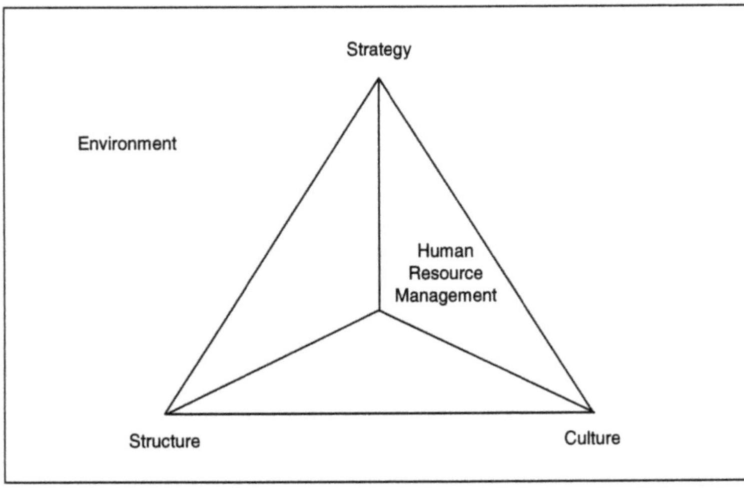

Figure 1.6: Dimensions of Merger & Acquisitions Management

Source: Rühli, Edwin (1996), p. 45.

The four management dimensions are of the same importance. The same applies to the objectives set within the management dimensions. Interdependencies exist between the objectives within the management dimensions, and between the management dimensions.[90] For management to be able to shape, steer and develop social systems in an efficient manner, the objectives pursued by it should be aligned logically with each other.[91] If they contradict each other, it is difficult to decide which objective to adapt to which. The objectives are also influenced by the firm's surrounding environment.[92] Impulses from its environment can force management to change some of its objectives.[93] Hence, the objectives pursued in the four management dimensions may be outdated from one day to the other.

M&A management objectives may be aimed for consciously or unconsciously. Moreover, they may be based on unanimous management decisions, or they may be proposed by some and opposed by other managers. No matter whether objectives are conscious, unconscious, unanimous or non unanimous, they imply human resource requirements that need to be coped with.

---

[90] Each objective can have an impact on each other objective, and each management dimension can influence each other management dimension.

[91] Cf. Rühli, Edwin (1996), p. 44.

[92] Cf. Rühli, Edwin (1996), p. 44. Systems (e.g. firms) absorb information from their environment(s) (translation by the author, original: "System-Umwelt-Paradigma"). Cf. Krieger, David J. (1996), pp. 17, 39f.

[93] This is in line with the new St. Gallen management framework. Cf. Rüegg-Stürm, Johannes (2003), pp. 39ff.

M&A management is the shaping, steering and development of two formerly independent social systems/of one formerly dependent social system (in case of a spin-off) in line with certain objectives. It is assumed to take place based on objectives in four different dimensions – strategy, structure, culture and human resource management.

1.5 Human Resource Due Diligence Concept

As illustrated in figure 1.7, the Human Resource Due Diligence Concept[94] consists of three steps. These three steps have been identified based on the Performance Measurement Model by Rose, who states that firms should follow eight steps when aiming to measure and improve organisational performance.[95]

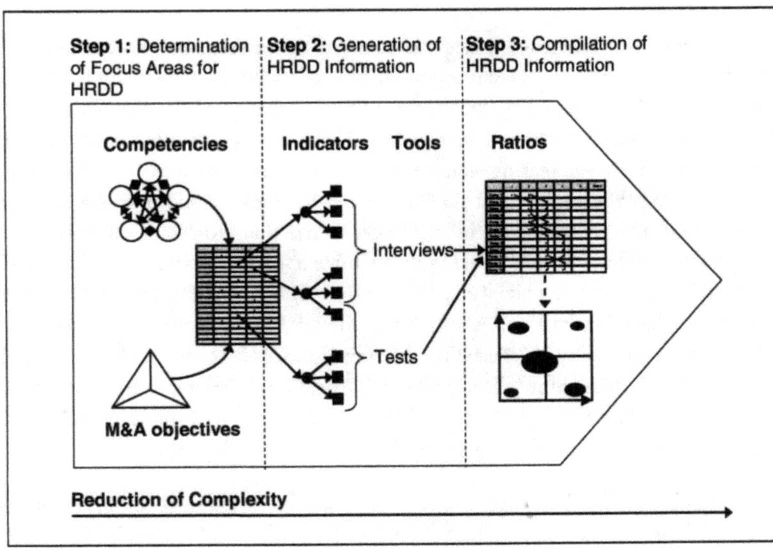

Figure 1.7: Human Resource Due Diligence Concept

94 Referred to as the Human Resource Due Diligence Concept, the HRDD Concept or the Concept.

95 Cf. Gleich, Ronald (2001), p. 67, quoted after Rose 1995. The eight steps to be undertaken when aiming to measure and improve organisational performance are: 1. Determination of performance categories 2. Development of performance objectives, 3. Identification of performance indicators 4. Deduction of elements of measure, 5. Definition of factors influencing the parameter values of controlling ratios 6. Determination of desired parameter values of ratios 7. Definition of types of ratios 8. Development of specific ratios. Step 1 of the HRDD Concept contains the second, third, fifth and sixth step of the Performance Measurement Model, whereas step 2 of the concept is reflected in the fourth step of Rose's model, and step 3 is represented in the seventh and eighth step. The first step of Rose's model has been taken already in chapter 1, when defining the understanding of M&A management for this study based on its research gap.

(1) **Step 1 – Determination of Focus Areas for HRDD:** Step 1 determines what competences to consider as highly relevant in HRDD, depending on the M&A objectives underlying a transaction.[96] A desired competence profile is developed, which serves as a basis for conducting Human Resource Due Diligence (chapter 2).

(2) **Step 2: Generation of HRDD Information:** In step 2, HRDD is carried out. To generate HRDD information in line with the focus areas from step 1, first, indicators are developed which serve to break down competences into measurable attributes.[97] Second, these indicators are applied to evaluation tools (chapter 3).

(3) **Step 3: Compilation of HRDD Information:** Step 3 of the HRDD Concept compiles the HRDD information generated in step 2, through use of controlling ratios, as a basis for further management activities[98] (chapter 4).

The Human Resource Due Diligence Concept is based on the assumption that for M&A management to be able to follow its objectives, it needs to cope with the complexity underlying M&A transactions.[99] This complexity, results from the fact that in M&A transactions, two formerly independent social systems join together. There are two possible approaches to coping with complexity – increasing complexity and reducing complexity.[100] Increasing complexity can be important to account for the number of elements and interdependencies between these elements characteristic of an M&A transaction. Reducing complexity is necessary for management to be able to act in line with its objectives. In step 1 of the HRDD Concept, a certain degree of complexity is first created. The potentially important competences and M&A objectives that serve as a basis for all three steps of the concept are elaborated on. Then complexity is reduced by determining focus areas for HRDD. In step 2, complexity is reduced once more when generating HRDD information based on certain indicators and tools, in line with the focus areas determined in step 1. In step 3, complexity is again reduced by compiling the results from HRDD through controlling ratios.

The Human Resource Due Diligence Concept is based on a heuristic problem-solving approach. Even though three steps to be undertaken by professionals when performing a management-objective oriented HRDD are suggested in the following three chapters, these three steps still leave room for professionals to dispose of. This implies that, when applying

---

[96] It is assumed that human behavior can be adapted to the context in which it is performed (situationism). Cf. Amelang, Manfred/Bartussek, Dieter (1997), pp. 5ff.

[97] Cf. Boudreau, John W. (1998), p. 14.

[98] Cf. Weismüller, Albert (1997), p. 892 for the use of condensed information.

[99] A precondition for coping with complexity is that management has information at hand about its business. Cf. Kaplan, Robert S./Norton, David P. (2001), p. 306. Cf. Picot, Gerhard, quoted in: Adelsberger, Heimo H./Stallkamp, Markus. In: Reichmann, Thomas (Ed.) (2003), p. 22. Biethahn, Jörg/Huch, Burkhard (1994), pp. 18f. For reasons for generating information in an M&A context, cf. Spremann, Klaus (1999), pp. 562ff. Strasser, Brigitte (2000) (entire book).

[100] Cf. Ulrich, Hans (2001), p. 118ff.

the HRDD Concept, the solution in content used by a firm is firm-specific, not only following the concept's suggestions but also being based on management's preferences.

1.6 Layout of the Thesis

Chapter 1.5 presented the Human Resource Due Diligence Concept, which consists of three steps: determination of focus areas for HRDD, generation of HRDD information and compilation of the generated HRDD information. Chapter 2 contains step 1 of the HRDD Concept. Focus areas for HRDD are developed based on different underlying M&A objectives. In chapter 3, representing step 2 of the HRDD Concept, based on the developed focus areas from chapter 2, indicators and tools for HRDD are elaborated on that can be used when actually generating HRDD information. In chapter 4, it is illustrated how to compile the HRDD information generated in step 2. Controlling ratios and human resource portfolios are the basis for the compilation of HRDD information. After creating the HRDD Concept in chapters 2 to 4, chapter 5 complements this HRDD Concept with empirical-singular insights from an expert survey. The three steps of the HRDD Concept are referred to one after the other, the propositions of the professionals concerning these 3 steps are explained, and implications for the HRDD Concept are derived. Chapter 6 is meant to illustrate the application of the Concept to business practice, based on two retrospective case studies about M&A transactions. Advantages from the application of the Concept are referred to by comparing the propositions of the Concept to the HRDD actually conducted in the two transactions. Chapter 7 consists of a résumé and critical discussion of the insights of this thesis, and of an outlook into future research questions.

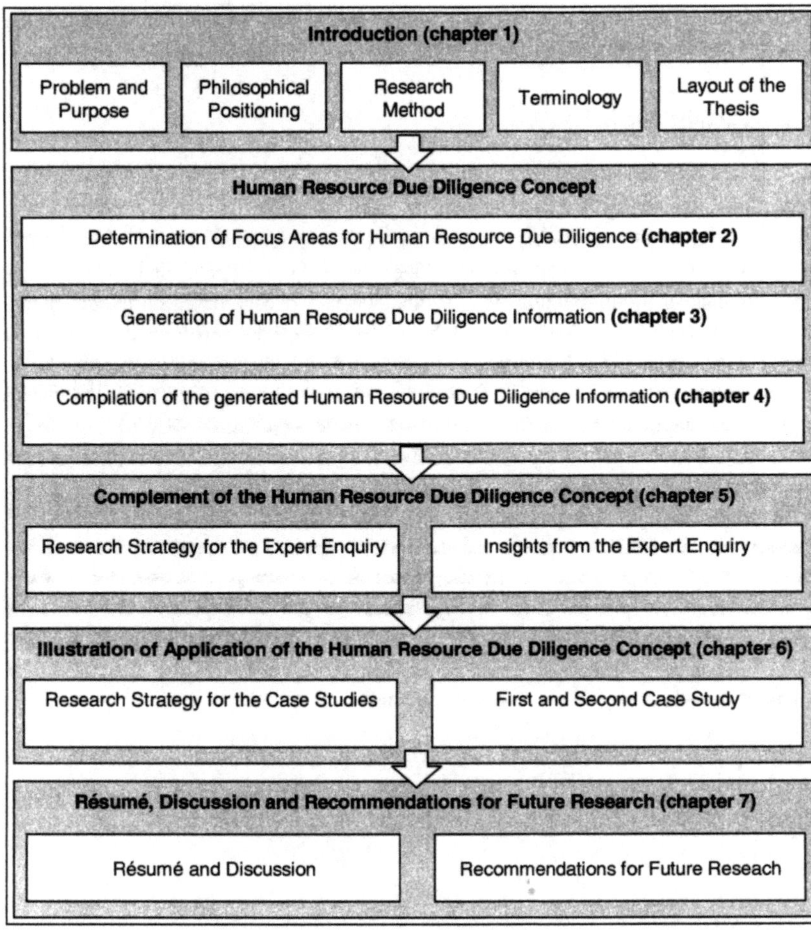

Figure 1.8: Layout of the Thesis

2 Determination of Focus Areas for Human Resource Due Diligence

In step 1 of the HRDD Concept, focus areas for Human Resource Due Diligence are determined (see figure 2.1). To determine these focus areas, first, competences are deduced from psychological literature and M&A literature (chapter 2.1) and second, the relevance of these competences is investigated for different underlying M&A objectives (chapter 2.2).

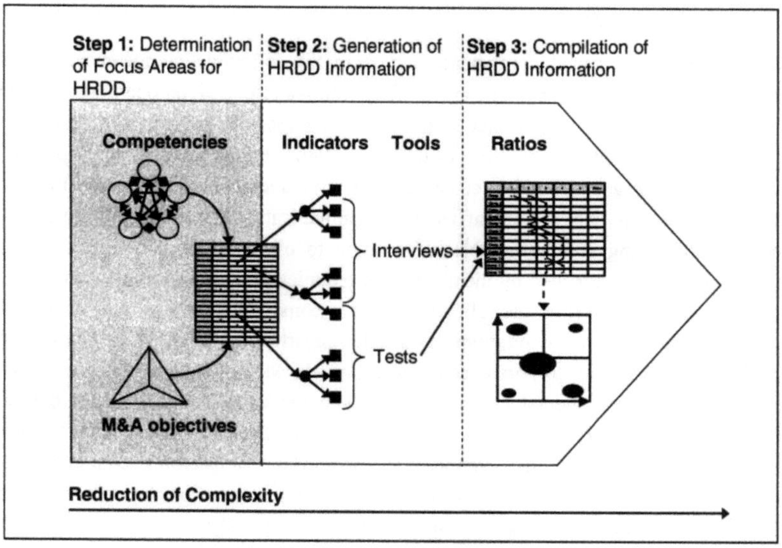

Figure 2.1: Determination of Focus Areas for Human Resource Due Diligence

2.1 Possible Focus Areas for Human Resource Due Diligence

To arrive at possible focus areas for Human Resource Due Diligence, it is first investigated which competences are named the most frequently in psychological literature (chapter 2.1.1). Given the practical research goal of this thesis, the potential focus areas for HRDD are supposed to be applicable to a large number of M&A transactions. Second, potential reasons for the relevance of these competences in M&A transactions are appraised, based on a review of M&A literature (chapter 2.1.2).

2.1.1 Possible Competences for the Human Resource Due Diligence Concept

To arrive at a catalogue of competences to be included in the M&A literature review, psychological literature has been reviewed. Possible competences have been discovered and allocated to the competence groups in figure 1.4.[101] Definitions of the selected competences as found in psychological literature are provided in the following, if necessary, slightly amended for the purpose of this thesis.

2.1.1.1 Social Competence

The literature review of social competence put forth the following competences: Needs adjournment, uncertainty, communication, conflict, motivation, and co-operation competence.[102] Needs adjournment competence is defined as competence in deferring one's own needs for the good of a larger whole/the firm.[103] Uncertainty competence means a person's competence in accepting and dealing constructively with uncertainty, both from his own perspective and from the firm's point of view.[104] Communication competence is a person's competence in delivering comprehensible information to other persons or groups and of receiving the information intended by them. Each communication has an informational and a relational component.[105] In a firm, the following types of communication can take place: self-communication, dialogues, team communication, inter-departmental communication, presentations and discussions, and corporate communication. In the following, dialogues, team communication, inter-departmental communication, and presentations and discussions are referred to, for all these types refer to the individual level and are considered relevant for the subsequent argumentation. Conflict competence encompasses a person's competence in preventing, stimulating and solving conflicts. This study concentrates on the competence in solving conflict, since this competence seems to be most frequently required. Accordingly, conflict competence refers to a person's competence in coping with (already existing/erupted) conflicts in a constructive manner for all parties involved, whilst pursuing their own goals.[106] Motivation competence is defined as a person's competence in influencing others/a group

---

101 The following selection criteria have been used: number of appearances in the psychological literature (at least two), fit with the competence definition of this study, and conceivability with the competence groups delimited for this thesis.

102 The following literature sources have been reviewed. Argyle, Michael (1972), p. 327. Baacke, Dieter (1973), pp. 287 – 292. Berkel, Karl. In: Sarges, Werner (Ed.) (2000), p. 420. Blaschke, Dieter (1987), p. 51. Bungard, Walter. In: Sarges, Werner (Ed.) (2000), p. 407. Deutscher Manager-Verband e.V. (2003) (entire book). Faix, Werner G./Laier, Angelika (1994), pp. 62ff. Fittkau, Bruno. In: Sarges, Werner (Ed.) (2000), p. 386. Gerig, Valentin (1998), p. 244. Hubner, Ulrich (1985), pp. 116, 135. Kempf, Wilhelm In: Frey, Dieter/Greif, Siegfried (1987), p. 328. Lang, Rudolf W. (2000), pp. 398 – 542. Marggraf, Claudia. In: Marggraf, Claudia (Ed.) (1995), p. 75. Ortwig, Harald (2002) (entire book). Robbins, Stephen P. (2003), p. 314. Schuler, Heinz/ Barthelme, Dorothea. In: Seyfried, Brigitte (Ed.) (1995), p. 82. Wellhöfer, Peter R. (2004), p. 4. Wunderer, Rolf (2003), p. 5.

103 Cf. Faix, Werner G./Laier, Angelika (1994), pp. 62ff.

104 Ditto.

105 Cf. Hubner, Ulrich (1985), pp. 116, 135. Fittkau, Bruno. In: Sarges, Werner (Ed.) (2000), p. 386. Baacke, Dieter (1973), pp. 287ff. For different definitions of the term communication competence cf. Kempf, Wilhelm In: Frey, Dieter/Greif, Siegfried (1987), p. 328. Lang, Rudolf W. (2000), pp. 398ff.

106 Cf. Berkel, Karl. In: Sarges, Werner (Ed.) (2000), p. 420. Similarly cf. Kempf, Wilhelm. In: Frey, Dieter/Greif, Siegfried (1987), p. 328. Lang, Rudolf W. (2000), pp. 398ff. For details on different types of conflicts, cf. Glasl, Friedrich (1999) (entire book).

toward certain behaviour.[107] Co-operation competence refers to a person's competence in joining his forces with those of others. It is often referred to as the opposite of competition. Co-operation is frequently accompanied by joint decision-making.[108]

2.1.1.2 Systems Competence

The following competences have been found in the review of psychological literature as components of systems competence: innovation, internal, market, socio-cultural, and complexity competence.[109] Innovation competence means the competence in re-thinking existing patterns of behaviour and of detecting new solutions.[110] Innovation competence can encompass product and process innovations.[111] Both these types of innovations are considered in the subsequent argumentation. Internal competence refers to the competence in understanding the elements of and interdependencies between the firm's internal structures. Moreover, internal competence means the competence in comprehending the impact implied by changes to structural elements and interdependencies.[112] Market competence means competence in understanding the current and potential future states of the firm's market(s).[113] Socio-cultural competence relates to competence in comprehending and dealing constructively with socio-cultural differences. Socio-cultural differences encompass differences in managerial principles, legislation, education systems, languages and political systems.[114] Differences in managerial principles, legislation and languages are considered, in this study.[115] Complexity competence signifies competence in constructively dealing with complex and networked problems by making adequate selections.[116] Hence, it means competence in structuring and condensing complex problems to make them manageable.[117]

---

[107] Cf. Robbins, Stephen P. (2003), p. 314. Robbins uses the term "leadership". Similarly cf. Hubner, Ulrich (1985), pp. 116, 135. Cornelli, Gerhard/Rosenstiel, Lutz von (2001), p. 6.

[108] Cf. Bungard, Walter. In: Sarges, Werner (Ed.) (2000), p. 407.

[109] The following literature sources have been reviewed. Behler, Steffen (2002), pp. 78ff. Berghaus, Margot (2003), p. 23. Gerig, Valentin (1998), pp. 152 – 160. Girod, Bernd/Rabenstein, Rudolf/Stenger, Alexander (2003), p. 7. Kalpaka, Annita (1998), p. 593. Katz, Robert L. (1974), pp. 92f. Krause, Detlef (2001), p. 7. Kriz, Willy Christian (2000), p. 14. Luhmann, Niklas (1984), pp. 35ff. Manteufel, Andreas/Schiepek, Günter (1993), p. 25. Milling, Peter. In: Milling, Peter (Ed.) (2002), p. 15. Pollack, Walter/Pirk, Dieter: (2001), p. 41. Reither, Frank (1997), p. 12. Schiepek, Günter. In: Reiter, Ludwig (Ed.) (1997), pp. 190f. Staudt, Erich/ Rehbein, Monika (1988), pp. 42 – 67. Thommen, Jean-Paul (2004b), p. 599. Willke, Helmut (2000), p. 53.

[110] Cf. Gerig, Valentin (1998), pp. 152 – 160. Similarly cf. Behler, Steffen (2002), pp. 78ff.

[111] Cf. Liepmann, Detlev/König, Ferdinand/Stübig, Jacob. In: Marggraf, Claudia (Ed.) (1995), pp. 141f.

[112] Cf. Backhausen, Wilhelm/Thommen, Jean-Paul (2004b), p. 226.

[113] Cf. Behler, Steffen (2002), pp. 78ff.

[114] Cf. Staudt, Erich/Rehbein, Monika (1988), pp. 42 – 67. Kalpaka, Annita (1998), p. 590.

[115] The reason for focusing on these is that such differences are likely to play a role in many M&A transactions, which enhances the suitability of the Concept for business practice.

[116] In case of complex, networked and severe problems, selections need to be made. Cf. Thommen, Jean-Paul (2004b), p. 342.

[117] Cf. Milling, Peter. In: Milling, Peter (Ed.) (2002), p. 15.

2.1.1.3 *Specialist Competence*

The review of psychological literature for competences to be allocated to the competence group of specialist competence resulted in the following competences: functional and process competence.[118] Functional competence means the competence used for the correct fulfilment of functional tasks in firms, such as e.g. marketing, finance, human resource management, controlling, production and logistics tasks.[119] Process competence refers to competence in comprehending and being able to accomplish business processes as a whole.[120]

2.1.1.4 *Methods Competence*

Based on the literature review, the following competences have been found for the competence group of methods competence: planning, problem-solving, organisation and decision-making competence.[121] Planning competence relates to a person's ability to establish a time, quality and resource frame for the accomplishment of tasks.[122] Problem-solving competence is referred to as the ability to make use of business administration methods when solving business-related problems.[123] A person has a problem if he is supposed to transform the status quo into a desired state, without knowing how. The less information there is at hand about the desired state and about the ways of arriving at it, the more difficult it is to deal with a problem.[124] Organisation competence is defined as competence in structuring the tasks inherent in a firm (by dividing the firm's entire task spectrum into subtasks), and of integrating these subtasks.[125] Decision-making competence means competence in choosing one (or more) out of a multitude of alternative courses of action, based on the systematic review and evaluation of information. Decisions are always related to certain principles against which the consequences of a chosen course of action are appraised.[126]

---

118 The following literature sources have been reviewed. Blaschke, Dieter (1987), p. 51. Behler, Steffen (2002), pp. 78ff. Gerig, Valentin (1998), p. 137. Jetter, Wolfgang (1996), p. 14. Mayrshofer, Daniela/Kröger, Hubertus A. (2001), p. 18. Osterloh, Margit/Frost, Jetta (2003), pp. 31ff. Schneider, Helmut (1992), p. 51. Staudt, Erich/Rehbein, Monika (1988), p. 95. Thommen, Jean-Paul. In: Thommen, Jean-Paul (Ed.) (1995), p. 17.

119 Cf. Thommen, Jean-Paul. In: Thommen, Jean-Paul (Ed.) (1995), p. 17.

120 Cf. Osterloh, Margit /Frost, Jetta (2003), p. 32.

121 The following literature sources have been reviewed. Behler, Steffen (2002), pp. 78ff. Deutscher Manager-Verband e.V. (2003) (entire book). Jungermann, Helmut. In: Sarges, Werner (Ed.) (2000), pp. 247ff. Lang, Rudolf W. (2000), pp. 57 – 186. Müller, Burkhard (1995), p. 39. Putz-Osterloh, Wiebke. In: Sarges, Werner (Ed.) (2000), p. 241. Reetz, Lothar. In: Reetz, Lothar /Reitmann, Thomas (Eds.) (1990), pp. 22ff. Selzer, Helmut M. In: Schweizer, Gerd/Selzer, Helmut M. (Eds.) (2001), pp. 15 – 20. Thommen, Jean-Paul. In: Thommen, Jean-Paul (Ed.) (1995), p. 17. Ueckert, Hans. In: Sarges, Werner (Ed.) (2000), p. 255.

122 Cf. Ueckert, Hans. In: Sarges, Werner (Ed.) (2000), p. 256.

123 Cf. Thommen, Jean-Paul (Ed.) (1995), p. 17.

124 Cf. Putz-Osterloh, Wiebke. In: Sarges, Werner (Ed.) (2000), p. 241 quoted after Klix, Friedhart and Dörner, Dietrich. Heuristic and not facts knowledge (competence) is needed to show problem solving competence. Cf. Putz-Osterloh, Wiebke. In: Sarges, Werner (Ed.) (2000), p. 243.

125 Own definition, based on Ueckert, Hans. In: Sarges, Werner (Ed.) (2000), p. 256. Thommen, Jean-Paul (2002), p. 1006.

126 Cf. Jungermann, Helmut. In: Sarges, Werner (Ed.) (2000), pp. 247 – 253. Ueckert, Hans. In: Sarges, Werner (Ed.) (2000), p. 255.

2.1.1.5 Change Competence

In academic literature, hardly any competences can be found for change competence. The literature review indicated the following competences: technical change and social change competence.[127] Technical change competence means competence in adapting to new technical, i.e. task-related requirements. Social change competence means competence in adapting to new social requirements, for instance those implied by new social relationships or a new cultural environment.[128]

2.1.2 Competences Selected for the Human Resource Due Diligence Concept

A review of nearly fifty human resource-related sources[129] in the M&A literature has demonstrated that the following competences can be relevant in M&A in general: Uncertainty, communication, conflict, motivation, co-operation, innovation, internal, market, socio-

---

[127] The following literature sources have been reviewed. Dr. Wieselhuber und Partner Unternehmensberatung (2003) p. 77. Große-Oetringhaus, Wigand F. (1993), p. 275. Kaiser, Arnim (1992), p. 13. Kobi, Jean-Marcel (1999), p. 97. Krüger, Wilfried. In: Krüger, Wilfried (Ed.) (2000), p. 21. Mary, Michael/Nordholt, Henny (2004), pp. 60 – 67. Vahs, Dietmar (2003), p. 2.

[128] Cf. Kobi, Jean-Marcel (1999), p. 97. Both definitions are derived from the same literature source.

[129] The following literature sources have been reviewed. Birkinshaw, Julian/Bresman, Henrik/Hakanson, Lars (2000), pp. 400ff. Blake, Robert R./Mouton, Jane S. (1985), pp. 41 – 56. Böer, Frank-Michael/Stottmeister, Gerd (2001), w.p. Bramson, Ruth N. (2000), p. 65. Buono, Anthony F./Bowditch, James L. (1989), pp. 13, 15f, 18. Buono, Anthony F./Bowditch, James L./Lewis, John W. (1985), pp. 477ff. De Voge, Sylvia/Shiraki, Jeffrey (2000), pp. 30f. Deering, Anne/Dilts, Robert/Russell, Julian (2002), p. 35. Dickmann, Michael (2002), pp. 60ff. Dooley, Kevin J./Zimmermann, Brenda J. (w.y.), p. 28. Friederichs, Peter (1999), p. 337. Galpin, Timothy J./Herndon, Mark (2000), p. 8. Gaughan, Patrick A. (2002), pp. 171ff. Gerpott, Torsten J. (1993), p. 106. Gerpott, Torsten J. (1994), p. 5. Gutknecht, John E./Keys, J. Bernard (1993), p. 31. Gut-Villa, Cornelia (1997), pp. 81, 134. Homburg, Christian (2000), pp. 80f. Howell, Robert A. (1970), pp. 68f. Ivancevich, John M./Schweiger, David M./Power, Frank R. (1987), pp. 21f. Ivancevich, John M./Schweiger, David M./Power, Frank R. (1989), p. 20. Jansen, Stephan A./Pohlmann, Niko (2000), p. 30. Kay, Ira T./Shelton, Mike (2000) pp. 27f. Lubatkin, Michael/Schweiger, David M./Weber, Yaakov (1999), p. 55. Lüdi, Markus/Eicken, Sabine (2000), p. 11. Mace, Myles L./Montgomery, George G. (1962) (entire book). Marks, Mitchell Lee/Mirvis, Philip H. (1985), p. 50ff. Marks, Mitchell Lee/Mirvis, Philip H. (1992), p. 29. Mc Leod, Douglas (2001), pp. 6f. McKay, Jim/Qureshi, Imran (2001), p. 37. Mirvis, Philip H. (1985), p. 66. Müller-Stewens, Günter (1991). In: Ackermann, Karl-Friedrich/Scholz, Hartmut (Eds.), pp. 159ff. Napier, Nancy K. (1989), p. 277. Neumann, Petra/Rumpf, Bernd-Michael (1998), pp. 58, 62. Pablo, Amy (1994), p. 804. Ranft, Annette L./Lord, Michael D. (2000), p. 300. Risberg, Anette (2001), p. 60. Salecker, Jürgen (1995), pp. 165ff. Schlieper-Damrich, Rolf (2000), p. 41. Schreier, Claus (2001) (entire book). Schweiger, David M./De Nisi, Angelo S. (1991) (entire article). Schweiger, David M./Ivancevich, John M. (1985), p. 44. Schweiger, David M./Ivancevich, John M./Power, Frank R. (1987), p. 128. Steinöcker, Reinhard (1998), p. 165. Töpfer, Armin (2000), pp. 13, 15. Uder, Helmuth L./Kramarsch, Michael H. (2001), pp. 328f. Werner, Markus (1999), p. 33. Wirtgen, Jörg (1999), p. 6. Wood, Judy (1992), p. 48. Zwahlen, Beat (1994), p. 276. So far, hardly any competence grids are used in academic research to describe the human resource requirements of M&A transactions. Therefore, the relevance of the different competences in M&A needed to be derived "indirectly", from the description of human resource problems and human resource success factors in M&A. The criteria for identifying the competences from the M&A literature reviewed have been the competence group definitions from chapter 1.4.4 and the competence definitions from chapter 2.1.1. The contributions originate from mixed sources – some from refereed journals, others from non-refereed journals, and thirds from books and edited books. Moreover, the contributions show different publication dates, covering the past forty years of M&A research. The mixture of sources and publication dates can be explained by the multidimensional perspective of analysis of this study, which requires a varied argumentation.

cultural, complexity, planning, problem-solving, organisation, decision-making, functional, process, social change and technical change competence (see figure 2.2). The two criteria for selecting M&A relevant competences have been their number of appearances in the M&A literature reviewed and their perceived relevance to M&A transactions.

The reasons for the potential relevance of the respective competences according to the M&A literature review are presented in the following.[130] Needs adjournment competence appeared only once in the M&A literature review[131] and is therefore excluded from further analysis.

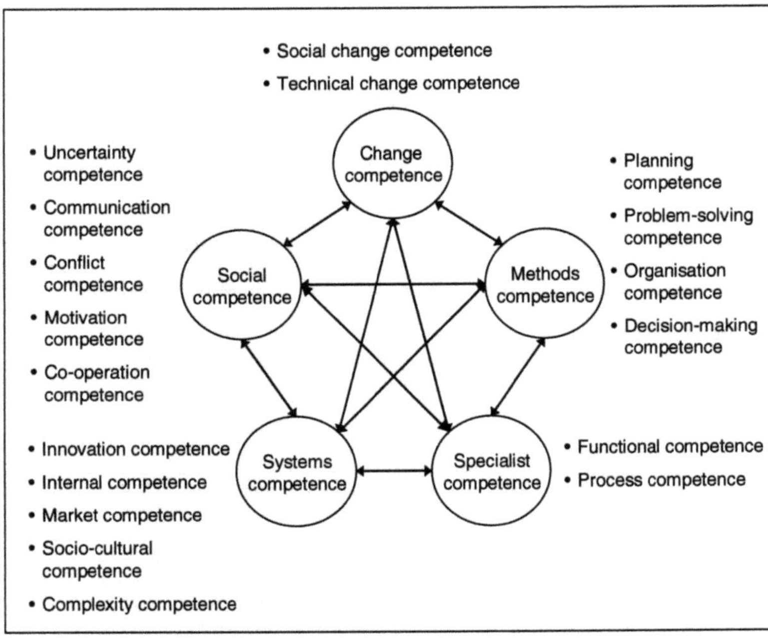

Figure 2.2: Competences reflected in the M&A literature reviewed

Source: based on Backhausen, Wilhelm/Thommen, Jean-Paul (2004), p. 226f.

2.1.2.1 Social Competence

The following social competences can be of importance in M&A – uncertainty, communication, conflict, motivation and co-operation competence. **Uncertainty competence** can be

[130] Many of the reasons for the relevance of the competences are derived from studies, which are written from certain theoretical perspectives. Thus, despite the non theoretical perspective of this thesis, theoretical explanations underlie the argumentation.

[131] The criterion for including a competence into the Concept was that it appeared at least twice in the literature reviewed.

required in M&A, since such transactions often imply changes to organisational structures, human resource policies and practices, strategy and corporate culture. Given these changes, there can be uncertainty about e.g. staffing, compensation and benefits, performance criteria, reporting relationships, and individuals' status and recognition in the new firm.[132] **Communication competence** can be demanded in M&A for four reasons. First it can be needed to reduce uncertainty through information[133] and second, for social relationships to be established.[134] Third, communication competence can be required to enable a competence transfer between the M&A parties.[135] Fourth, the relevance of communication competence can be due to a general augmentation in communication density upon completion of an M&A transaction, due to an increased number of interdependencies. As Buono/Bowditch put it, in M&A, "...the potential for dysfunctional interactions and outcomes, and personal and organisational conflicts is... quite high."[136] **Conflict competence** is a precondition for conflicts to be resolved in a constructive manner.[137] One reason for the high conflict potential in M&A is that the transaction parties' employees can be used to different patterns of behaviour. Also, role and status fights can be a reason for conflicts to emerge within and between the formerly independent firms as well as at different levels in the hierarchy. In M&A, **motivation competence** can be an important social competence (especially for management) to possess. The reason for this is that following an M&A transaction, employees require support in dealing constructively with changes implied by a new strategy, new structures, a new culture and a new human resource management.[138] They should be encouraged to have trust in and show commitment to the new firm.[139] **Co-operation competence** can be required in the context of Mergers & Acquisitions, e.g. if cross-organisational teams are established between the formerly independent firms.[140] Moreover, co-operation competence can be important in M&A, if the transaction parties' employees show different patterns of co-operation.[141]

---

[132] Cf. Breitstein, Joanna (2001), p. 98. Marks, Mitchell Lee/Mirvin, Philip H. (1992), p. 29. Risberg, Anette (2001), p. 60. Kay, Ira T./Shelton, Mike (2000), pp. 27f. Gut-Villa, Cornelia (1997), p. 134. Ivancevich, John M./Schweiger, David M./Power, Frank R. (1989), p. 20. Wood, Judy (1992), p. 48. Zwahlen, Beat (1994), p. 276. For supportive non-M&A related literature sources cf. Cf. Klimecki, Rüdiger/Gmür, Markus (2001), pp. 60f based on Cyert, Richard M./March, James G. (1995). Fisch, Jan Hendrik (2003), p. 216.

[133] Cf. Buono, Anthony F./Bowditch, James L. (1989), p. 16.

[134] Cf. Dooley, Kevin J./Zimmermann, Brenda J. (w.Y.), p. 28. Salecker, Jürgen (1995), pp. 165f.

[135] Cf. Salecker, Jürgen (1995), pp. 165ff.

[136] Buono, Anthony F./Bowditch, James L. (1989), p. 13. Similarly cf. Mirvis, Philip H. (1985), p. 66. Marks, Mitchell Lee/Mirvis, Philip H. (1985), pp. 50ff.

[137] Cf. Blake, Robert R./Mouton, Jane S. (1985), pp. 41 – 56.

[138] Cf. Gutknecht, John E./Keys, J. Bernard (1993), p. 31. Schlieper-Damrich, Rolf (2000), p. 41. Schweiger, David M./De Nisi, Angelo S. (1991) (entire article). Werner, Markus (1999), p. 33. Lubatkin, Michael/ Schweiger, David M./Weber, Yaakov (1999), p. 55. Gerpott, Torsten J. (1994), p. 5. Wirtgen, Jörg (1999), p. 6.

[139] Cf. De Voge, Sylvia/Shiraki, Jeffrey (2000), p. 31. Neumann, Petra/Rumpf, Bernd-Michael (1998), p. 58.

[140] Cf. Gut-Villa, Cornelia (1997), p. 81.

[141] Cf. Buono, Anthony F./Bowditch, James L. (1989), p. 18. Gut-Villa, Cornelia (1997), p. 81.

2.1.2.2 Systems Competence

As illustrated in figure 2.2, according to the literature review, the following systems competences can be of importance in M&A – innovation, internal, market, socio-cultural and complexity competence. **Innovation competence** can be of relevance in the context of M&A for two reasons. First, it can be important in a transaction accompanied by an organisational restructuring. In such a case, process (and structural) innovations are especially relevant.[142] Second, it can be important for strategic reasons, as innovation competence makes employees hard to substitute. In this case, product innovations are given particular attention to.[143] **Internal competence** can be extremely valuable in an M&A context. There are two reasons for this – first, in order to enhance organisational changes following an M&A. Maybe employees are needed, who can familiarise employees of the other firm with interdependencies and specifics of their transaction parties' internal structures.[144] Second, internal competence can be demanded when assessing whether new structures accord with former characteristics of the firms' structures.[145] **Market competence** can be of use in M&A not only for supporting the firm's new strategic positioning, especially if old markets are abandoned.[146] Also, market competence can be important for achievinge strategic positioning on an operative level.[147] **Socio-cultural competence** can be valuable in M&A, since differences between the transaction parties, deriving from their socio-cultural backgrounds, can require a culture sensitive social intercourse of their employees.[148] **Complexity competence** can be crucial in the context of M&A transactions, since the number of elements and interdependencies between these elements can increase upon completion of such transactions.[149] Moreover, the dynamics of the existing interdependencies can augment.[150] In M&A transactions, management must be able to cope with many different problems at one time. It must focus on the most important ones to make transactions successful.[151]

2.1.2.3 Specialist Competence

The following specialist competences can be of relevance in M&A – functional- and process competence. There are two reasons for the relevance of **functional competence** in M&A transactions, which are similar to the reasons for the relevance of process competence. First, the importance of functional competence can be explained by its potential relevance (or the

---

[142] Cf. Steinöcker, Reinhard (1998), p. 165.
[143] Cf. Gut-Villa, Cornelia (1997), p. 81. Pablo, Amy (1994), p. 804 quoted after Hitt, Hoskisson and Ireland.
[144] Cf. Gaughan, Patrick A. (2002), pp. 171ff.
[145] Cf. Böer, Frank-Michael/Stottmeister, Gerd (2001), w.p.
[146] Cf. Töpfer, Armin (2000), p. 13.
[147] Cf. Homburg, Christian (2000), pp. 80f.
[148] Cf. Schreier, Claus (2001) (entire book). Buono, Anthony F./Bowditch, James L./Lewis, John W. (1985), pp. 477ff.
[149] This can lead to an information overload, which implies barriers to the absorption and procession of information. Cf. Probst, Gilbert J.B./Deussen, Arne/Eppler, Martin J./Raub, Steffen P. (2000), p. 23.
[150] For example if the firms involved in an M&A transaction decide to carry out an organizational restructuring upon its completion. Cf. Koch, Tomas (2001), p. 168.
[151] Cf. Mace, Myles L./Montgomery, George G. (1962) (entire book). Töpfer, Armin (2000), p. 15.

relevance of certain functions of the M&A parties' value chains) to the competitive advantage of the new firm.[152] If certain functions of the value chain are essential to competitive advantage, the nature of the businesses participating in an M&A transaction determines which function(s). Second, functional competence can be important to enhance the efficiency of the new firm upon completion of an M&A transaction. Where certain functions should be managed as efficiently as possible, functional competence is vital (whilst maintaining a certain quality standard).[153] As for functional competence, the significance of **process competence** can be explained from a strategic perspective, namely by the strategic orientation towards processes of many of today's businesses. These processes are presumed to be relevant when strategically positioning a new firm after an M&A transaction. Moreover, the efficiency of many firms strongly depends on the functioning of their processes.[154]

2.1.2.4 Methods Competence

As illustrated in figure 2.2, the following methods competences can be of substance in M&A – planning, problem-solving, organisation and decision-making competence. **Planning competence** can be required for two reasons in. First, it may be necessary to prepare operative changes – short and middle term[155] – to be undertaken in order to achieve M&A objectives.[156] Second, planning competence can be demanded to prepare the strategic changes envisaged after a transaction.[157] **Problem-solving competence** may be required in an M&A context when operative, cultural or human resource management problems follow from a transaction.[158] In the context of M&A, **organisation competence** may be needed to ensure the well-functioning of operative restructurings envisaged by M&A management.[159] **Decision-making competence** may be of significance in M&A due to an increased number of decisions to be made in such transactions, compared to every day business.[160]

2.1.2.5 Change Competence

Figure 2.2 shows that according to the literature review, the following change competences can be of importance in M&A – technical change and social change competence. **Technical change competence** can be required in M&A due to the frequency and urgency with which

---

[152] Cf. Ranft, Annette L./Lord, Michael D. (2000), p. 300. Kay, Ira T./Shelton, Mike (2000) p. 28. Müller-Stewens, Günter (1991). In: Ackermann, Karl-Friedrich/Scholz, Hartmut (Eds.), pp. 159ff. Bramson, Ruth N. (2000), p. 65. Dickmann, Michael (2002), pp. 60ff. Pfeffer, Jeffrey (1994) (entire book).

[153] Cf. Mc Leod, Douglas (2001), pp. 6f. Redman, Tom/Mathews, Brian P. (1998), p. 58.

[154] Cf. Birkinshaw, Julian/Bresman, Henrik/Hakanson, Lars (2000), pp. 400ff. Similarly cf. Galpin, Timothy J./Herndon, Mark (2000), p. 8.

[155] M&A management activities can be of short or middle term nature. Cf. chapter 1.4.5.

[156] Cf. McKay, Jim/Qureshi, Imran (2001), p. 37.

[157] Cf. Uder, Helmuth L./Kramarsch, Michael H. (2001), pp. 328f.

[158] Cf. De Voge, Sylvia/Shiraki, Jeffrey (2000), p. 30. Deering, Anne/Dilts, Robert/Russell, Julian (2002), p. 35.

[159] Cf. Uder, Helmuth L./Kramarsch, Michael H. (2001), pp. 328f. Howell, Robert A. (1970), pp. 68f.

[160] Cf. Schweiger, David M./Ivancevich, John M./Power, Frank R. (1987), p. 128. Neumann, Petra/Rumpf, Bernd-Michael (1998), p. 62.

new technical requirements arise in the context of such transactions.[161] **Social change competence** can be relevant, as M&A transactions can imply social changes, such as new roles and assignments, new jobs, modified working conditions, new colleagues, superiors and collaborators, changes in organisational status and in corporate culture.[162]

2.2 Focus Areas in line with Merger & Acquisition Management Objectives

The competences in figure 2.2 are assumed to be of varying relevance depending on the objectives underlying an M&A transaction.[163] In the following, a selected number of M&A objectives[164], which are free of intersections with each other, are elaborated on regarding the competence requirements that result from them.[165] Interdependencies between the M&A management objectives within each management dimension and in between the management dimensions are discussed.[166]

---

161 Cf. Schweiger, David M./Ivancevich, John M. (1987), p. 47. Napier, Nancy K. (1989), p. 277.

162 Cf. Buono, Anthony F./Bowditch, James L. (1989), p. 15. Ivancevich, John M./Schweiger, David M./Power, Frank R. (1987), pp. 21f. Jansen, Stephan A./Pohlmann, Niko (2000), p. 30. Gerpott, Torsten J. (1993), p. 106.

163 Cf. Cascio, Wayne F./Sweet, Donald H. (1988), pp. 2 – 62.

164 The selection of these M&A management objectives has been made based on a review of roughly fifty M&A literature sources (other than the ones in chapter 2.1.2). The following literature sources have been reviewed. Ansoff, Igor H. (1957), p. 115ff. Bamberger, Burkhard (1994), pp. 202 – 204. Blasko, Matej/Netter, Jeffrey M./Sinkey, Joseph F. (2000), p. 79. Buono, Anthony F./Bowditch, James L. (1989), p. 143. Cartwright, Sue/Cooper, Cary L. (1996), pp. 10ff. Clever, Holger (1993), pp. 11, 16. Copeland, Thomas E./Weston, Fred J. (1992), p. 682. Datta, Deepak K. (1991), pp. 283ff. Datta, Deepak K./Grant, John H. (1990), p. 32. Deiser, Roland (1994), p. 380. Dielmann, Klaus (1997), p. 479. Eccles, Robert G./Lanes, Kersten L./Wilson, Thomas C. (2000), p. 84. Gaughan, Patrick A. (2002), pp. 111 – 157. Gerpott, Torsten J. (1993), p. 63. Gut-Villa, Cornelia (1997), p. 67. Haspeslagh, Philippe C./Jemison, David B. (1991), p. 145. Haspeslagh, Philippe C./Jemison, David B. (1992), p. 174. Hofstede, Gerd (1983), pp. 78ff. Ivancevich, John M./Schweiger, David M./Power, Frank R. (1989), p. 30. Jaeger, Michael (2001), pp. 24, 75. Jansen, Stephan A. (2001), pp. 70 – 107. Jansen, Stephan A. (2002), p. 10. Koch, Tomas (2001), pp. 167f. Lajoux, Alexandra Reed (1998), p. 35. Larsson, Rikard/Finkelstein, Sydney (1999), p. 4. Lüdi, Markus/Eicken, Sabine (2000a), pp. 11, 12, 14f. Nahavandi, Afsaneh/Malekzadeh, Ali R. (1988), pp. 82f. Nahavandi, Afsaneh/Malekzadeh, Ali R. (1994), pp. 295f. Napier, Nancy K. (1989), p. 280. Pablo, Amy (1994), pp. 806 – 809. Pritchett, Price (1985), pp. 5ff. Reineke, Björn (2001), pp. 71 – 89. Salecker, Jürgen (1995), pp. 13, 15, 27. Schmidt, Sascha L./Schettler, Marc A. (1999), p. 313. Schweiger, David M./Ivancevich, John M./Power, Frank R. (1987), p. 131. Shrivastava, Paul (1986), pp. 68ff. Steinöcker, Reinhard (1998), pp. 10, 118. Töpfer, Armin (2000), p. 11. Uder, Helmuth L./Kramarsch, Michael H. (2001), pp. 3ff. Vahs, Dietmar/Wuth, Steffen (2001), p. 671. Vogel, Dieter (2002), pp. 149, 257ff, 261f. Werner, Markus (1999), pp. 333f. Wirtgen, Jörg (1999), p. 7. Wood, Judy (1992), pp. 48, 51ff. Zwahlen, Beat (1994), pp. 23, 60 – 86, 266f. Three criteria were used to select M&A objectives for the subsequent argumentation. First, their frequency of appearance in the literature reviewed, second, their use for enhancing the multidimensional perspective of analysis of this study, and third, their expected impact on the human resource requirements in an M&A transaction were considered. The rationale for putting the most frequently named objectives first has been the practical research goal of this study. Mixtures of sources and publication dates have been the underlying principles for the literature review. This has been done to enhance part of the practical research goal of this thesis (broad applicability).

165 To reduce the subjectivity of the assignment of competences to M&A objectives, a second person has repeated the assignment. More than 90% of all assignments made by the second person were identical to those made for the HRDD Concept.

166 This is done due to the systemic philosophical positioning of this thesis and the resulting holistic, circular way of thinking. Cf. Ulrich, Hans (2001), pp. 118ff.

Those competences which are considered as highly relevant are referred to in terms of the reasons for their importance when a specific M&A objective is pursued.[167] The M&A management objectives referred to in the following represent extremes which have consciously been selected from the M&A literature reviewed. After having defined which competences out of the catalogue in figure 2.2 are of high relevance to which M&A objective and why, determinants of the competences' parameter-value are defined for each M&A objective. This is in order to take the variety of nuances which business practice can choose when defining its M&A objectives into consideration.[168]

The competences can also be of different relevance, depending on the employee groups that are at the centre of attention. Some competences are solely relevant for employees at lower levels in the hierarchy and others for managers, either of one or of both firms. Some competences are relevant in the short term, whereas others are required in the middle term. Differences in the time horizon of the human resource requirements are alluded to. Finally, the relevance of the competences can depend on whether Human Resource Due Diligence is conducted in a merger, in an acquisition or in a spin off. Differences are highlighted, if applicable.

2.2.1 Focus Areas in line with Strategic Objectives

Strategic management deals with the long term development of the firm.[169] Two types of strategic M&A management objectives are examined in the following paragraphs as regards their impact on the relevance of the competences from figure 2.2, namely internal objectives (chapter 2.2.1.1) and external objectives (chapter 2.2.1.2). The first type of objectives deals with firms' internal value creation. The reason for selecting the first type of management objectives has been its frequency of appearance in the M&A literature reviewed. The second type of strategic M&A objectives has been chosen to broaden the perspective on strategic management taken in this thesis by an external one.[170] Hence, the rationale for selecting the second type of objectives has been to vary argumentation and not to account for its frequency of appearance in the M&A literature reviewed. After defining focus areas for HRDD related to both types of M&A management objectives, interdependencies between the Strategic M&A management objectives are discussed (chapter 2.2.1.3).

---

[167] To do so, the general reasons for the relevance of the different competences in an M&A context, as presented in chapter 2.1.2, are applied to different M&A objectives. To facilitate the presentation of step 1 of the Concept, only highly and less relevant competences are distinguished in the subsequent argumentation. Still, in real M&A transactions, no dichotomy exists, but instead, desired parameter values need to be assigned to all competences.

[168] Cf. chapter 1.3.2 practical research goal of this study.

[169] Cf. chapter 1.4.5.

[170] Two classical views of corporate strategy are often distinguished in academic literature – the market and the resource based view. According to Müller-Stewens/Lechner, strategic management deals with the design of strategic measures of the firm, it's positioning towards external stakeholders (including competitors) and patterns of internal value creation. Cf. Müller-Stewens, Günter/Lechner, Christoph (2003), p. 3.

2.2.1.1 Focus Areas in line with Internal Strategic Objectives

Internal objectives for carrying out M&A encompass objectives related to value creation within the firm.[171] Different internal objectives for engaging in an M&A transaction have been found in the M&A literature reviewed. This thesis follows the categorisation by Jaeger, as he depicts the most frequently named objectives, namely[172]

(1) Synergy objective,

(2) Financial return objective,

(3) Resource access objective and

(4) Status objective.

(1) One reason for firms to enter into an M&A transaction is to become more efficient[173] by utilising synergies. Synergies are achieved if the sum of a whole exceeds the sum of its components.[174] According to Ansoff, M&A can imply that the total performance of a new firm is higher than the sum of the potential performances of the individual firms if they had remained independent.[175] Attaining this performance edge requires the realisation of synergies. Synergies are assumed to comprise all efficiency effects that can be brought about upon completion of an M&A transaction through economies of scope.[176]

Three different types of synergies can be distinguished – operating, financial and management synergies. Operating synergies bring about efficiency effects if similar functions of the M&A parties' value chains are combined. Financial synergies lead to more advantageous borrowing conditions on the capital market. Management synergies allow one to use the most cost efficient management team and management system upon completion of an M&A.[177] In the following, operating synergies are at the core, since they are a frequently named type of synergies[178], and are assumed to imply the most human resource requirements out of the three types.

If operating synergies are supposed to be achieved upon completion of an M&A transaction, employees are required to support the realisation of these synergies. To be able to support the realisation of the efficiency effects, employees should possess the following competences – motivation, innovation, internal, functional, process, planning, and decision-making competence. The substance of **motivation competence** can be

---

171 Cf. Clever, Holger (1993), p. 16.
172 Cf. Jaeger, Michael (2001), p. 24.
173 Efficiency is defined as the ability of pursuing business activities at low cost using few resources. Cf. Thommen, Jean-Paul (2004b), p. 178.
174 Cf. Thommen, Jean-Paul (2004b), p. 599.
175 Cf. Ansoff, Igor H. (1965), pp. 50f.
176 Cf. Sandler, Guido G. (1991, pp. 4ff.
177 Cf. Jaeger, Michael (2001), p. 21.
178 Cf. Blasko, Matej/Netter, Jeffrey M./Sinkey, Joseph F. (2000), p. 79.

explained by the fact that synergistic M&A transaction are often accompanied by a downsizing.[179] Human resources, like as all other resources, can be economised by combining certain stages of the M&A parties' value chains. To prevent negative motivation effects of downsizing for those remaining with the new firm, managers are required to enthuse employees at lower levels for the new firm.[180] **Innovation competence** is relevant to support the efficiency effects to be brought about by a consolidation of similar functions in the M&A parties' value chains. For instance, the realisation of synergies can presuppose process innovations.[181] In synergetic M&A, **internal competence** eases the combination of (parts of) the M&A parties' value chains. The value chains of the M&A transaction parties need to be well known and respected in order for operating synergies to be attained.[182] It must be considered how the various functions of the firms depend on one another and how changes in one part affect the others. **Functional competence** is also required if synergies are aimed at in M&A. This is due to the efficiency effects of functional competence. When operating synergies are pursued by combining similar functions of the M&A parties' value chains, employees with a maximum of functional competence must be identified. In this way, the efficiency of the new firm can be superior to the efficiency of the formerly independent firms, for the selected functions. The same characteristics also apply to **process competence**. Its importance can be explained by its potential positive effect on the efficiency of the new firm's processes. **Planning competence** is needed for establishing a time, quality and cost framework for the realisation of synergies. The timing of synergy realisation has an effect on its success, as the accrued costs of synergy realisation should not exceed the benefits from it.[183] Quality means that the realised synergies should be equal to the ones aimed at. When deciding for which functions of the firms' value chains synergies are supposed to be realised and in which way, **decision-making competence** is important.

The human resource requirements presented above relate to all employees to whom the aim of realising synergies applies. Sometimes firms involved in an M&A transaction intend to realise economies of scope only for certain stages in their value chains, but sometimes, all stages of their value chains can be concerned. The more enthusiastically the synergies are aimed at, the higher the significance of the competences mentioned above. Regarding the time horizons of the competences, presumably motivation, internal, planning, and decision-making competence are required in the short term. Innovation, functional, and process competence are demanded more in the middle term.

---

179 Often, operating synergies imply staff reductions. Cf. Vogel, Dieter H. (2002), p. 37.

180 Cf. Salecker, Jürgen (1995), p. 8. Salecker mentions the importance of communicating with employees. Given the competence definitions of this thesis, the quotation is used to underline the importance of motivation competence.

181 Cf. Liepmann, Detlev/König, Ferdinand/Stübig, Jacob. In: Marggraf, Claudia (Ed.) (1995), p. 142. Eccles, Robert G./Lanes, Kersten L./Wilson, Thomas C. (2000), p. 84.

182 Cf. Sandler, Guido G. (1991), p. 20.

183 When synergies are reached, often, social cost implied by them can outweigh the efficiency effects in a transaction. Cf. Vogel, Dieter H. (2002), p. 37.

(2) Another possible internal objective underlying M&A transactions is to produce a financial return. Firms are sometimes acquired (and integrated), because an investor assumes that they possess a short or middle term value creation potential. By contrast, firms are sometimes sold, because an investor doubts their (further) value creation potential.[184]

If the underlying objective of an M&A is financial, employees are required to support the realisation of value creation. The following competences are relevant in financial M&A – motivation, innovation, internal, market, functional, process, planning, and decision-making competence. The importance of **motivation competence** can be explained by the fact that the target firm's managers need to support potential strategic changes brought about by an investor. Only if managers facilitate these changes, can a value creation potential be turned into an actual value increases.[185] Moreover, **innovation competence** is crucial in financial M&A. On the one hand, process innovations may be required to enhance the efficiency of the firm upon completion of the acquisition. On the other hand, product innovations can be useful to foster the firm's competitive position and hence increase its value. In financial M&A, **internal competence** is necessary for the investor to understand how the functions of the target firm depend on each other. By considering the characteristics of internal structures when introducing value creation measures, changes in one function are prevented from unexpectedly affecting another.[186] The relevance of **market competence** is twofold. First, employees with market competence support the investor in determining the short or middle term strategy of the firm after the M&A. Second, the adequacy of all the operative measures that need to be introduced can be appraised, given this strategy. Thus, the less the investor knows about the market the firm is active in, the more important market competence is.[187] **Functional competence** is also required if one assumes that a financial return is aimed for in an M&A. The reason for this lies in the significance of functional competence for competitive advantage. Certain functions of the target firm can be fundamental to the competitive advantage of the new firm. If the strategy of the target firm – as it was prior to the M&A transaction – is retained, the major functions are likely to be known to its managers. If the strategy of the firm is changed upon completion of the M&A, the major functions may have to be newly defined. The same applies to process competence as to functional competence. The substance of **process competence** can be explained by the relevance of certain business processes for the competitive advantage of the new firm upon completion of the M&A transactions. Employees with **planning competence** are needed in financial M&A for two purposes. First, they are relevant when a new strategy is/must be formulated upon

[184] Large holding companies can e.g. invest their free cash flows by purchasing new subsidiaries. Cf. Copeland, Thomas E./Weston, Fred J. (1992), p. 682.

[185] This can also imply that, for the good of the financial investment, certain managers who are unwilling to enthuse employees for the new firm, should leave. Cf. Bergh, Donald D. (2001), p. 620.

[186] Given the fact that many financial investors pursue a – as Siehl/Smith/Omura put it – pillage and plunder strategy, internal competence is often required to keep (harmful) changes to internal structures to a minimum. Cf. Siehl, Caren/Smith, Dayle/Kissinger Omura, Ann (1990), p. 51.

[187] Cf. Gaughan, Patrick A. (2002), pp. 130f.

completion of an M&A. Second, they are vital when determining operative measures to be pursued to implement the new strategy in the middle and in the short term (transition measures). **Decision-making competence** is significant when selecting a strategy from several alternative strategies upon completion of an M&A, but also when choosing measures to put the selected strategy into action. Without decision-making competence, the choice of a strategy and of measures could be based on one-sided considerations.[188]

These human resource requirements apply to all employees whose behaviour is important for enhancing value creation upon completion of a financial M&A. The higher the intended increase of the firm's value, the more important the competences are. Motivation, internal, planning, and decision-making competence are presumably rather required in the short term, and innovation, market, functional, and process competence rather in the middle term.

If a financial M&A takes place for de-investment purposes, employees of the firm that undertakes the spin off are required to support the sale. The same human resource requirements as for a financial merger or acquisition result from the need to support the spin off, but in part for different reasons. The significance of motivation competence can be explained by the fact that a spin off may possibly be interpreted as a failure by the investor's employees. Someone is required to motivate them to identify with the new investment opportunities. Innovation competence can be relevant in order to smoothly separate the formerly integrated firms from each other. Internal competence is necessary for the financial investor to prevent important functions of its own business from disappearing with the spin off.[189] If the financial investor aims to remain in the market the firm to be spun off is active in, it should be ensured that market competence does not disappear. At the same time, limiting the market of the spin off can lead to failure of the newly created firm and thereby damage the reputation of the seller. The reputation of the seller is also endangered if the buyer is equipped with too little functional and/or process competence. Employees with planning competence are important when determining operative measures to implement a spin off, but also when planning for the future strategy of the investor. The reasons for the relevance of decision-making competence in spin offs are identical to the reasons for its relevance in mergers or acquisitions.

(3) Firms involved in resource-related M&A transactions aim at acquiring resources that are necessary to create competitive advantage and dispose of such resources that are unimportant for it.[190] The rationale for deciding to purchase resources in an M&A transaction instead of producing them internally can be that the estimated costs of

---

[188] Cf. Schweiger, David M./Ivancevich, John M./Power, Frank R. (1987), p. 128.

[189] Cf. Jansen, Stephan A. (2001), pp. 104ff. Jansen does not explicitly refer to financial investors, but according to him, one potential reason for carrying out an M&A transaction is to focus on core competences.

[190] Cf. Haspeslagh, Phillipe C./Jemison, David B. (1991), pp. 107ff. Grant, Robert M. (1991), pp. 119ff. Wright, Patrick M./Rowland, Kendrith M./Ferris, Gerald R. (1994), p. 307. Müller, Werner R. In: Bruhn, Manfred (Ed.) (1998), p. 241. Barney, James B. (1991), pp. 105f.

producing the resources exceed the purchase price.[191] The other way around, one reason for firms to sell off resources to other firms in an M&A can lie in the fact that other firms are able to use these better than the firm itself.

Resources can be of a tangible or intangible nature. Examples of tangible resources include real estate, plants, machines and inventories. Intangible resources encompass knowledge, skills, patents and licences.[192] In this thesis, intangible resources – namely knowledge and skills – are the focus of attention.[193] If an M&A takes place for the resource access objective, employees are required to make the desired transfer of knowledge and skills possible.

The following human resource requirements result from the need to support the resource transfer. To enable a successful transfer of knowledge and skills between the firms involved in an M&A, **communication competence** is of high importance. The reason for this is the higher communication density due to additional communication channels between the different functions of the formerly independent firms. Communication competence encourages the exchange of difficult-to-transfer aspects of knowledge and skills – for instance tacit knowledge – are exchanged between the employees of both firms.[194]) Inter-firm teams may be created in between those functions where a knowledge and skill transfer is supposed to take place. **Co-operation competence** is a prerequisite for these teams to be successful. If an M&A transaction takes place for resource access reasons and the resources to be transferred are knowledge and skills, **innovation competence** can be of great importance. Often, firms do not differ in the way they sell already existing products, but in their innovation rates.[195] Therefore, when carrying out a resource access M&A, it should be evaluated whether employees are innovative. The value of the knowledge and skills that are transmitted and further made use of upon completion of an M&A also depends on the market they are used for. If the market evolves faster than the transaction parties of an M&A, (old) knowledge may no longer be of use to obtain competitive advantage.[196] Therefore, **market competence** is relevant in resource access M&A to verify the significance of the to-be-acquired knowledge and skills. **Planning competence** is needed in resource access M&A to assess which functions knowledge and skills shall be transferred to. Moreover, planning competence helps define possible measures to bring about the desired resource transfer, and determine a time and quality horizon for it. When plans are made, **decision-making** competence is required to choose between alternative functions of and measures for a resource transfer. If M&A

---

[191] Cf. Williamson, Oliver E. (1990), p. 194. Wirtz, Bernd W. (2003), pp. 25ff. In that case, the transaction parties must fit strategically with each other. Cf. Shelton, Lois M. (1988), pp. 279f.

[192] Cf. Gerpott, Torsten J. (1993), pp. 85ff. Gerpott distinguishes between management skills, tangible resources and functional knowledge. On knowledge, cf. Süverkrüp, Christian (1990) (entire book).

[193] The reason for this is the Human Resource Due Diligence definition of this study. Cf. chapter 1.4.3.

[194] Cf. Ranft, Annette L./Lord, Michael D. (2000), p. 297.

[195] Cf. Liepmann, Detlev/König, Ferdinand/Stübig, Jacob. In: Marggraf, Claudia (Ed.) (1995), p. 144. According to Liepmann/König/Stübig, innovation culture makes innovative firms stand out against others.

[196] Cf. Teece, David J./Pisano, Gary/Shuen, Amy (1997), pp. 509f.

take place for resource access reasons and the resources to be transferred are knowledge and skills, **technical change competence** can be of great importance. Given the decreasing half-life time of knowledge, knowledge or skills purchased today are often outdated tomorrow.[197]

The above-mentioned human resource requirements apply to employees of both firms, and can be relevant at different levels in the firms' hierarchies. Planning and decision-making competence are presumably most relevant at high levels in the hierarchies. Market, planning, and decision-making competence are needed in the short term, and communication, co-operation, innovation, and technical change competence are required in the middle term.

If an M&A takes place to dispose of resources, employees are required to show broadly the same competences as in resource access transactions. They must fulfil these requirements for the resource transfer to be attractive to the potential buyer. Transferring worthless resources would benefit neither the seller nor the buyer.[198] Innovation, market, and technical change competence should be shaped in a way to benefit the buyer. At the same time, the seller must ensure that he does not sell off resources that carry competences which might have been relevant for the future.

The degree of importance of the above competences can differ depending on the direction of the M&A transaction that is referred to. The following directions for M&A transactions were mentioned in the M&A literature reviewed – horizontal, vertical and conglomerate.[199] Horizontal transactions are carried out between two competitors that operate in very similar businesses on the same market and at the same stage in the value chain. In vertical M&A, transaction parties are active in the same kind of business, but the business of one firm operates at a stage further up or down the value chain compared to the other firm. Conglomerate transactions are carried out between two firms that are active in two unrelated businesses.[200] It is assumed that the knowledge and skills gap between the transaction parties is the lowest in horizontal and the highest in conglomerate transactions. Accordingly, the competences are least relevant in horizontal and most relevant in conglomerate transactions, at least from a strategic perspective. From a structural perspective, the competences may carry different weight.

(4) Apart from the objectives outlined above, M&A transactions can be pursued due to personal (non value creating) management objectives. Several different types of personal management objectives have been distinguished in the M&A literature reviewed. In the following, the most frequently named objective – the status objective – is considered.

---

197 Translation by the author, original: "Halbwertszeit des Wissens". Cf. Albath, Andreas (2002), p. 14.

198 The seller would lose his reputation, and the buyer would not be able to make use of the resources in the intended way.

199 Cf. Clever, Holger (1993a), p. 11. Zwahlen, Beat (1994), p. 23.

200 Cf. Clever, Holger (1993a), p. 11.

M&A sometimes take place, because management intends to increase its own status and influence by augmenting the size of the firm it represents.[201] In M&A transactions that take place due to management's aim of increasing its own status, employees are required to show uncertainty and motivation competence. Given the fact that no value creation is aimed for in an M&A transaction that takes place for status reasons, the usefulness of the transaction from a strategic perspective may be limited.[202] Hence the future of the firms involved in such transactions can be described as unclear, which is why **uncertainty competence** is required. Uncertainty is worsened from the perspective of employees at lower levels, if managers fail to communicate effectively with them. The relevance of **motivation competence** can be traced back to the lack of a strategic rationale behind a status transaction and the communication gap potentially caused by managers. Given the uncertainty that employees at lower levels of the firms involved in an M&A face, managers must be able to keep their employees committed despite uncertainty. This can include competence in making employees at lower levels accept the M&A transaction without understanding its background.[203]

Table 2.1 summarises which competences are considered highly relevant for which internal strategic objective.

Internal Strategic Objectives / Competence	Synergy Objective	Financial Return Objective	Resource Access Objective	Status Objective
Uncertainty Competence				•
Communication Competence			•	
Conflict Competence				
Motivation Competence	•	•		•
Co-operation Competence			•	
Innovation Competence	•	•	•	
Internal Competence	•	•		
Market Competence		•	•	
Socio-cultural Competence				
Complexity Competence				
Functional Competence	•	•		
Process Competence	•	•		
Planning Competence	•	•	•	
Problem-solving Competence				
Organisation Competence				
Decision-making Competence	•	•	•	
Social Change Competence				
Technical Change Competence			•	

Table 2.1: Competences and Internal M&A Management Objectives

201 Cf. Jaeger, Michael (2001), p. 25.
202 Cf. Töpfer, Armin (2000), p. 11.
203 Cf. Donahue, Kristen B. (2001), p. 1. According to Donahue, otherwise many change efforts can fall victim to politics.

2.2.1.2 *Focus Areas in line with External Strategic Objectives*

Besides internal objectives, a firm can also pursue external strategic objectives when carrying out an M&A transaction.[204] These relate to the firm's envisaged positioning on the markets it is active on. Different categorisations for external objectives have been found in the M&A literature reviewed. This thesis follows the categorisation by Ansoff, since it contains the most cited M&A objectives in the literature reviewed. Ansoff distinguishes between four external strategic objectives (see figure 2.3), namely

(1) Diversification objective,

(2) Market development objective,

(3) Market penetration objective and

(4) Product development objective.

Markets / Products	Current	Future
Current	Market Penetration	Market Development
Future	Product Development	Diversification

Figure 2.3: Product Market Matrix

Source: Ansoff, Igor H. (1957), p. 115ff.

(1) One reason for M&A transaction to occur is that the firms involved aim to enter new markets. Firms that conduct M&A transactions for diversification reasons aim to absorb new products into their product portfolio.[205] Often, firms aim to spread their business risk to a broader range of products, which can be done by accommodating additional ones in new markets.[206] Alternatives to diversification through M&A their own research & development activities or joint ventures.[207] If firms decide to enter into an M&A transaction, this can – as for the resource access objective – be explained by transaction cost theory. Employees are required to ensure the success of diversification, expressed as a successful absorption of additional products from new markets into the M&A parties' product portfolios. To enable the integration of additional products, **innovation competence** should be considered in Human Resource Due Diligence. This is because obtaining the production facilities of another firm through an M&A is no guarantee of a successful product development in the future, especially not on unknown markets. Therefore, innovation competence is of high strategic importance. This is especially the case, since firms that pursue diversification M&A are often not acquainted with the other transaction party's products. Besides innovation competence, **market competence** is also required. It is

[204] Cf. Clever, Holger (1993), p. 16.
[205] Cf. Ansoff, Igor H. (1957), p. 115ff.
[206] Cf. Thommen, Jean-Paul (2004b), p. 165.
[207] Cf. Wirtz, Bernd W. (2003), pp. 14f.

necessary to determine the strategic positioning of the newly acquired products on their markets. Moreover, market competence can be useful in forecasting and steering the future development of these products. If certain functions of the M&A parties' business are what makes the transaction parties' products successful, **functional competence** is critical in HRDD because of the specific functions that it is related to. In this context, benchmarking can be an appropriate way of determining why the functions of one business are more successful than those of another. The same can also apply to **process competence** as to functional competence when the specifics of the newly obtained products are based on particular processes.

The specialist competences mentioned above, which are important if the diversification objective is pursued, are relevant at those levels in the hierarchy at which specialists for the acquired products can be found. The same applies to innovation competence. Market competence is of interest at rather higher levels in the hierarchy. All competences are crucial in the middle term, and none is in the short term.

In the case of a spin-off, the same competences as for a merger or an acquisition should be concentrated on in Human Resource Due Diligence. However, in a spin off, the aim of competence analysis is not to ensure successful product absorption. Instead, the competences are vital for investigating to make sure that the transaction party receives only the competences it is supposed to and no other. When undertaking a spin off, transferring the wrong competences to the buyer can result in a loss of competences that are important for the future.

(2) Besides aiming to enter new unrelated markets, firms sometimes also decide to carry out M&A to develop their current markets.[208] This can be done by introducing existing products on new (foreign) markets, by making new applications of existing products accessible or by tapping new customer groups.[209] To achieve the market development objective, employees must contribute to the success of the measures described. Accordingly, the following competences should be taken into consideration in Human Resource Due Diligence when the market development objective is aimed for. **Innovation competence** can be relevant, though not as defined in chapter 2.1.1 (product or process innovations). Instead, it can be a precondition for finding new applications for existing products. **Market competence** is central in HRDD, since knowing about the competitive situation on potential future markets can be considered indispensable for M&A success. Understanding customers' needs in terms of demand for further product applications can also be considered a key factor. Finally, market segmentation and the corresponding customer (group) preferences are highly important. To enable the entry into new markets, the introduction of new product applications and the contacting of new customer groups, **functional competence** is decisive. In particular, employees in those functions of the M&A

[208] Cf. Ansoff, Igor H. (1957), p. 115ff.
[209] Ditto.

parties' value chains which are indispensable for the success of market development should be evaluated in Human Resource Due Diligence.[210] **Process competence** can also be important, for instance if new product applications require the introduction of processes different from old ones. Moreover, approaching new customer groups can require an entirely different customer relationship management from targeting old customer groups.[211] Upon completion of an M&A transaction, plans must be set up how to position the new firm strategically against its competitors (**planning competence**) in order to achieve the market development objectives. Besides, alternative measures need to be weighed against each other to best reach the strategic objective (decision-making competence). **Decision-making competence** is beneficial when evaluating the adequacy of alternative measures. For instance decision-making rules can help one arrive at a result.[212]

The above mentioned competences are seen as highly relevant in market development transactions and can be required from employees at all levels. Market competence alone is presumably relevant at a rather higher level in the hierarchy, since its strategic importance is at the core. Planning and decision-making competence are required in the short term, whereas innovation, market, functional, and process competence are essential primarily in the middle term.

In the case of spin offs, as for acquisitions and mergers, innovation, market competence, all specialist competences, planning, and decision-making competence are vital. If a firm disposes of a part of itself in order to abandon existing market segments, to abolish existing product variations or to leave certain geographical areas, this implies the following for Human Resource Due Diligence: it must be ensured that only those innovation, market and specialist competences disappear that are required for the future development of the parts which it is intended to abandon. A spin off may easily be carried out without recognising that, for instance, important innovation competences needed for remaining in core markets are lost when certain employees leave the firm.

(3) Market penetration refers to a type of M&A transaction motivated by the aim of being more intensely active than before on existing markets.[213] These transactions take place between firms that are active in the same market (segments). Higher market penetration can be achieved by increasing the number of products sold per customer or by increasing the number of buyers.[214] A prerequisite for market penetration M&A to be feasible is that the M&A parties offer the same types of products and have the same customers. The success of market penetration M&A can be measured in the market share of the new firm after the M&A in comparison to the market shares of the firms prior to the M&A. Two human resource requirements are particularly important for such M&A transactions. First,

---

210 Depending on the industry, these functions can be sales, production and/or research and development.
211 Cf. Thommen, Jean-Paul (2002), p. 179.
212 Cf. Jungermann, Helmut. In: Sarges, Werner (Ed.) (2000), p. 248.
213 Cf. Ansoff, Igor H. (1957), p. 115ff.
214 Ditto.

in order to coordinate the activities of the new firm after completion of the transaction, plans should be set up (**planning competence**). A coordination of activities involves setting up a joint strategy to prevent resource-consuming overlaps between the formerly independent firms. Second, **decision-making competence** is needed to suitably choose between alternative ways of coordinating future activities[215], e.g. when determining who is in charge of which new customer(s). A sale of market share is rare, which is why the relevance of the competences in spin offs is not discussed. The above-named competences are presumably most relevant for managers, for they are required to plan and decide how to realise the market penetration objective. Both competences are essential in the short term.

(4) The fourth M&A objective mentioned in Ansoff's product market matrix is product development. In some cases, firms decide to carry out M&A to be able to launch new products on existing markets.[216] Presumably, an M&A is carried out instead of developing new products internally, due to a too long and/or too costly product development process. Hence, product development is successful if, after completion of the transaction, new products can be introduced timely. The costs of an M&A should also be lower than the costs of product development. As a prerequisite to the attainment of the product development objective, the following competences should be considered. First, **innovation competence** should be assessed in Human Resource Due Diligence, since existing markets can only be supplied with new products if the competences underlying these products are (still) available. Moreover, innovation competence is important for future product developments (if the market is subject to fast changes). Second, **market competence** is central in product development M&A, since a firm aiming to (continuously) launch new products must understand its customers' needs. Innovation competence is mostly needed at lower levels in the hierarchy, whereas market competence can be important at all levels. Given the need for timely product innovations, both competences are decisive in the short term.

As can be seen from table 2.2, none of the highlighted competences is crucial for all of the four external strategic objectives. Presuming the objective is diversification, market development and product development, innovation and market competence are highly valued, whereas supposing the objective is market penetration, planning and decision-making are vital.

---

[215] Cf. Ueckert, Hans. In: Sarges, Werner (Ed.) (2000), pp. 255f.
[216] Cf. Ansoff, Igor H. (1957), p. 115ff.

External Strategic Objectives / Competence	Diversification Objective	Market Development Objective	Market Penetration Objective	Product Development Objective
Uncertainty Competence				
Communication Competence				
Conflict Competence				
Motivation Competence				
Co-operation Competence				
Innovation Competence	•	•		•
Internal Competence				
Market Competence	•	•		•
Socio-cultural Competence				
Complexity Competence				
Functional Competence	•	•		
Process Competence	•	•		
Planning Competence		•	•	
Problem-solving Competence				
Organisation Competence				
Decision-making Competence		•	•	
Social Change Competence				
Technical Change Competence				

Table 2.2: Competences and External M&A Management Objectives

2.2.1.3 Interdependencies between Strategic Objectives

As stated in the introduction of chapter 2, there are interdependencies between the strategic management objectives. Internal and external types of M&A objectives are often pursued simultaneously. Different views on the long term development of the firm after the M&A are taken when defining internal and external objectives. Ideally, the parties involved in an M&A transaction should know about the new firm's external objectives when deciding on appropriate internal objectives and vice versa. Knowing what customers want is a precondition for developing suitable resources internally. At the same time, internal strengths must be known to be able to position the new firm on future markets. Internal and external objectives should be in line with each other for management to reach its objectives the best possible. Still, in business practice, internal and external objectives may also contradict each other, especially if management objectives are not set unanimously. Alternatively, firms may consciously set themselves internal objectives, and thereby unconsciously set themselves external objectives, which ensue logically from the internal objectives. Competence requirements that ensue from both types of objectives should be considered in HRDD.

As illustrated when defining focus areas for HRDD for the different internal and external objectives, there are differences in the competence groups that are considered relevant. In the case of internal objectives, the entire spectrum of competence groups is vital in HRDD. At the same time, supposing external objectives, Human Resource Due Diligence should focus on systems, specialist, and methods competence. Direct implications for every day work can be deduced from internal M&A objectives, whereas not from external objectives, which explains the different focus areas that ensue from both types of objectives. However, given the fact that internal M&A objectives should be in line with external objectives, it may ensue that the M&A parties collaborate operationally when market development is aimed for. Hence, indirectly, also social and change competence can be important. Still, there are also alternatives to collaboration: if the M&A parties possess very different knowledge, they can split up the market between them. Sometimes, the same competences are required for internal and external M&A objectives, but due to different reasons. The focus areas for HRDD which result from these objectives can e.g. relate to several employee groups or time horizons. Also, the different reasons for the relevance of the competences may be reflected in different indicators that are developed for the generation of HRDD information.

No matter whether internal and external objectives are in line, contradict each other and/or are unconsciously aimed for, when defining focus areas for HRDD a maximum of competences should be considered. This is necessary to account for the specifics of the M&A transaction, in which the HRDD concept is applied.

2.2.2 Focus Areas in line with Structural Objectives

Structure refers to organisational, rather technical aspects of management.[217] Organisational structure can be subdivided into formal and informal structure.[218] Formal organisational structure refers to the desired division of labour within a firm and has an impact on the behavioural requirements imposed on the members of an organisation. Informal organisational structure describes the actual division of labour within the same firm, which can differ from what is desired. This thesis focuses on formal organisation structure, since concrete management objectives presumably relate to it more frequently than to (often unintended) informal structure.[219] Three types of structural management objectives are examined in the following paragraphs as regards their impact on the relevance of the human resource requirements in figure 2.2, namely macro structure objectives (chapter 2.2.2.1), micro structure objectives (chapter 2.2.2.2) and task spectra objectives (chapter 2.2.2.3).

The first type of objectives refers to the way in which the firms are supposed to coexist on an organisational level after completion of the M&A transaction. The reason for selecting the first type of structural M&A management objectives is its frequency of appearance in the M&A literature reviewed. The second type of structural M&A objective concentrates on the coexistence of specific parts of the organisation, such as business units or departments. It has also been chosen due to its frequency of appearance in the M&A literature reviewed. The

217 Cf. chapter 1.4.5.
218 Cf. Thommen, Jean-Paul (2002), p. 1046.
219 Cf. Staehle, Wolfgang H. (1999), p. 466. Moreover, objectives related to informal structure are to some extent covered by cultural M&A management objectives.

third type of objective focuses on the level of individual employees. The reason for selecting this objective has partly been its appearance in the M&A literature reviewed and partly its assumed impact on human resource requirements. By covering the three structural management objectives, three different levels of abstraction are considered for working out the requirements to be imposed on employees. In this way, the relevance of the competences in figure 2.2 is investigated from three different perspectives, which is consistent with the multidimensional perspective of analysis in this study. Upon the determination of focus areas for HRDD related to the three types of structural M&A management objectives, interdependencies between these types of objectives are illustrated (chapter 2.2.2.4).

2.2.2.1 Focus Areas in line with Objectives related to Macro Structure

From the M&A literature reviewed, two opposing options have been selected which the firms involved in M&A transactions can pursue on the level of macro structure upon completion of a transaction.[220] These options are

(1) Consolidation objective and

(2) Autonomy objective.

(1) One objective often pursued by firms when involved in M&A is to consolidate their organisations.[221] The reason can be to enhance the manageability of the new firm.[222] There are several different degrees of consolidation. Consolidation can cover entire firms or certain parts of them. In the following, consolidation accompanied by the birth of an entirely new organisation is referred to.[223]

If consolidation is aimed at upon completion of an M&A, employees are required to support the achievement of this, which requires them to possess especially the following competences – communication, motivation, co-operation, complexity, functional, process, and problem-solving competence. The significance of **communication competence** can be explained by an increase in communication density upon completion of the M&A. If two firms' former organisations become part of a new one, the number of elements and

---

220 Cf. Vogel, Dieter (2002), pp. 257ff. Salecker, Jürgen (1995), p. 13. Haspeslagh, Philippe C./Jemison, David B. (1991), p. 145. Haspeslagh, Philippe C./Jemison, David B. (1992), p. 174. Werner, Markus (1999), p. 333. Wood, Judy (1992), pp. 51ff. Reed Lajoux, Alexandra (1998), p. 35. Steinöcker, Reinhard (1998), p. 118. Uder, Helmuth L./Kramarsch, Michael H. (2001), pp. 3ff. None of these authors named the two extremes concentrated on in this study, only, but also further options. To prevent the argumentation in this study from being repetitive, the two extremes are considered, and further options, that can be in place in business practice, are discussed briefly.

221 Cf. Salecker, Jürgen (1995), p. 13. Reed Lajoux, Alexandra (1998), p. 35. Steinöcker, Reinhard (1998), p. 118. Uder, Helmuth L./Kramarsch, Michael H. (2001), pp. 3ff.

222 Cf. Thommen, Jean-Paul (2002), p. 1007.

223 This is because if certain parts of the M&A parties are consolidated, the same human resource requirements are assumed to ensue for employees who work in the consolidated parts as in case of complete consolidation.

relations between these elements is likely to increase. Hence, the number of potential communication partners increases and accordingly, the importance of communication competence can be explained. Communication related to matters of fact is presumed to be important in the case of organisational consolidation to ensure information flows between the firms. **Motivation competence** is required if the consolidation objective is pursued, since thorough changes to the firms' organisations are implied. Employees at lower levels must be supported in dealing with the changes they face e.g. if they bring about a re-definition of roles and statuses.[224] If the organisational structures of the M&A parties are melted into one, both firms' employees are automatically asked to join forces. Formally defining a joint macro organisation is not sufficient for employees to be able to work with this structure. Therefore, **co-operation competence** is required. As mentioned for communication competence, the number of interdependencies and the dynamics of these interdependencies increases in consolidation M&A. To be able to create an organisational structure that helps to reduce complexity, managers must possess **complexity competence**. What is more, all employees are required to be able to deal with dynamic, multiple interdependencies in their every day work. Often similar functions of the M&A parties' value chains are subject to consolidation.[225] It is important to assess **functional competence** to make sure that those employees who are most suitable for a specific function are identified. The same can also apply to **process competence** assuming that the M&A parties are organised in terms of processes. Operational problems caused by malfunction of the new macro structure may possibly need to be solved. The most suitable way of combining the two organisations is usually not known upon completion of an M&A. The less clear the desired new macro structure, the more difficult it is to turn the status quo into the desired status. Employees with **problem-solving competence** can contribute to successful consolidation.

All competences – except motivation competence – that have been assigned high importance in consolidation M&A are relevant for all of the new firm's employees. Motivation competence applies to managers primarily, as well as the type of complexity competence required to create a new macro structure. Communication, motivation, co-operation, and complexity competence are essential to cope with transition in the short term, whilst functional, process, and problem-solving competence are more needed in the middle term.

In the case of a spin off, the same competences as in a merger or an acquisition are imperative in Human Resource Due Diligence, apart from communication, co-operation, and problem-solving competence. In a spin off, the motivation of employees at lower levels is also important to successfully detach the firms from each other. Moreover, complexity must be dealt with when determining which parts of the firm should be detached and which should be kept. It is important to assess specialist competence in Human Resource Due Diligence to make sure that no important functional or process

[224] This can be a difficult task, if there is resistance to change. Cf. Lawrence, Paul R. (1954), p. 50.
[225] Cf. Vogel, Dieter (2002), pp. 257ff.

specialists are lost. Communication competence is of less relevance in spin offs, since a part of a firm is detached and supposed to work independently. The same applies to co-operation competence. Problem-solving competence is required in order to ensure that the desired de-merged organisation can be achieved.

In the case of partial consolidation, two frequent options are to consolidate corporate centres or to consolidate subsidiaries.[226] In both cases, the same human resource requirements are relevant as for full integration. The only difference is that if partial integration is aimed at, the competences named apply solely to the employees working in the corporate centres or in the subsidiaries.

(2) Besides macro organisation consolidation, firms involved in an M&A transaction sometimes aim to give one transaction party (usually the target firm) as much autonomy as possible.[227] They can therefore decide to integrate the transaction party into a holding company.[228] Two generic types of holding companies can be distinguished.[229] These types differ according to the degree of autonomy they give to their subsidiaries. Financial holdings administrate participations in firms, but do not influence the management of their subsidiaries in any way, neither strategically nor operationally. Management holdings participate in the strategic management of their subsidiaries, but refrain from influencing their business operations.[230] Hence, subsidiaries are given a high degree of economic autonomy. In the following, management holdings are at the centre of attention, to prevent intersections with the financial return objective.

For the autonomy objective to be achieved upon completion of an M&A, managers are required to show communication and co-operation competence. They need to show co-operation competence, since the development of the new firm is determined by managers in the management holding and by managers in the subsidiaries. These two groups of managers must join forces for the good of the new firm. Joint decision-making about strategic questions can only work if managers show **co-operation competence**. The significance of **communication competence** can, similarly to co-operation competence, be explained by the strategic link between the parent company and its subsidiary(ies). Most probably for managers, communication competence serves to ensure an efficient exchange of information. Besides matters of fact, the relational component of communication can also play its part in a well functioning parent subsidiary relationship.[231] In the case of a spin off, co-operation and communication competence of subsidiary and holding managers are also important to ensure a smooth separation of the firms from each other. Both co-operation and communication competence are vital in the middle term.

---

[226] Cf. Wood, Judy (1992), pp. 51ff.
[227] Cf. Steinöcker, Reinhard (1998), p. 118.
[228] Cf. Uder, Helmuth L./Kramarsch, Michael H. (2001), pp. 3ff.
[229] Cf. Thommen, Jean-Paul (2002), pp. 1073f. Other authors may define financial holdings differently.
[230] Cf. Thommen, Jean-Paul (2002), p. 1074.
[231] Cf. Salecker, Jürgen (1995), pp. 165ff.

Table 2.3 contains the condensed results of a competence analysis for the consolidation and for the autonomy objective. As can be seen from the right column of the table, autonomy implies that only managers are required to show certain competences.

Macro Structure Objectives / Competence	Consolidation Objective	Autonomy Objective
Uncertainty Competence		
Communication Competence	•	•
Conflict Competence		
Motivation Competence	•	
Co-operation Competence	•	•
Innovation Competence		
Internal Competence		
Market Competence		
Socio-cultural Competence		
Complexity Competence	•	
Functional Competence	•	
Process Competence	•	
Planning Competence		
Problem-solving Competence	•	
Organisation Competence		
Decision-making Competence		
Social Change Competence		
Technical Change Competence		

Table 2.3: Competences and M&A Management Objectives related to Macro Structure

2.2.2.2 Focus Areas in line with Objectives related to Micro Structure

Besides defining objectives related to macro structure, firms often define M&A objectives related to micro structure, e.g. structures and processes at business unit or department level, in the context of M&A transactions. In the M&A literature reviewed, two options have been defined to describe how structures and/or processes of M&A parties can coexist upon completion of a transaction.[232] A third option[233] has been added to these two options, resulting in

(1) Reinvention objective,

(2) Linkage objective and

(3) Preservation objective.

---

[232] The reinvention and the preservation objective have been defined in the M&A literature reviewed. Cf. Wood, Judy (1992), p. 48. Koch, Tomas (2001), pp. 167f. Shrivastava, Paul (1986), pp. 68ff.

[233] The rationale for defining the linkage objective was its presumed relevance in business practice. Different human resource requirements from those for the other two options are assumed to be implied if one supposes that there will be a linkage.

(1) M&A management may envisage inventing completely new structures and processes at the business unit or department level upon completion of an M&A.[234] Reinvention means that the former structures and/or processes of the transaction parties cease to exist, and an entirely new micro structure is build. The rationale underlying reinvention is often – as presumed for this study – to create a joint, lean organisation.[235]

If reinvention is aimed at upon completion of an M&A transaction, employees are required to support its realisation. To be able to support reinvention, employees need to show all the competences in the competence grid. Only conflict, market, socio-cultural, and technical change competence seem to be of minor importance. Given the fact that in the case of reinvention, former micro organisation disappears, employees' promotion prospects can cease to exist. Moreover, individual status and recognition can be jeopardised due to **uncertainty (competence)** about the shape of the future organisation. Also, the importance of certain positions can be questioned as a consequence of reinvention. Finally, it may be unclear where departments or business units (and hence also individual positions) will be located in the future. The substance of **communication competence** can be explained by an increase in communication density when reinvention is aimed at. This increase is due to the increasing number of interdependencies as well as the increasing relevance of exchanging information in those parts of the firm that in the short run do not possess any structures and processes. To prevent employees at lower levels from being caught in a leadership vacuum when structural leadership ceases to exist, personal leadership must compensate for the missing structural framework.[236] Hence, **motivation competence** is of high relevance. **Co-operation competence** is required, since both firms' employees are required to work together. Joint decision-making enhances the efficiency of the new firm. Process innovations can be vital to successful reinvention. Therefore, **innovation competence** is critical for employees who will presumably be active in those departments or business units that are subject to changes. The number of interdependencies can, but need not increase in the middle run due to reinvention. In the short run, however, this number presumably does increase due to the necessity of trying out potentially suitable new structures and processes. Moreover, the interdependencies between the elements of the new social system are ever-changing upon completion of an M&A accompanied by reinvention (**complexity competence**). **Functional competence** should also be part of Human Resource Due Diligence. First, because employees' functional competence can determine the suitability of alternative new structures and processes. Second, since functional competence is a prerequisite for the efficiency of these new structures and processes. The same applies to **process competence** as to functional competence. For reinvention to be achieved, plans must be made about when and how and with what kinds of resources changes to micro

[234] Cf. Wood, Judy (1992), p. 48. Koch, Tomas (2001), p. 168.
[235] Cf. Wood, Judy (1992), p. 48. Koch, Tomas (2001), p. 168. Still, the strategic changes that can be implied by the reinvention objective are not at the core of this chapter.
[236] Cf. Weibler, Jürgen (2001), p. 126.

organisation shall take place (**planning competence**). For instance, it can become necessary to determine what steps are supposed to be taken to enable a smooth transition. Moreover, one must find out whose assistance is required to support these steps. Reinvention involves substituting the former organisational structures and processes of the M&A parties by new ones. To be able to work towards an entirely new organisation, it must be determined what the new organisation should be.[237] Hence employees' **problem-solving competence** is of high significance to make sure that reinvention works. The relevance of **organisation competence** derives from the fact that the reinvention objective requires a redistribution of the tasks inherent in (parts of) the M&A parties' organisations. Moreover, it involves the integration of the firms' tasks. If alternative new organisations need to be assessed as regards their suitability for the new firm, **decision-making competence** helps to base this evaluation on adequate suitability criteria. M&A transactions followed by reinvention often result in changes among colleagues, collaborators or superiors as a natural consequence of changes to the structure of and to linkages between organisational units.[238] This implies that employees should be able to deal with **social change(s) (competence)**. Apart from communication and co-operation competence, all the above-named competences are required shortly after completion of an M&A transaction, to make reinvention work.

These human resource requirements apply to all employees, except for motivation competence which is especially relevant at higher levels in the new firm's hierarchy. In the case of a spin off, the same competences as in a merger or in an acquisition are demanded. These competences are relevant to ensure that employees of the old firm are able to cope with reinvention. Reinvention is assumed to take place in those parts of the old firm that are affected by the spin off.

(2) Besides deciding to entirely recreate organisational micro structure after an M&A, management may possibly aim at linking the existing structures and processes of the transaction parties with each other. Linkage means that the former structures and processes of the transaction parties are combined to form new ones.[239] There are different ways of linking existing structures and processes, which differ according to the proportion of structures and processes retained from each firm.[240] In the following, it is assumed that the same shares are taken from each firm. Possible rationales underlying linkage can be to take the best of the transaction parties' micro structures, or to prevent the organisational chaos that can result from reinvention.

---

[237] Cf. Putz-Osterloh, Wiebke. In: Sarges, Werner (Ed.) (2000), p. 241.

[238] Cf. Shrivastava, Paul (1986), pp. 68ff.

[239] However, linkage is not possible in all M&A transactions. If the M&A parties' structures and processes are too different from each other, a reinvention can be inevitable. Cf. Salecker, Jürgen (1995), p. 27.

[240] Cf. Uder, Helmuth L./Kramarsch, Michael H. (2001), pp. 3ff. Wood, Judy (1992), pp. 51ff. Werner, Markus (1999), p. 333.

Human resources are required to support the achievement of the linkage objective, which is why the following competences should be assigned high importance in Human Resource Due Diligence. **Communication competence** should be considered, since interfaces must be established between the formerly independent firms when linkage is aimed at. Hence, communication density increases, which explains the relevance of communication competence. The establishment of interfaces between the M&A parties results in the necessity of not solely uniting structures and processes in a formal manner. Instead, well functioning joint decision-making is important to enhance the efficiency of the new organisation. **Co-operation competence** is a precondition for linkages to work. When structures and processes are analysed as a pre-stage to the establishment of linkages, **internal competence** can serve to create an understanding of the transaction parties' former organisations. Such an understanding is necessary to possess – partly to prevent discontinuities in every day business and partly to support decisions about alternative new structures. Given the above-mentioned interfaces being established between certain departments or business units of the transaction parties, **complexity competence** is required. This is necessary to be able to cope with the increased number of interdependencies between the firms. Employees still have to know whom to address on what subjects, and managers must be able to steer the organisation despite complexity. As for reinvention, in the case of the linkage objective plans also need to be made about how, when and with what resources linkages shall be created (**planning competence**). **Problem-solving competence** is relevant both to establishing a new organisation, whose (optimum) shape is unpredictable, and for troubleshooting if a first linkage attempt is ineffective. If alternative linkage approaches are assessed as regards their suitability for the new firm, **decision-making competence** is important to make sure that this assessment is based on suitable criteria. Social changes such as changes among colleagues, collaborators and superiors are implied for such employees who work at the interfaces between the transaction parties (**social change competence**).

All these competences apply to all employees who are supposed to work at the interfaces between the formerly independent firms. In the case of a spin off, the same human resource requirements are implied as in a merger or an acquisition, except for planning and decision-making competence. It is assumed that interfaces between the formerly dependent firms are maintained upon completion of the spin off. Hence, the spun off firm still works for/with the firm it previously was part of whilst remaining independent in an economic sense. Planning and decision-making competence are of limited relevance in a linkage spin off, since linkages to the sold part of the firm are simply maintained and no new ones are established. Internal, planning, problem-solving, decision-making, and social change competence are critical in the short term, whereas communication, co-operation, and complexity competence are indispensable for the linkage objective to be achieved in the middle term.

(3) Sometimes Mergers & Acquisitions have no implications for the structures and processes of the firms involved in them, e.g. when a financial holding company acquires a new subsidiary.[241] The transaction parties' former structures and processes are maintained in the aftermath of the M&A transaction. A reason for preservation can be that the transaction parties need not work together operationally upon completion of the transaction.[242] No human resource requirements are induced to enable preservation, since the micro structures of the transaction parties are retained. Hence, no specific competences are required for employees to be able to deal with preservation. In the case of a spin off, no new human resource requirements follow either. A part of a firm is sold off to become independent and no linkages with the former parent company are maintained. This fact illustrates that no M&A induced competences are required to be able to deal with the new micro structures.

In table 2.4, the focus areas for Human Resource Due Diligence presuming the reinvention objective are compared to those for the linkage and for the preservation objective.

Micro Structure Objectives / Competence	Reinvention Objective	Linkage Objective	Preservation Objective
Uncertainty Competence	•		
Communication Competence	•	•	
Conflict Competence			
Motivation Competence	•		
Co-operation Competence	•	•	
Innovation Competence	•		
Internal Competence		•	
Market Competence			
Socio-cultural Competence			
Complexity Competence	•	•	
Functional Competence	•		
Process Competence	•		
Planning Competence	•	•	
Problem-solving Competence	•	•	
Organisation Competence	•		
Decision-making Competence	•	•	
Social Change Competence	•	•	
Technical Change Competence			

Table 2.4: Competences and M&A Management Objectives related to Micro Structure

[241] Cf. Haspeslagh, Philippe C./Jemison, David B. (1991), p. 145.
[242] Cf. Vogel, Dieter (2002), pp. 257ff.

2.2.2.3 Focus Areas in line with Objectives related to Task Spectra

The third level of abstraction on which structural M&A objectives are investigated in this thesis is the level of individuals. Two different objectives related to individuals' tasks spectra have been discovered in the M&A literature reviewed, namely

(1) Renewal objective and

(2) Conservation objective.[243]

(1) As a consequence of an M&A transaction, M&A management may decide to create new task spectra for all or some of the new firm's employees.[244] Renewal can have the same impact for both former firms' employees, but also a higher impact for the one firm's employees than for the other firm's. Accordingly, those employees on whom (the most) human resource requirements are imposed should be evaluated in HRDD. Two options when renewing task spectra are to enlarge existing task spectra with additional tasks or to expand them with new, more sophisticated tasks. In the following, the latter option is concentrated on. The former option is not referred to since enlarging existing task spectra does not result in any new human resource requirements.[245]

The following competences should be treated as highly relevant in Human Resource Due Diligence in the case of a renewal – functional, process, planning, problem-solving, organisation, decision-making, and technical change competence. **Functional competence** is important because of its second component – competence in contributing to tasks of superiors in a useful manner. When tasks spectra are expanded, higher-ranked tasks are to be performed by the same employee. The same applies to **process competence**. In the case of a renewal, employees should be able to carry out super-ordinate processes of the same quality as former subordinate processes. The accomplishment of new super-ordinate tasks may require employees to establish a time and resource framework. Previous, less complicated tasks possibly did not require the employee to plan in advance, but more sophisticated tasks can do so – so **planning competence** is required. Expanded tasks can also demand that the employee works towards a set goal without knowing the path to this goal. Their own solutions must be found to pave the way to this goal. This requires **problem-solving competence**. **Organisation competence** can be required if there is a renewal, as the fulfilment of expanded tasks often implies the involvement of more than one person.[246] Hence the person whose tasks have been expanded must be able to split

---

243 Cf. Ivancevich, John M./Schweiger, David M./Power, Frank R. (1989), p. 30. Deiser, Roland (1994), p. 380.

244 Cf. Deiser, Roland (1994), p. 380.

245 The subsequent argumentation refers to the extreme case where employees are required to fulfill new, more sophisticated tasks, since most human resource requirements are assumed to ensue in that case. Still, one might argue that even if existing task spectra are enlarged with additional tasks, at least complexity competence becomes relevant.

246 This is e.g. the case if employees are suddenly allowed to take on leadership tasks.

these tasks up into several subtasks, and if necessary, arrange for their completion. If alternative courses of action lead to the accomplishment of the expanded tasks, the individual should be able to weigh these alternative courses. Moreover, he needs to be capable of making a selection from the alternatives at hand. The nature of the decisions that are made depends on the part of the new firm which the person is active in (**decision-making competence**). **Technical change competence** is important, since new, more sophisticated tasks require employees to get acquainted with them quickly.

These competences apply to all employees who are concerned in the renewal. An exception is motivation competence, which is primarily important for managers and not for employees at lower levels. The closer the new, expanded tasks are to the tasks a person had before, the lower the importance of the competences mentioned above. The opposite is true, if the new tasks are very different from the tasks a person had before. In the case of a spin off, the same competences as in a merger or an acquisition should be considered. This means that employees of the old firm that sells off a part can be required to cope with new, more sophisticated tasks. All the previously named competences are vital in the middle term; they are not needed for transition, but must be shown when working with new task spectra in the new firm.

(2) Apart from renewing the task spectra of all or some of the new firm's employees, M&A management can also decide to conserve all task spectra.[247] The possible reason for the conservation objective is that no new human resource requirements are implied in a transaction. Alternatively, though this seldom happens, M&A management can decide to consciously conserve task spectra – even though a reinvention would be useful – to reduce M&A induced stress. No matter what reason leads M&A management to conservation, Human Resource Due Diligence need not specifically focus on any competence. Social competences are not required more than they were prior to the M&A – employees can proceed as they did before. Moreover, they are not required to understand the system surrounding them better than they did prior to the M&A transaction. Specialist competence refers to the depth and breadth of specialist knowledge demanded in M&A. No further depth or breadth is required in the aftermath of a transaction followed by a conservation of task spectra. The same applies to methods and change competence. The same as for Mergers & Acquisitions also counts for spin offs. If task spectra are conserved at the firm doing the spin off, no new requirements are implied for its employees. Between the two extremes of renewal and conservation, it is often the case that the M&A transaction results in enlarged task spectra for certain employee groups.[248] If so, functional and process competences are fundamental in Human Resource Due Diligence. This is to see whether the employees concerned have competences broad enough to deal with the requirements of the enlarged tasks they face.

---

[247] Cf. Ivancevich, John M./Schweiger, David M./Power, Frank R. (1989), p. 30.
[248] Cf. Koch, Tomas (2001), pp. 167f.

As can be understood from table 2.5, the renewal objective implies that employees are required to show specialist, methods, and technical change competence. Assuming conservation, no new competences are demanded at all.

Competence \ Task Spectra Objectives	Renewal Objective	Conservation Objective
Uncertainty Competence		
Communication Competence		
Conflict Competence		
Motivation Competence		
Co-operation Competence		
Innovation Competence		
Internal Competence		
Market Competence		
Socio-cultural Competence		
Complexity Competence		
Functional Competence	•	
Process Competence	•	
Planning Competence	•	
Problem-solving Competence	•	
Organisation Competence	•	
Decision-making Competence	•	
Social Change Competence		
Technical Change Competence	•	

Table 2.5: Competences and M&A Management Objectives related to Task Spectra

2.2.2.4 Interdependencies between Structural Objectives

The three types of structural management objectives refer to different levels of abstraction: individual level, group/departmental level and organisational level. All three types of objectives may be logically intertwined, but they need not be. M&A management may e.g. aim to renew task spectra whilst changing structures and processes, as well as whilst retaining structures and processes as they are. M&A management may pursue objectives on all three levels of abstraction or on one or two of the three levels, only. Even if no conscious M&A objectives are aimed for at a certain level of abstraction, this level should be considered to cover all relevant competence requirements induced by structural objectives in HRDD.

There are differences in the types of competences that are considered relevant for the different types of structural management objectives. In case of macro structure objectives, specialist, and social competence in particular should be considered in Human Resource Due Diligence. Supposing micro structure objectives, Human Resource Due Diligence should focus on all five competence groups, the reason for this being that direct implications for every day work can be inferred from this type of objectives. Task spectra objectives imply a focus on specialist and methods competence in Human Resource Due Diligence.

2.2.3 Focus Areas in line with Cultural Objectives

The third perspective of the extended trilogy of the Zurich management framework considers management from a cultural perspective. The term culture stands for all norms and values that influence the appearance of a firm.[249] According to Schein, a firm's culture can be subdivided into different layers, certain of which are visible whereas others are hidden.[250] The characteristics of the corporate culture considered in the following are visible.[251] Corporate culture serves to orientate, coordinate and motivate the members of the organisation.[252] It is assumed that culture is developed, meaning that it can be shaped in a certain way.[253] Firms not only have a culture, but are also part of a larger national culture surrounding them. Three types of cultural M&A management objectives are examined in the following as regards their impact on the relevance of the human resource requirements from figure 2.2, namely corporate culture objectives (chapter 2.2.3.1), leadership objectives (chapter 2.2.3.2) and national culture objectives (chapter 2.2.3.3).

The three types of cultural M&A management objectives differ according to the level of abstraction they presuppose. The first type of objectives refers to the way in which the M&A parties are supposed to continue in terms of corporate culture upon completion of M&A. The reason for selecting the first type of cultural M&A management objectives is its frequency of appearance in the M&A literature reviewed. The second type of cultural M&A objective concentrates on the nature of the leadership relationships desired between managers and their collaborators. Leadership relationships are shaped by manager's decision-making approach, by control- and communication patterns. This second objective has also been chosen due to its frequency of appearance in the M&A literature reviewed.[254] The third type of objective focuses on firms' surrounding national culture. The reason for selecting this objective has partly been its appearance in the M&A literature reviewed and partly its assumed impact on the relevance of the human resource requirements. By referring to these three cultural management objectives, requirements imposed on employees are deduced based on insights on three different levels of abstraction. After developing focus areas for HRDD which result from cultural M&A objectives, interdependencies between the three types of cultural objectives are discussed (chapter 2.2.3.4).

---

[249] Cf. Thommen, Jean-Paul (2002), p. 1161.

[250] These layers are: values and basic assumptions, norms and standards, artifacts and symbols. Cf. Schein, Edgar H. (1986), p. 14. For different elements of corporate culture cf. Buono, Anthony F./Bowditch, James L./Lewis, John W. (1985), pp. 480f.

[251] Cf. Nahavandi, Afsaneh/Malekzadeh, Ali R. (1988), p. 80. Examples of visible elements of corporate culture are mission statement and leadership principles.

[252] Cf. Olbrich, Michael (1999), p. 26. Rühli, Edwin (1996), p. 44 states a different purpose for corporate culture. The definition of Olbrich is used, since it is more in line with the managerial perspective of this study.

[253] Cf. Schein, Edgar H. (1984), p. 4. Fatzer, Gerhard (2002), p. 52. In this thesis, it is assumed that culture is developed, not discovered.

[254] Cf. Sackmann, Sonja A. (2002), p. 25.

2.2.3.1 Focus Areas in line with Objectives related to Corporate Culture

M&A objectives related to corporate culture refer to the desired composition of the corporate culture of the new firm. Different objectives related to corporate culture have been found in the M&A literature reviewed. This thesis basically follows the categorisation by Nahavandi /Malekzadeh.[255] However, one of their four culture-related objectives is not considered here – deculturation. This is, because the other three cultural management objectives (integration, assimilation and segregation – see below) were often mentioned in the M&A literature reviewed, whereas the last was not.[256] When pursuing M&A objectives related to corporate culture, the transaction parties can aim at three different objectives. These are

(1) Integration objective,

(2) Assimilation objective and

(3) Segregation objective.

(1) Upon completion of an M&A, M&A management may possibly decide that one of the transaction parties' corporate cultures shall cease to exist.[257] This means that one firm's corporate culture remains whereas the other firm's employees are supposed to adapt to that corporate culture.[258] To enable integration, the employees of the firm that is to be integrated must be prepared to adapt to the other firm's corporate culture. It is therefore important to assess communication, motivation, and social change competence in HRDD. For integration to work, the employees of the integrated firm should show **communication competence**. The reason for this is that M&A transaction parties can be used to very different patterns of communication. To make the M&A work, the employees of the integrated firm need to adopt the other firm's patterns of communication. This adoption requires assistance from the integrating firm's employees. Therefore communication competence should also be assessed for them. To support the integrated firm's employees in dealing with the modified patterns of communication they face, **motivation competence** is required. Both the integrating and the integrated firm's managers should facilitate cultural changes. Integration is accompanied by changes to the patterns of behaviour underlying every-day work for the employees of the integrated firm. Moreover, they can be required to adapt to different kinds of relationships with colleagues, superiors and collaborators. Finally, the persons they work with may change as well[259] – not only the nature of the firm's internal relationships, therefore requiring **social change competence**.

---

[255] Cf. Nahavandi, Afsaneh/Malekzadeh, Ali R. (1994), pp. 294ff. Nahavandi, Afsaneh/Malekzadeh, Ali R. (1988), p. 83.

[256] In 80% of the M&A literature sources reviewed on corporate culture, the above three objectives were mentioned (though always worded differently).

[257] Cf. Nahavandi, Afsaneh/Malekzadeh, Ali R. (1994), pp. 294ff. Nahavandi, Afsaneh/Malekzadeh, Ali R. (1988), p. 83.

[258] Cf. Stahl, Günter K. (2001), p. 63.

[259] Cf. Ivancevich, John M./Schweiger, David M./Power, Frank R. (1987), pp. 21f.

The above competences are potentially important at all levels in the integrated firm's hierarchy, apart from motivation competence, which is solely relevant for managers. Communication competence is decisive for both firms' employees and motivation competence especially for both firms' managers. All three competences can be critical in both the short and in the middle term.

The more differences there are between the transaction parties' corporate cultures, the more important the above mentioned competences.[260] Corporate culture typologies can be used to illustrate the differences between M&A parties' corporate cultures. The typology of Deal and Kennedy is frequently mentioned in business administration literature.[261] According to Deal and Kennedy, corporate cultures can be differentiated according to the underlying riskiness of business decisions/activities one the one hand. On the other hand, they can be differentiated according to the speed with which feedback is received about the success of business decisions. Following these two distinction criteria, four different types of corporate cultures can be identified – namely macho cultures (high risk, fast feedback cultures), work hard/play hard cultures (low risk, fast feedback cultures), bet your company cultures (high risk, slow feedback cultures) and process cultures (low risk, slow feedback cultures). Great differences can be found between the four types of cultures.[262] In M&A between firms whose corporate cultures can be associated with different types according to the Deal and Kennedy typology, the above mentioned competences are crucial. Still, their relative importance can be expressed more concretely by taking other cultural characteristics into account. One danger with using cultural typologies is that the complex phenomenon of corporate culture is oversimplified. This can lead to faulty assumptions and hence to a faulty focus in HRDD. Therefore, prior to performing HRDD, firms involved in M&A transactions are recommended to carry out an analysis of their corporate culture(s) using at least two cultural typologies.

(2) Besides integrating one firm's culture, M&A management can also aim at corporate cultural assimilation upon completion of an M&A transaction. Assimilation means that the M&A transaction parties join their corporate cultures to form a new one.[263] This new culture consists of elements of both firms' former corporate cultures (best-of-both

---

[260] Assuming that corporate cultures which are similar to each other can be combined more easily than those which are different from each other. Cf. Cartwright, Sue/Cooper, Cary L. (1996), p. 10. Greengard, Samuel (1999), p. 71. Siehl, Caren/Ledford, Gerald/Silverman, Richard/Fay, Peter (1988), p. 56. According to Chatterjee/Lubatkin /Schweiger, cultural differences between the transaction parties in related mergers can even be correlated with shareholder value. Cf. Chatterjee, Sayan/Lubatkin, Michael H./Schweiger, David M./Weber, Yaakov (1992), p. 330. A study by Stahl/Voigt illustrates, however, that variables other than the degree of cultural differences can have an impact on M&A performance supposing major cultural differences. The most important variable seems to be the degree of (DP: organisational) relatedness of the M&A parties. Cf. Stahl, Günter K./Voigt, Andreas (2004), p. I1.

[261] Cf. e.g. Thommen, Jean-Paul (2002), p. 1163.

[262] Cf. Deal, Terrence E./Kennedy, Allen A. (1999), pp. 12ff.

[263] Cf. Nahavandi, Afsaneh/Malekzadeh, Ali R. (1994), pp. 294ff. Nahavandi, Afsaneh/Malekzadeh, Ali R. (1988), p. 83.

approach).[264] Such a type of cultural coexistence can be observed where transaction parties aim to benefit from their respective strengths and their former cultures are different but do not clash.[265] In order to enable assimilation, both firms' employees must give up part of their norms and values and accept new ones.[266] Communication, conflict, motivation, and social change competence should be at the core of Human Resource Due Diligence. To make sure that information flows and new relationships are established between the M&A parties' employees, **communication competence** is of high relevance. Like integration, assimilation can also require people to overcome communication barriers caused by cultural differences. Given the best-of-both approach of cultural coexistence, firm A's employees have to adapt to firm B's patterns of communication in certain fields. However, in other fields, party B's employees must accept party A's patterns. The process of understanding and adopting each other's patterns of communication can result in conflicts. This does not only apply for communication patterns but also for many other patterns of behaviour (including roles and states). Both firms' employees must possess **conflict competence** to constructively deal with disagreements. Successful conflict resolution requires that a constructive manner of combining both firms' patterns of behaviour is found.[267] To support collaborators in dealing with the modified patterns of behaviour, **motivation competence** is required. Both firms' managers should facilitate the cultural changes. Assimilation is accompanied by changes to the patterns of behaviour of both firms' employees. This is because the transaction parties' different corporate cultures are combined to form a new (patchwork) culture. Relationships with colleagues, superiors and collaborators can also be affected, hence the significance of **social change competence.**

Managers in particular should possess motivation competence. The other competences should ideally be assessed for all of the transaction parties' employees. If cultural assimilation does not take place in all parts of the new firm to the same extent, a distinction should be made in HRDD with respect to this fact. To support assimilation, the above-mentioned competences are important in the short term.

The more differences there are between the transaction parties' corporate cultures, the more important the competences mentioned above are. For assimilation, corporate culture typologies can also serve to map the differences between the firms' cultures. Corporate cultures belonging to different fields of the typologies are probably quite different from each other. The importance of the competences to employees from both firms depends on the proportion of cultural elements taken from each firm. In the case of a spin off, assimilation cannot take place, since one firm becomes independent from another.

---

264 Cf. Höher, Friederike/Koall, Iris (2002), p. 70.
265 Cf. Zwahlen, Beat (1994), pp. 266f.
266 Cf. Simon, Hermann (1999), p. 97.
267 Cf. Bastien, David T. In: Ven, Andrew H. van de/Angle, Harold L./Poole, Marshall Scott (Eds.) (1989), pp. 367ff.

(3) Segregation means that the M&A parties' corporate cultures coexist independently of each other upon completion of an M&A transaction.[268] Both (all) transaction parties stay with their own norms and values. Apparently, no human resource requirements need to be fulfilled for segregation to work, since both firms proceed as they did before in terms of culture. Thus, they adhere to their previous patterns of behaviour. Only if additional M&A objectives in the other M&A management dimensions are considered – for instance micro structure objectives – can competences for Human Resource Due Diligence can be deduced. Presumably, the segregation objective is inconsistent with structural linkage. It is difficult working together whilst maintaining two different cultures.

In the case of a spin-off, a formerly dependent part of a firm can be required to establish a culture of its own. To be able to do so, it might be useful to segregate it from the parent culture, so that its employees can e.g. develop their own patterns of behaviour.

The highly relevant competences resulting from the integration, the assimilation and the segregation objective are illustrated in table 2.6. As can be seen from the table, supposing the objective is integration, the integrated firm's employees should mainly show the highlighted competences.

Corporate Culture Objectives / Competence	Integration Objective	Assimilation Objective	Seggregation Objective
Uncertainty Competence			
Communication Competence	•	•	
Conflict Competence		•	
Motivation Competence	•	•	
Co-operation Competence			
Innovation Competence			
Internal Competence			
Market Competence			
Socio-cultural Competence			
Complexity Competence			
Functional Competence			
Process Competence			
Planning Competence			
Problem-solving Competence			
Organisation Competence			
Decision-making Competence			
Social Change Competence	•	•	
Technical Change Competence			

Table 2.6: Competences and M&A Management Objectives related to Corporate Culture

[268] Cf. Nahavandi, Afsaneh/Malekzadeh, Ali R. (1994), pp. 294ff. Nahavandi, Afsaneh/Malekzadeh, Ali R. (1988), p. 83. Jaeger, Michael (2001), p. 75.

2.2.3.2 Focus Areas in line with Objectives related to Leadership Style

Besides pursuing objectives related to corporate cultures, M&A management sometimes intends to influence the nature of leadership relationships in the new firm.[269] The reason for this is that leadership relationships are a reflection of the corporate culture predominant in a firm. By prescribing a leadership style that is supposed to be used in a firm, manager-collaborator relationships and hence patterns of co-operation are influenced. In the M&A literature reviewed, only one M&A objective related to leadership style has been found: to create a joint leadership style for the new firm.[270] However, this does not seem to be the only possible objective – M&A management can also pursue others. In the following, three types of leadership-related objectives are considered regarding their impact on the relevance of the competences, namely

(1) Absorption objective,

(2) Creation objective and

(3) Coexistence objective.

(1) M&A management may want the employees of one of the firms to adapt to the manager-subordinate relationships characteristic of the other firm. Hence, one firm's leadership style is absorbed by the other firm's. A rationale underlying absorption can be that one firm's manager-subordinate relationships are considered especially to favour what it is planned to do with the new firm in the future. If the absorption objective is to be achieved, employees must contribute to this objective. The following highly important human resource requirements ensue in case of absorption: communication, motivation, and co-operation competence. **Communication competence** is demanded since different leadership styles go along with different patterns of communication. The employees of the firm that maintains its leadership style should be prepared for a different approach to giving information and sharing opinions with colleagues, superiors and collaborators from the absorbed firm. In contrast, the employees of the firm whose leadership style is absorbed must be able to adopt new patterns of information and opinion exchange. To prevent the absorbed firm's employees at lower levels in particular from reacting with de-motivation to the change of patterns of communication and co-operation, **motivation competence** is required. Besides having to motivate the absorbed firm's employees at lower levels, managers also need to make sure that their collaborators originating from the absorbing firm are prepared for the changes. They may possibly react with de-motivation due to impatience or intolerance.[271] Different leadership styles mean not only different patterns of communication but also different control and decision-making patterns (**co-operation**

[269] Cf. Shrivastava, Paul (1986), pp. 68ff.

[270] Cf. Dielmann, Klaus (1997), p. 479. Shrivastava, Paul (1986), pp. 68ff.

[271] Cf. Lüdi, Markus/Eicken, Sabine (2000), p. 11.

competence). As for communication competence, the absorbing firm's employees must accept the clash of patterns. Simultaneously, the absorbed firm's employees need to adopt new patterns.

These competences are potentially important at all levels in the hierarchy. The only exemption is motivation competence which is especially relevant at relatively high levels in the new firm's hierarchy. The degree of importance of the above-mentioned competences depends on the differences between the leadership styles of the M&A parties.[272] Two extreme types of leadership styles are often distinguished in business administration literature – an authoritative and a co-operative leadership style.[273] Between these two extremes, many different nuances can be found in business practice. However, for illustration purposes, the two extremes are at the core, here. An authoritative leadership style is characterised by a concentration of decision-making in the hands of managers. Communication takes place by collaborators reporting to their superiors. Collaborators are given very little room for their own creativity and are subject to tight control patterns.[274] In the case of a co-operative leadership style, the roles of manager and employee are differently shaped. Employees participate in decision-making or even take decisions on their own. They are given a high degree of responsibility. Control is substituted by the definition and pursuit of joint objectives between superiors and collaborators.[275] As can be seen from the description of the two leadership styles, they require very different competences. Employees must be specialists at what they do and good at following instructions if an authoritative leadership style is used. Assuming a co-operative leadership style, collaborators must take decisions themselves and handle large parts of their work on their own. In M&A transactions between firms whose leadership styles differ as described above – or even if they differ less than described above – the competences mentioned are strongly required. Nevertheless, the degree of relevance can be expressed more in detail by taking other leadership style nuances into account. All three competences are vital in the short term, to facilitate the achievement of the absorption objective.

(2) Besides having one firm's leadership style absorb the other, M&A management can aim at creating a new joint leadership style upon completion of an M&A transaction.[276] In such case, new kinds of manager-collaborator relationships are created for the new firm. These relationships can – and this is most probable – be based on both firms' former leadership styles or be entirely new. For the further argumentation, it does not matter which possibility is chosen. What matters is that both firms' leadership styles cease to exist and are substituted by a new kind of manager-collaborator behaviour. This implies changes for

[272] Cf. Henkel, Martin (1994), p. 31. According to Henkel, different (leadership) positions require different competences. As for the corporate culture objectives, it is assumed that similar leadership styles can be brought together more easily than different ones. Cf. also Lüdi, Markus/Eicken, Sabine (2000a), p. 11.

[273] Cf. Pfützner, Robert (1994), pp. 27ff. Simons, Robert (1995), p. 88.

[274] Cf. Thommen, Jean-Paul (2002), pp. 1168ff.

[275] Ditto.

[276] Cf. Dielmann, Klaus (1997), p. 479.

the employees of both firms. The rationale for creating a new leadership style can be to facilitate the development of a new joint corporate culture in contrast to a patchwork one.[277] To achieve this objective, the same human resource requirements as for absorption are crucial. However, this time the requirements apply to both firms' employees in the same way. **Communication competence** is required, since different leadership styles go along with different patterns of communication. Employees must adopt new patterns of information and opinion sharing, as prescribed by the definition of the new leadership style. Managers should possess **motivation competence** if a new joint leadership style is aimed at in an M&A, to support their collaborators in acquainting themselves with the new leader-subordinate relationships. This can include explaining the advantages of modified decision-making and control patterns to them. Different leadership styles mean not only different patterns of communication but also different control and decision-making patterns. As for communication competence, all employees need to adopt the new patterns (**co-operation competence**). All the required competences are relevant in the short term.

(3) The third leadership objective referred to in this thesis is the coexistence objective. M&A management may decide that both transaction parties' leadership styles shall be maintained after the M&A[278], no matter whether they are different from each other or not. No specific human resource requirements result if the coexistence objective is aimed for. Neither of the firms' employees faces any changes to the nature of their manager collaborator relationship.

If M&A management aims at having the transaction parties' leadership styles coexist, the competences in table 2.7 should be concentrated on in Human Resource Due Diligence for both firms' employees. Presuming the objective is absorption, however, the same competences are essential only for the absorbed firm's employees.

[277] Cf. Shrivastava, Paul (1986), pp. 68ff.
[278] Cf. Datta, Deepak K. (1991), p. 283.

Leadership Objectives / Competence	Absorption Objective	Coexistence Objective	Creation Objective
Uncertainty Competence			
Communication Competence	•	•	
Conflict Competence			
Motivation Competence	•	•	
Co-operation Competence	•	•	
Innovation Competence			
Internal Competence			
Market Competence			
Socio-cultural Competence			
Complexity Competence			
Functional Competence			
Process Competence			
Planning Competence			
Problem-solving Competence			
Organisation Competence			
Decision-making Competence			
Social Change Competence			
Technical Change Competence			

Table 2.7: Competences and M&A Management Objectives related to Leadership Style[279]

2.2.3.3 Focus Areas in line with Objectives related to National Culture

The third type of cultural M&A management objectives relates to the transaction parties' national cultures. According to the M&A literature reviewed, cultural differences arising from differences between the transaction parties' national cultures should always be considered in cross-border M&A transactions.[280] Yet, this needs not always be the case, unless the transaction parties' employees are required to work together post completion. Accordingly, two objectives related to national culture are elaborated on in the following, namely

(1) Commutation objective and

(2) Insulation objective.

(1) M&A management sometimes decides to facilitate intercultural commutation – meaning exchange – between the transaction parties' employees upon completion of an M&A. One reason for this can be the necessity of working together upon completion of an M&A, presuming that the inability to work together will lead to inefficiencies. For commutation

[279] If the coexistence objective is aimed for, the human resource requirements are not identical to those which become relevant if the absorption objective is pursued. If the absorption objective is aimed for, the competences in table 2.7 are highly relevant for employees of the firm whose leadership style ceases to exist, whereas if the coexistence objective is pursued, they are highly relevant for all employees.

[280] Cf. Jansen, Stephan A. (2002), p. 10. Blasko, Matej/Netter, Jeffrey M./Sinkey, Joseph F. (2000), p. 79.

to work, employees should especially fulfil the following requirements: They should show communication, conflict, and socio-cultural competence. Commutation requires that both firms' employees work together constructively, which is conditional to them understanding each other. Therefore, **communication competence** is crucial, as national cultures differ in e.g. to their patterns of communication. Communication competence includes competence in providing comprehensible information to others and understanding information from others the way it is meant. Besides serving the exchange of information, communication competence also ensures that both firm's employees are able to form relationships. Language skills can be an important component of communication competence when the commutation objective is pursued. **Conflict competence** is required to ensure that conflicts due to different patterns of behaviour between national cultures are handled in a constructive manner. In a constructive manner from an M&A management perspective means in a way that will achieve the commutation objective. Knowing the respective other firm's socio-cultural background is a precondition for successful communication and the resolution of conflicts. Without knowing the reasons for cultural differences, successful commutation may be difficult to reach in the long run (**socio-cultural competence**).[281]

These competence considerations apply to all employees. In contrast to corporate culture, it probably is almost impossible to change national cultures and hence not possible to absorb one firm's underlying national culture. However, the extreme case that all employees of both firms are required to work together after the M&A is generally not the case. Rather, certain employee groups can be required to show such competences, whereas others – who do no interact with the other firm's employees – are not. Given the fact that intercultural commutation persists once it has been decided upon in an M&A transaction, all the above-named competences are essential in the middle term. The more different the national cultures of the transaction parties, the greater the importance of these competences will be. National cultural typologies can be used to discover to what extent the two firms differ from each other. The most cited national culture typology in business administration literature is probably that of Hofstede. He argues that national culture differ according to their parameter value in the following four criteria – uncertainty avoidance, masculinity/femininity, power distance and individualism/collectivism.[282] The larger the differences in the M&A parties' national culture are in the four categories, the more important the above competences are.

(2) The second way of reacting to differences between the M&A parties' national cultures is by keeping the two firms independent of each other. If the insulation objective is pursued, no interaction is supposed to be encouraged between the firms' employees. One reason for pursuing the insulation objective is that interaction is not necessary for M&A objectives to

[281] Cf. Blasko, Matej/Netter, Jeffrey M./Sinkey, Joseph F. (2000), p. 93. In the DaimlerChrysler merger, cultural differences would hinder the realization of synergies, unless management succeeded in coping with them.

[282] Cf. Hofstede, Gerd (1983), pp. 80ff.

be achieved. It seems as if no specific human resource requirements need to be fulfilled in the case of insulation. Still, it should be noted that even when a financial investor is the acquirer, a certain degree of interaction at the executive level will likely take place.[283] Thus, in the case of interaction between the firms' managers, the competences outlined above can also be important when following the insulation objective.

Table 2.8 summarises which competences should be focused on in Human Resource Due Diligence for the commutation objective and which for the insulation objective.

National Culture Objectives / Competence	Commutation Objective	Insulation Objective
Uncertainty Competence		
Communication Competence	•	
Conflict Competence	•	
Motivation Competence		
Co-operation Competence		
Innovation Competence		
Internal Competence		
Market Competence		
Socio-cultural Competence	•	
Complexity Competence		
Functional Competence		
Process Competence		
Planning Competence		
Problem-solving Competence		
Organisation Competence		
Decision-making Competence		
Social Change Competence		
Technical Change Competence		

Table 2.8: Competences and M&A Management Objectives related to National Culture

2.2.3.4 *Interdependencies between Cultural Objectives*

The three types of cultural management objectives all relate to the new firm's norms and values. Based on these norms and values, M&A objectives may be aimed for on an interpersonal level (leadership objectives) and on an organisational level (corporate and national culture objectives). The cultural M&A objectives do not overlap: certain types of objectives may be pursued even though other(s) are not. Especially cultural management objectives may be aimed for unconsciously, still implying competence requirements.

Communication competence is relevant in the case of the commutation, the absorption and the integration objective. However, the reasons for the significance of communication compe-

[283] Cf. commutation objective.

tence differ, depending on the underlying M&A objective. For the commutation objective, communication competence is crucial to ensure that employees are able to exchange information and build relationships across different national cultures. In the case of the absorption objective, the employees of the firm whose leadership style is absorbed must be able to adopt new patterns of information exchange. Finally for the integration objective to be achieved, the employees of the integrated firm in particular must adopt the other firm's patterns of communication. The different reasons for the importance of the highly relevant have an impact on step 2 of the HRDD, namely on the definition of indicators for HRDD.

2.2.4 Focus Areas in line with Human Resource Management Objectives

Besides strategic, structural and cultural management, M&A management also comprises a human resource dimension. As mentioned in chapter 1.4.5, human resource management means all activities performed to shape, steer and develop the firm's human resources.[284] Three types of human resource management objectives in M&A are examined in the following paragraphs as regards their impact on the relevance of the human resource requirements in figure 2.2, namely objectives related to human resource strategies (chapter 2.2.4.1), objectives related to human resource policies and practices (chapter 2.2.4.2) and objectives related to human resource organisation (chapter 2.2.4.3). The three types of objectives differ according to the level of abstraction they assume.

The first type of objective refers to the way in which the M&A parties' human resource strategies are supposed to coexist upon completion of an M&A. The first type of M&A management objectives has been selected, based on the assumption that human resource strategy shapes the human resource requirements of an M&A transaction.[285] The second type of human resource management objective concentrates on the desired coexistence of (selected) human resource policies and practices of the transaction parties. It has been chosen due to its frequency of appearance in the M&A literature reviewed. The third type of objective focuses on the firms' human resource organisations. The reason for selecting this objective has been its appearance in the M&A literature reviewed. By covering these three M&A management objectives, human resource requirements are inferred based on three different levels of abstraction, which is in line with the multidimensional perspective of analysis in this study.[286] Chapter 2.2.4.4 addresses interdependencies between the three human resource management objectives in M&A.

---

284 Cf. Hilb, Martin (2002), pp. 12f. Cf. chapter 1.4.5.

285 This assumption has been made despite the fact that the M&A literature reviewed did not contain any hints about human resource strategy objectives in such transactions.

286 Cf. chapter 1.3.1.

2.2.4.1 Focus Areas in line with Human Resource Strategy Objectives

In the M&A literature reviewed, no M&A objectives related to human resource strategy have been referred to. However, such objectives should form part of the HRDD Concept, for the reason named in the previous paragraph, that the new firm's human resource strategy strongly shapes future human resource requirements. Therefore, the following two M&A objectives related to human resource strategies have been defined

(1) Aggregation objective and

(2) Independence objective.

(1) The M&A transaction parties can decide to aggregate their human resource strategies upon completion of an M&A transaction. In the case of aggregation, the firms' human resource strategies are combined to form a joint human resource strategy. One reason for pursuing this objective can be to arrive at joint activities to shape, steer and develop the new firm's human resources. The following human resource requirements ensue supposing aggregation: communication, conflict, motivation, co-operation, innovation, functional, process, social change, and technical change competence. The importance of **communication competence** can be explained by the modified patterns of communication potentially resulting from aggregation. If the M&A parties unite their human resource strategies, the relative significance of communication competence may increase as a result of modified human resource requirements. Patterns of behaviour, not only in terms of communication but also in more general terms, can be subject to change. Conflicts can result from these changes.[287] Hence, **conflict competence** is required to ensure that conflicts are solved constructively in accordance with the objectives of the new firm. Aggregating the human resource strategies of the firms involved in an M&A transaction demands that employees are able to deal with the changes implied by aggregation. New behavioural requirements imposed on employees underline this necessity. Hence, the relevance of **motivation competence,** to support employees at lower levels in dealing with the changes. Besides new patterns of communication, new patterns of co-operation can also be the result of an aggregation of human resource strategies. **Co-operation competence** is required to ensure that the new firm's employees are able to cope with the new co-operation demands. For the successful aggregation of two formerly independent human resource strategies, **innovation competence** can be demanded. This is if the new human resource strategy fosters employee innovations more strongly than or differently from the firms' former human resource strategies.[288] Functional specialists can be required upon completion of an M&A transaction, depending on the concrete human resource strategy pursued. If this strategy highlights the significance of specialists, **functional competence** can serve as a basis for finding specialists for the new firm amongst existing employees.

[287] Cf. Buono, Anthony F./Bowditch, James L. (1989), p. 13.
[288] Cf. Klimecki, Rüdiger/Gmür, Markus (2001), pp. 377f.

The same applies to **process competence**. Given the potential social changes implied by aggregation, **social change competence** is relevant. Aggregation can result in changing relationships e.g. with collaborators, superiors and colleagues. Technical changes can follow from combining human resource strategies. A new human resource strategy may be associated with an increasing necessity of coping with new technical requirements in terms of human resource (**technical change competence**). These competences apply to all employees, except for motivation competence, which is likely to be most relevant at high levels in a hierarchy.

In many M&A transactions, aggregation means that uneven proportions of the transaction parties' human resource strategies are retained. Hence, one firm's human resource strategy may possibly dominate the new firm's human resource strategy. In such cases, the human resource requirements are most relevant for the employees of the firm whose human resource strategy is dominated. This is because these employees are most required to adapt to changes inherent in the new human resource strategy. The dominating firm's employees hardly face any changes at all. All highly relevant competences are important in the middle term – consequences resulting from the aggregation of human resource strategies presumably manifest themselves mostly in the middle term.

The relative importance of the above-mentioned human resource requirements depends on the similarity of the human resource strategies of the transaction parties. Four extreme human resource strategies can be distinguished – the well-rehearsed team, the perfect machine, the intelligent organism and the creative evolution. These differ according to the human resource management approach and according to the market strategy they presuppose.[289] Between these four extremes, many different nuances can be found in business practice.[290] However, for illustration purposes, the four extremes are referred to here. The well-rehearsed team is characterised by expertise, harmony, reliability, consistency, continuity and loyalty. The perfect machine features discipline, subordination, and smooth interaction and exchange relationships. The intelligent organism defines itself by development, growth, renewal, creativity and pride. The creative evolution distinguishes itself by competition, fast changes, challenges to the status quo and a fun culture.[291] The four extremes require very different competences. In the case of the well-rehearsed team, functional and process competences are highly important to ensure that each employee plays his expert part in the team. In the case of the perfect machine, co-operation, communication, and motivation competence are required to facilitate smooth interaction and exchange relationships. Employees who work for the intelligent organism must be innovative and technically flexible. In the case of the creative evolution, all methods competences as well as internal competence are valued to ensure that changes to the status quo are well-prepared. In M&A between firms whose human resource strategies differ,

[289] Cf. Gmür, Markus/Thommen, Jean-Paul (2005) (forthcoming).
[290] Ditto.
[291] Ditto.

the above mentioned competences are crucial. Their relative relevance can be expressed in more detail by taking further nuances into account.

In the case of a spin off, the same competences as in a merger or an acquisition should be part of HRDD. The only difference to the above argumentation is that in a spin off, the above competences should be assessed to see whether the seller's employees show the competences demanded to further develop the remaining business.

(2) Apart from deciding to aggregate their human resource strategies, M&A transaction parties can choose to maintain their human resource strategies independent from each other upon completion of a transaction. Hence, if the independence objective is pursued, the firms' human resource strategies coexist. A reason for pursuing the independence objective can be that joint human resource management activities are unnecessary for objectives in other M&A management dimensions to be attained.[292] No specific human resource requirements are implied whatsoever when the independence objective is followed. This also goes for spin offs where the seller retains their human resource strategy.

As illustrated in table 2.9, when M&A management pursues the aggregation objective, it is crucial to consider social, specialist, and change competence in HRDD. If both human resource strategies are supposed to coexist independently from each other, no competences need to be assessed at all.

Human Resource Strategy Objectives / Competence	Aggregation Objective	Independence Objective
Uncertainty Competence		
Communication Competence	•	
Conflict Competence	•	
Motivation Competence	•	
Co-operation Competence	•	
Innovation Competence	•	
Internal Competence		
Market Competence		
Socio-cultural Competence		
Complexity Competence		
Functional Competence	•	
Process Competence	•	
Planning Competence		
Problem-solving Competence		
Organisation Competence		
Decision-making Competence		
Social Change Competence	•	
Technical Change Competence	•	

Table 2.9: Competences and Human Resource Strategy Objectives in M&A

[292] Cf. chapter 1.4.5.

2.2.4.2 *Focus Areas in line with Human Resource Policy and Practice Objectives*

M&A management can also encompass objectives related to human resource policies and practices. The M&A literature review demonstrated that firms can pursue two extreme objectives related to human resource policies and practices.[293] These are

(1) Amalgamation objective and

(2) Self-containment objective.

In the M&A literature, certain human resource policies and practices are frequently discussed, namely compensation and benefits[294], and performance policies.[295] For this reason, these human resource policies and practices are referred to when examples of the relevance of the competences are given in the subsequent argumentation.

(1) The transaction parties may agree to unite their human resource policies and practices after completion.[296] Hence, in the case of amalgamation, the firms' human resource policies and practices are combined. A reason for pursuing the amalgamation objective can be to reach common ground for the transaction parties to work on. Amalgamation can also be chosen for financial reasons.[297] Finally, it can support the achievement of M&A management objectives in other management dimensions.[298] The following competences are critical assuming that amalgamation is the objective – uncertainty, communication, conflict, motivation, co-operation, innovation, market, socio-cultural, functional, process, planning, problem-solving, organisation, decision-making, and technical change competence. If the transaction parties combine their compensation and benefits and performance policies, employees' **uncertainty competence** can be challenged. This is because previously established policies and practices cease to exist. The new firm's employees may be required to accept a new base salary, a new policy on variable pay etc. They can also be asked to deal with new criteria according to which their performance in the new firm is appraised. The need for assessing **communication competence** can be explained by new behavioural expectations imposed on employees. If a new performance policy requires that collaborators report to their managers more frequently, this fact implies communication requirements for both superiors and collaborators. Should new behavioural requirements result in an increase in conflict potential, employees' **conflict competence** is highly valued. This is the case if the new performance policies conflict with one of the

---

[293] Cf. Lüdi, Markus/Eicken, Sabine (2000a), p. 12. Napier, Nancy K. (1989), p. 280. Both these objectives have been selected due to their frequency of appearance in the M&A literature.

[294] Cf. Bickford, Lawrence (1997), p. 54. Overton, Bruce B. (1991), p. 40. Teall, John L. (1992), p. 60. Wiltz, Stefan (1999), p. 17.

[295] Cf. Pritchett, Price (1985), pp. 5ff. Schweiger, David M./Ivancevich, John M./Power, Frank R. (1987), p. 131.

[296] Cf. Lüdi, Markus/Eicken, Sabine (2000a), p. 12.

[297] Possibly, joining the firms' human resource policies and practices is cheaper than maintaining them.

[298] Cf. chapter 1.4.5 interdependencies in between the management dimensions.

firm's former performance policies. Changes to compensation and benefits, and performance policies can require that employees are supported in dealing with these changes. **Motivation competence** is therefore a prerequisite for the required support to be provided. Moreover, new performance criteria can also result in new behavioural requirements in other fields. For instance, the required patterns of co-operation can be subject to change. **Co-operation competence** can be important in dealing with new approaches to information sharing. Changes to performance criteria can also relate to the degree of innovativeness required of employees, which is why it is possibly important to investigate **innovation competence** in HRDD. The same applies to **market competence, socio-cultural and specialist competence** which can be integral to new performance appraisal criteria.[299] **Planning competence** can be significant for two reasons. First, to plan for the intended amalgamation to be attained. Second, as part of new performance criteria, as it is for specialist competence. The same two factors explain the potential relevance of **problem-solving, organisation and decision-making competence**. If the new performance criteria include the necessity of adapting to new technical requirements, **technical change competence** is essential.

All these competences are relevant at all levels in the new firm's hierarchy. The only exemptions are motivation competence and all methods competences, which are likely to be most relevant at higher levels of the new firm's hierarchy. The same applies to methods competences. So far, it has implicitly been presumed that the M&A parties give up their former human resource policies and practices to the same extent. However, in many M&A transactions, one party dominates the amalgamation, whereas the other firm's human resource policies and practices are less important for the new firm. This should be considered in HRDD in the case of amalgamation. The human resource requirements outlined above apply especially to the employees of the dominated firm. The relative importance of the competences depends on the degree of similarity between the firms' former human resource policies and practices.[300] If human resource policies and practices used to be similar to each other, the above competences are less important than in the case of formerly widely differing ones. Of the above-named competences, planning, decision-making, organisation, and problem-solving competence are essential in the short term. All social competences, innovation, market, and socio-cultural competence, as well as specialist, and technical change competence are needed in the middle term. What matters in a spin off is whether the old firm's employees are able to deal with the requirements imposed by the human resource policies and practices of the seller. The same competences as in a merger or an acquisition should be assessed in HRDD.

(2) In the case of self-containment, the human resource management policies and practices of the transaction parties coexist independently of each other.[301] A possible motive for self-

[299] Cf. Hentze, Joachim/Kammel, Andreas (2001), p. 293.
[300] Cf. Cummings, Larry L. (1984), p. 38.
[301] Cf. Lüdi, Markus/Eicken, Sabine (2000a), p. 12.

containment can be to keep motivation high or to support the attainment of M&A objectives in other dimensions. No human resource requirements ensue from self-containment, for the M&A parties do not change their human resource policies and practices in any way. The same applies to spin offs as to mergers and acquisitions, for the same reason as in mergers and acquisitions.

Table 2.10 contains the focus areas for HRDD for the two alternatives of amalgamation and self-containment related to the transaction parties' human resource policies and practices.

HR Policy & Practice Objectives / Competence	Amalgamation Objective	Self-containment Objective
Uncertainty Competence	•	
Communication Competence	•	
Conflict Competence	•	
Motivation Competence	•	
Co-operation Competence	•	
Innovation Competence	•	
Internal Competence		
Market Competence	•	
Socio-cultural Competence	•	
Complexity Competence		
Functional Competence	•	
Process Competence	•	
Planning Competence	•	
Problem-solving Competence	•	
Organisation Competence	•	
Decision-making Competence	•	
Social Change Competence		
Technical Change Competence	•	

Table 2.10: Competences and Human Resource Policy and Practice Objectives in M&A

2.2.4.3 *Focus Areas in line with Human Resource Organisation Objectives*

The third type of human resource management objective in M&A relates to the human resource organisations of the M&A parties. Human resource organisation mirrors how human resource management is institutionalised within a firm, which in turn influences the manner in which employees are dealt with in a firm.[302] According to the M&A literature reviewed, two extreme objectives[303] – which have been chosen due to their appearance in the M&A literature reviewed – are the following.

[302] Cf. Scholz, Christian (Ed.) (1999), p. 427.
[303] Cf. Lüdi, Markus/Eicken, Sabine (2000a), pp. 14f.

(1) Collaboration objective and

(2) Impartiality objective.

(1) Collaboration means that the firms' human resource organisations are consolidated, i.e. the human resource management departments of the M&A parties are melted into one.[304] Possible rationales underlying collaboration can be to reduce human resource management costs or learn from each other in terms of human resource management. A consequence of bringing together human resource management departments is usually fewer human resource managers as a percentage of the total workforce. The following competences are therefore vital in Human Resource Due Diligence: uncertainty, motivation, and social change competence. Collaboration is often followed by downsizing in the human resource management department, indicating that the intensity of supervision of employees by human resource managers is likely to decrease. As a consequence, human resource managers have less time and resources to devote to individuals, which can lead to aggravated **uncertainty**. Given this uncertainty, managers are required to show **motivation competence** to aid employees at lower levels in dealing with it. Often, uncertainty concerns not only employees at lower levels but also managers. Hence, motivation competence can mean supporting collaborators in dealing with unpredictable changes, which is why **social change competence** is also important for managers.[305]

These competences apply to all employees, except motivation competence.[306] As for human resource policies and practices, it does matter whether the new human resource management department is equally composed of human resource managers from both former firms or not. Presumably, in some M&A transactions one firm dominates the other when configuring the new human resource organisation. Dominance can be expressed in the number of human resource managers originating from one firm. It can be deduced from whether the new human resource organisation is entirely new or a relict of one of the transaction parties' former human resource management departments. In either case, the human resource requirements mentioned above are less relevant for the dominant firms' employees. This is because the dominated firms' employees are faced with new human resource managers and/or with a new human resource organisation, whereas the dominating firms' are not. Social change competence is demanded in the short term, but uncertainty and motivation competence in the middle term.

Besides the dominance or non-dominance of one firm's human resource organisation, the degree of changes resulting from an M&A transaction should be considered. In the case of major changes, staff reductions and significant modifications to human resource organisation are probably implied. In the case of minor changes, changes to human resource

---

[304] Cf. Lüdi, Markus/Eicken, Sabine (2000a), pp. 14f.
[305] Even though the uncertainty they face is different from the uncertainty employees are confronted with.
[306] Cf. Katz, David M. (2000), p. 4. Mc Leod, Douglas (2001), pp. 58ff.

organisation may ensue. The above-named competences are fundamental and should be included in a Human Resource Due Diligence.

Employees are also required to tolerate uncertainty, be motivated and deal with social changes when part of their human resource management is sold off. A firm that sells off a part of itself can be required to cope with the fact that half of its human resource managers leave to the buyer.

(2) Impartiality implies maintaining the firms' former human resource organisations.[307] The reason for this could be that collaboration is not necessary for the M&A objectives in other M&A management dimensions to be attained. One motive for impartiality can also be (at least in the short run) to prevent confusion amongst employees.[308] Firms can keep their human resource organisations whilst having their organisations work together or whilst having them operate independently. In any case, impartiality does not result in specific human resource requirements. The reason for this being that there are no material changes in the intensity of supervision or the familiarity of employees with their human resource managers. However, for intensity of supervision to survive, impartiality must be accompanied by a constant size of the human resource management department, which seldom ensues. Therefore, uncertainty, motivation, and social change competence may need to be assessed in Human Resource Due Diligence, assuming that the size of the human resource organisation decreases. In the case of spin offs, the employees of the seller must deal with new requirements (the same as described above for mergers and acquisitions) when they lose part of their human resource managers to the sold-off firm.

Table 2.11 illustrates what M&A management should concentrate on in HRDD, presuming that the objective is collaboration and impartiality.

---

[307] Cf. Lüdi, Markus/Eicken, Sabine (2000a), pp. 14f.

[308] According to Friederichs, M&A transactions imply both good and bad changes for employees. A reason for pursuing the impartiality objective can be to minimise the bad changes. Cf. Friederichs, Peter (1999), p. 337.

Competence \ Human Resource Organisation Objectives	Collaboration Objective	Impartiality Objective
Uncertainty Competence	•	
Communication Competence		
Conflict Competence		
Motivation Competence	•	
Co-operation Competence		
Innovation Competence		
Internal Competence		
Market Competence		
Socio-cultural Competence		
Complexity Competence		
Functional Competence		
Process Competence		
Planning Competence		
Problem-solving Competence		
Organisation Competence		
Decision-making Competence		
Social Change Competence	•	
Technical Change Competence		

Table 2.11: Competences and Human Resource Organisation Objectives in M&A

2.2.4.4 Interdependencies between Human Resource Management Objectives

The three types of human resource management objectives are defined from three different perspectives: from a process (human resource strategy), from an instrumental (human resource policies and practices) and from an institutional perspective (human resource organisation). All three perspectives have an impact on the definition of focus areas for HRDD, since different competence requirements may ensure from them. These competence requirements are implied, no matter whether human resource management objectives are pursued consciously or unconsciously. Presumably, the three types of M&A objectives are not aimed for at the same point in time in most M&A transactions. Instead, human resource policy objectives may be aimed for in the short term, and the other two types of objectives in the middle term.

As can be seen from the definition of focus areas for HRDD, motivation competence may be required for all three types of human resource management objectives. However, the reasons for the relevance of motivation competence differ depending on the underlying M&A objective. The most diverse competence requirements ensue from human resource policy and practice objectives: direct implications for every day work can be deduced based on these.

2.2.5 Interdependencies between Merger & Acquisition Management Objectives

There are eight possible interdependencies between the dimensions of M&A management, since each dimension can have an impact on each other. By defining M&A objectives in one dimension, M&A management indirectly determines what objectives should ideally be pursued in the other dimensions, presuming that a logical alignment of the management dimensions is the aim.[309] Also in business practice, a logical alignment seems to be intended in some cases. For instance, according to Siehl/Smith/Omura, the synergy and the resource access objective often go along with the consolidation, the reinvention, the assimilation and the aggregation objective.[310] Still, there may be M&A transactions, where the management dimensions are not logically consistent with each other. Thus, all management objectives that have an impact on the focus areas for HRDD should be considered individually, if possible, so that no important competence information is overlooked.

[309] Cf. Fischer, Heinz/Steffens-Duch, Silvia (2001), p. 53. Vogel, Dieter H. (2002), pp. 254 – 262. Rockholtz, Carsten (1998), pp. 208 – 215. Sales, Amy/Mirvis, Philip H. (1984), pp. 108ff. Shrivastava, Paul (1986), pp. 75f. Hayes, Robert H. (1979), pp. 43f. Datta, Deepak K. (1991), pp. 283ff. Napier, Nancy K. (1989), p. 280.

[310] Cf. Siehl, Caren/Smith, Dayle/Kissinger Omura, Ann (1990), p. 52. Siehl/Smith/Omura call this type of M&A transaction "love and marriage".

3 Generation of Human Resource Due Diligence Information

After having determined focus areas for HRDD in step 1 of the HRDD Concept, step 2 deals with indicators and tools that can be used to actually generate the desired HRDD information (see figure 3.1). Indicators serve to break down especially those competencies which have been identified as highly relevant into measurable attributes (chapter 3.1). Evaluation tools are diagnostic means, through which the developed indicators can be assessed (chapter 3.2). To be able to deduce concrete indicators and tools for step 2 of the HRDD Concept, the M&A context in which HRDD is carried out, is supposed to be known to the analyst. Therefore, the following chapters contains general advice for the generation of HRDD information through indicators and tools, but still leave some room for professionals to dispose of when applying the concept.[311]

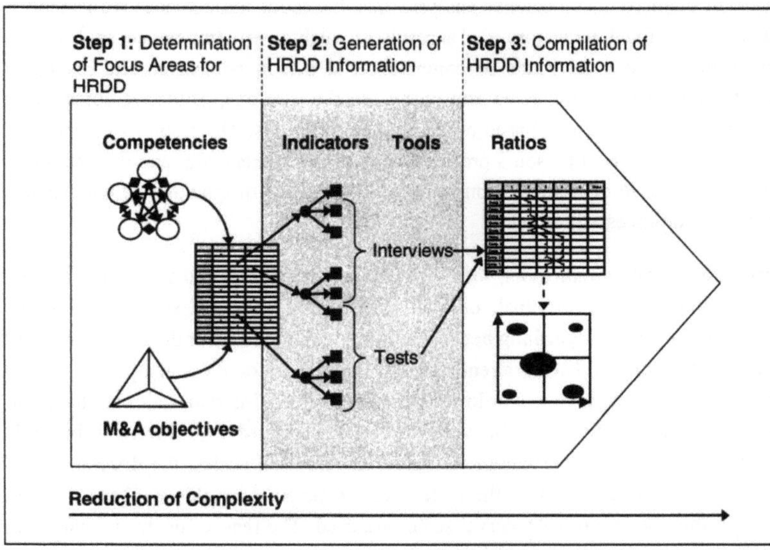

Figure 3.1: Generation of Human Resource Due Diligence Information

3.1 Indicators for Human Resource Due Diligence

In the following, appropriate types of indicators are derived for application to the HRDD Concept (chapter 3.1.1 and 3.1.2). Moreover, concrete indicators for the five competences are exemplified (chapter 3.1.3).

---

[311] This is in line with the research results, which this thesis is supposed to produce: a concept in content for a general problem. Cf. chapter 1.3.5.

3.1.1 Possible Types of Indicators for Human Resource Due Diligence

To determine types of indicators that could be considered for the HRDD Concept, psychological literature has been reviewed to find typical distinction criteria for human resource indicators.[312] Three different types of indicators, in line with three different distinction criteria, have been defined, namely measurability of the competences, the focal point of the analysis, and the time horizon of the indicators.

(1) As far as the **measurability** of competences is concerned, human resource indicators can be of either a qualitative or a quantitative nature.[313] Qualitative and quantitative competence analyses differ according to how the competences are assessed according to the nature of the results of analysis and according to how the results of analysis are processed. In the case of qualitative competence analysis, insights about competences are generated without any predefined indicators. As a result of qualitative competence analysis, an estimate is made about the kinds of competences a person possesses. The results of analysis are generally not processed any further. In the case of quantitative competence analysis, insights are generated based on predefined indicators. The result of competence analysis is an estimate of a person's proficiency or non-proficiency in, and the parameter value of predefined, to-be-assessed competences. The results of quantitative competence analysis are often processed further.[314]

When using quantitative indicators, four different scales can be used to express desired and actual competences – nominal, ordinal, interval and relational scales.[315] Nominal scales are suitable for distinguishing between objects with the same or different parameter values, and hence between two different states.[316] Ordinal scales allow analysis of objects differing between higher, identical or lower parameter values. Interval scales are based on the assumption that the difference between the ranks associated with different objects is identical to their differences in parameter value. In relational scales, the difference between two numbers is identical to the differences in parameter value between the two objects.[317] In this thesis, ordinal interval scales are used. The reason for this is that using the HRDD Concept is not about evaluating whether certain competences can be found in a

---

312 The following literature sources have been reviewed. Erpenbeck, John/Rosenstiel, Lutz von. In: Erpenbeck, John/Rosenstiel, Lutz von (Eds.) (2003), pp. IX – XL. Sarges, Werner. In: Sarges, Werner (Ed.) (2000), pp. 15f. Wottawa, Heinrich. In: Rosenstiel, Lutz von/Lang-von Wins, Thomas (2000), p. 33. Schuler, Heinz. In: Rosenstiel, Lutz von/Lang-von Wins, Thomas (2000), p. 65. Kanning, Uwe Peter. In: Kanning, Uwe Peter/Holling, Heinz (Eds.) (2002), pp. 60ff. Sarges, Werner. In: Rosenstiel, Lutz von/Lang-von Wins, Thomas (2000), p. 115. Sarges, Werner/Wottawa, Heinrich (Eds.) (2001), (entire book). Hossiep, Rüdiger. In: Rosenstiel, Lutz von/Lang-von Wins, Thomas (2000), p. 83.

313 Cf. Kane, Bob/Crawford, John/Grant, David (1999), p. 495.

314 Cf. Sarges, Werner. In: Sarges, Werner (Ed.) (2000), pp. 15f. Erpenbeck, John/Rosenstiel, Lutz von. In: Erpenbeck, John/ Rosenstiel, Lutz von (Eds.) (2003), pp. IX – XL distinguish between subjective and objective indicators.

315 Cf. Bortz, Jürgen/Döring, Nicola (2002), p. 73.

316 Nominal scales allow for binary measurements only. Cf. Bühner, Rolf (2000), pp. 24f.

317 Typical fields of application for ordinal interval scales are grades. Cf. Weber, Manfred (2002), pp. 18f. Baetge, Jörg (1998), p. 41.

person or not. Instead, it is appraised what parameter value (expressed in numbers) the person shows for certain competences. There are various relational scales – scales from 1 to 10, scales including 0.5 stages, scales including non-observable elements and Likert scales (ranging from 1 to 5). In this thesis, relational scales from 1 to 5 are used. There are three reasons for this. First, the indicators of the Human Resource Due Diligence Concept require that a person's competences are expressed on a sufficiently large scale to enable comparisons with other persons. Second, psychological literature argues that it is hardly feasible to assess a person in more detail than on a 1 to 5 scale. Gaps between one parameter value on a scale and another are defined on a comparative basis, which is why exact differences between e.g. a 2 and a 3 cannot be determined.[318] Third, the practical research goal of this thesis prohibits including non-observable items into the scale.

(2) The **focal point** of human resource indicators can be input-oriented, behavioural or output-oriented.[319] Input-oriented indicators assess competences by determining the predisposition a person has towards showing competent behaviour. A person's motivations, emotions, characteristics, education, knowledge, values/attitudes and cognitions can be subjected to a competence evaluation when taking an input-oriented perspective.[320] Behavioural indicators aim at determining a person's competences based on his actions or disposition to act.[321] Output-oriented indicators are based on the expectation that a person's competences can be deduced from the results generated.[322]

(3) Indicators for Human Resource Due Diligence can also differ according to the **time horizon** they refer to. They can be past-, present- or future-related. Past-related human resource indicators infer assumptions about a person's competences based on data that concern the past. Present-related indicators rely on data that are related to the present, whereas future-related indicators are grounded on data referring to the future.[323]

Figure 3.2 summarises the three distinction criteria. As can be seen, there is no hierarchy between the distinction criteria. This means that indicators can be of quantitative nature, input-oriented and past-related at the same time, i.e. twenty-four different types of indicators can be derived when combining all three distinction criteria with each other. Qualitative indicators can e.g. be combined with input-oriented, behavioural, output-oriented, past-, present- or future-related indicators.

---

318 Cf. Bühner, Rolf (2000), pp. 24f.
319 Cf. Wottawa, Heinrich. In: Rosenstiel, Lutz von/Lang-von Wins, Thomas (Eds.) (2000), p. 33.
320 Cf. Schuler, Heinz. In: Rosenstiel, Lutz von/Lang-von Wins, Thomas (Eds.) (2000), p. 65. Kanning, Uwe Peter. In: Kanning, Uwe Peter/Holling, Heinz (Eds.) (2002), pp. 61f. Sarges, Werner. In: Rosenstiel, Lutz von/Lang-von Wins, Thomas (Eds.) (2000), p. 115. Hossiep, Rüdiger. In: Rosenstiel, Lutz von/Lang-von Wins, Thomas (Eds.) (2000), p. 83.
321 Cf. Becker, Robert E./Heimberg, Richard Gordon. In: Bellack, Alan/Hersen, Michel (Eds.) (1988), pp. 370f.
322 Cf. Beer, Michael (1987), p. 290.
323 Cf. Sarges, Werner/Wottawa, Heinrich. In: Sarges, Werner/Wottawa, Heinrich (Eds.) (2001), pp. VIIf.

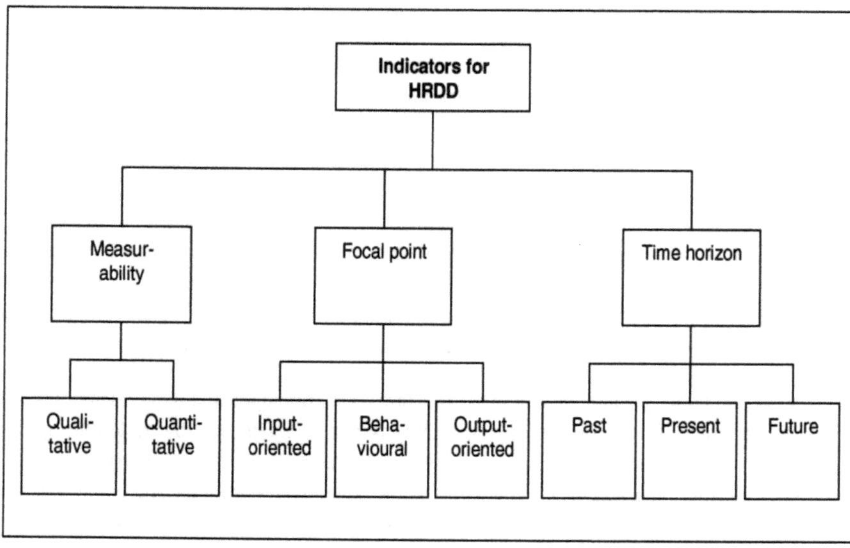

Figure 3.2: Types of Indicators for Human Resource Due Diligence according to the reviewed Psychological Literature

3.1.2 Types of Indicators Selected for the Human Resource Due Diligence Concept

Previous studies about Human Resource Due Diligence have dealt with future-related assessment tools, but not with indicators. Hence, the selection of indicators for HRDD Concept is entirely based on the assumptions of this thesis, and not on previous studies of HRDD.

(1) As regards the **measurability** of indicators for HRDD, quantitative indicators have been selected. The reason for including quantitative indicators into the HRDD Concept lies in the following. The Concept is supposed to reduce complexity for M&A management.[324] The aimed-for reduction of complexity is presumed to be best feasible, if quantitative indicators are applied, since relying on predefined, quantitative indicators already means making a selection, thereby reducing complexity.

(2) As regards the **focal point** of indicators for HRDD, behavioural indicators have been chosen, the reasons for this being the management objective-oriented perspective of analysis of this thesis, and the definition of competences as dispositions to act.[325] The input-oriented indicators are either not consistent with the management objective-oriented

[324] Cf. chapter 1.5.

[325] Cf. chapter 1.3.1 perspective of analysis, chapter 1.4.4 human resource requirement/competence definition.

perspective of analysis of this thesis or with the behavioural understanding of human resource requirements.[326] Output-oriented indicators are not considered either, due to the management objective-oriented perspective of analysis of this study. The HRDD Concept aims to clarify whether employees are likely to fulfil M&A-induced requirements in the future, and not to evaluate whether they have succeeded in meeting them in the past. Behavioural indicators are consistent with the perspective of analysis of this thesis and are therefore used in the further analysis.

(3) Human resource indicators integral to the Human Resource Due Diligence Concept must be related to the future. The reason for this **time horizon** is twofold. First, the management objective-oriented perspective of analysis requires a future-related perspective.[327] Second, future-related indicators are useful due to the potential dynamics of M&A management objectives.[328]

The indicators selected for the Human Resource Due Diligence Concept are summarised in figure 3.3. To sum up, for indicators to be suitable for the HRDD Concept, they should be quantitative, behavioural and future-related.

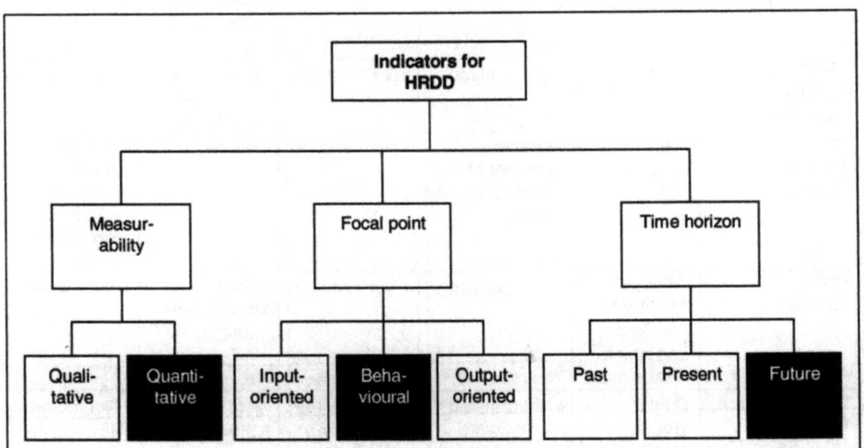

Figure 3.3: Types of Indicators for Human Resource Due Diligence selected for the Concept

---

326 Ditto.
327 Cf. chapter 1.3.1 perspective of analysis.
328 Cf. chapter 1.4.5.

3.1.3 Examples of Indicators for the Human Resource Due Diligence Concept

As can be seen from tables 4.1 to 4.5, in the following, concrete indicators are developed for each M&A objective[329] of the HRDD Concept. These indicators show two characteristics. First, they are defined based on the three types of indicators selected for the HRDD Concept – quantitative, behavioural, future-related indicators.[330] Second, they are defined in line with the focus areas for HRDD in chapter 2.2.

3.1.3.1 Social Competence

As shown in chapter 2.2, social competence is very important if certain M&A management objectives are aimed for. It can, but does not have to be assessed for other M&A objectives. There are certain M&A objectives for which social competence is not relevant.

Competence / Objective	Uncertainty Competence	Communication Competence	Conflict Competence	Motivation Competence	Co-operation Competence
Synergy Objective	• Not required	• Not required	• Not required	• **Enthuse for M&A despite downsizing**	• Not required
Financial Return Objective	• Not required	• Not required	• Not required	• Create optimism related to changes	• Not required
Resource Access Objective	• Not required	• Enable transfer of knowledge and skills	• Not required	• Not required	• Enable knowledge and skill transfer in inter-firm teams
Status Objective	• Accept M&A without knowing why it takes place	• Not required	• Not required	• Make collaborators support M&A	• Not required
Diversification Objective	• Not required	• Not required	• Not required	• Not required	• Not required
Market Development Objective	• Not required	• Not required	• Not required	• Not required	• Not required
Market Penetration Objective	• Not required	• Not required	• Not required	• Not required	• Not required
Product Development Objective	• Not required	• Not required	• Not required	• Not required	• Not required

329 Cf. chapter 2.2. The tables include indicators for those competences which are highly relevant for a certain M&A objective. For competences which are of minor or of conditional importance, no indicators are defined. This is to enhance the transparency of the argumentation.
330 Cf. Schuler, Heinz (2004), p. 443.

Competence / Objective	Uncertainty Competence	Communication Competence	Conflict Competence	Motivation Competence	Co-operation Competence
Consolidation Objective	• Not required	• Deal with increased number of communication partners	• Not required	• Help collaborators cope with organisational changes (e. g. new roles, states)	• Make joint macro structure work
Autonomy Objective	• Not required	• Exchange facts, establish parent/ subsidiary relationship	• Not required	• Not required	• Foster joint decision-making
Reinvention Objective	• Cope with uncertainty deriving from new micro structure	• Work with more communication partners, communicate more intensely	• Not required	• Compensate for missing leadership through structures and processes	• Enhance efficiency of new structures and processes
Linkage Objective	• Not required	• Exchange information at M&A parties' interfaces	• Not required	• Not required	• Take joint decisions at interfaces
Preservation Objective	• Not required	• Not required	• Not required	• Not required	• Not required
Renewal Objective	• Not required	• Not required	• Not required	• Not required	• Not required
Conservation Objective	• Not required	• Not required	• Not required	• Not required	• Not required
Integration Objective	• Not required	• Adopt other communication patterns, help others adopt own	• Not required	• Facilitate cultural changes for collaborators from integrated firm	• Not required
Assimilation Objective	• Not required	• Establish information flows and relationships with other firm's employees	• Deal with different patterns of behaviour	• Support collaborators in dealing with new patterns of behaviour	• Not required
Segregation Objective	• Not required	• Not required	• Not required	• Not required	• Not required

Competence / Objective	Uncertainty Competence	Communication Competence	Conflict Competence	Motivation Competence	Co-operation Competence
Absorption Objective	• Not required	• Adopt other firm's patterns of information and opinion sharing	• Not required	• Support collaborators from absorbed firm in dealing with changes, encourage collaborators from absorbing firm to be patient	• Adopt new patterns of behaviour (absorbed firm's employees), accept clash of patterns (all)
Coexistence Objective	• Not required	• Accept new patterns of information and opinion sharing	• Not required	• Help collaborators to acquaint themselves with new leader-subordinate relationships	• Adopt new patterns of behaviour
Creation Objective	• Not required	• Not required	• Not required	• Not required	• Not required
Commutation Objective	• Not required	• Provide comprehensible information to others and receive information in the intended way despite language barriers	• Deal constructively with conflicts caused by different patterns of behaviour, due to differences in national cultures	• Not required	• Not required
Insulation Objective	• Not required	• Not required	• Not required	• Not required	• Not required
Aggregation Objective	• Not required	• Communicate more effectively	• Deal constructively with conflicts caused by new behavioural requirements	• Help collaborators get along with new behavioural requirements	• Cope with new patterns of co-operation
Independence Objective	• Not required	• Not required	• Not required	• Not required	• Not required
Amalgamation Objective	• Accept uncertainty deriving from new compensation systems and performance criteria	• Get used to e.g. a higher communication density	• Negotiate constructively in the case of conflicts due to new behavioural requirements	• Enhance commitment of collaborators despite changes to policies and practices	• Change co-operation habits, e.g. introduce joint decision-making

Competence / Objective	Uncertainty Competence	Communication Competence	Conflict Competence	Motivation Competence	Co-operation Competence
Self Containment Objective	• Not required	• Not required	• Not required	• Not required	• Not required
Collaboration Objective	• Deal with uncertainty about where and how to proceed in the new firm	• Not required	• Not required	• Support collaborators in dealing with unpredictable changes	• Not required
Impartiality Objective	• Not required	• Not required	• Not required	• Not required	• Not required

Table 3.1: Human Resource Due Diligence Indicators for Social Competence

As can be seen from table 3.1, the indicators for HRDD for social competence are tailored to the reasons for their relevance, in line with the M&A management objectives from chapter 2.2. For instance, motivation competence in case of the synergy objective can be measured by evaluating managers' competence in enthusing collaborators for the new firm despite downsizing.[331]

3.1.3.2 Systems Competence

Table 3.2 focuses on indicators for HRDD for those M&A management objectives for which systems competence is demanded. As for social competence, the indicators for systems competence differ depending on the underlying M&A objectives. This implies that firms who want to make use of the HRDD Concept cannot apply a pattern solution, but must make adaptations in line with their objectives. For instance, internal competence in the financial return objective can be evaluated by observing the way in which former internal structures are respected when M&A changes are to be introduced.[332] In chapter 2.1.2, the general need for evaluating internal competence in M&A has been explained by the necessity of considering M&A parties' former internal structures when introducing changes.

Competence / Objective	Innovation Competence	Internal Competence	Market Competence	Socio-cultural Competence	Complexity Competence
Synergy Objective	• Foster synergies e. g. through process innovations	• Realise synergies in a responsible way	• Not required	• Not required	• Not required
Financial Return	• Enhance efficiency of	• **Consider specifics of**	• Take strategic	• Not required	• Not required

[331] Cf. highlighted indicator in table 3.1.
[332] Cf. highlighted indicator in table 3.2.

Competence / Objective	Innovation Competence	Internal Competence	Market Competence	Socio-cultural Competence	Complexity Competence
Objective	new firm, foster its competitive position (process and product innovations)	**Internal structures when introducing changes**	decisions, derive measures to realise these decisions		
Resource Access Objective	• Make new firm stand out against competitors through product innovations	• Not required	• Ensure significance of knowledge and skills to be transferred	• Not required	• Not required
Status Objective	• Not required	• Not required	• Not required	• Not required	• Not required
Diversification Objective	• Assure that innovation rates post M&A remain high	• Not required	• Position new firm in its market(s)	• Not required	• Not required
Market Development Objective	• Find new applications for existing products	• Not required	• Develop new products & applications, tap new customers	• Not required	• Not required
Market Penetration Objective	• Not required	• Not required	• Not required	• Not required	• Not required
Product Development Objective	• Invent new products	• Not required	• Not required	• Not required	• Not required
Consolidation Objective	• Not required	• Not required	• Not required	• Not required	• Create macro structure that reduces complexity, deal with every day complexity
Autonomy Objective	• Not required	• Not required	• Not required	• Not required	• Not required
Reinvention Objective	• Make process innovations	• Not required	• Not required	• Not required	• Cope with complexity caused by new micro structure
Linkage Objective	• Not required	• Avoid discontinuances post M&A, decide about new structures and processes	• Not required	• Not required	• Cope with new interdependencies

Competence / Objective	Innovation Competence	Internal Competence	Market Competence	Socio-cultural Competence	Complexity Competence
Preservation Objective	• Not required	• Not required	• Not required	• Not required	• Not required
Renewal Objective	• Not required	• Not required	• Not required	• Not required	• Not required
Conservation Objective	• Not required	• Not required	• Not required	• Not required	• Not required
Integration Objective	• Not required	• Not required	• Not required	• Not required	• Not required
Assimilation Objective	• Not required	• Not required	• Not required	• Not required	• Not required
Segregation Objective	• Not required	• Not required	• Not required	• Not required	• Not required
Absorption Objective	• Not required	• Not required	• Not required	• Not required	• Not required
Coexistence Objective	• Not required	• Not required	• Not required	• Not required	• Not required
Creation Objective	• Not required	• Not required	• Not required	• Not required	• Not required
Commutation Objective	• Not required	• Not required	• Not required	• Not required	• Not required
Insulation Objective	• Not required	• Not required	• Not required	• Not required	• Not required
Aggregation Objective	• Find a way of aggregating human resource strategies (process innovation)	• Not required	• Not required	• Not required	• Not required
Independence Objective	• Not required	• Not required	• Not required	• Not required	• Not required
Amalgamation Objective	• Show a generally higher degree of innovation	• Not required	• Be more market-oriented than before	• Be able to cope with people from different national cultures	• Not required
Self Containment Objective	• Not required	• Not required	• Not required	• Not required	• Not required
Collaboration Objective	• Not required	• Not required	• Not required	• Not required	• Not required
Impartiality Objective	• Not required	• Not required	• Not required	• Not required	• Not required

Table 3.2: Human Resource Due Diligence Indicators for Systems Competence

3.1.3.3 Specialist Competence

Table 3.3 summarises indicators for HRDD for specialist competence related to those M&A management objectives for which specialist competence is urgently required. Unlike the other four competences, the indicators for specialist competence hardly differ according to the underlying M&A objectives.[333] The highlighted indicator for functional competence for the reinvention objective is e.g. similar to the functional indicator for the aggregation objective.[334] If the type of tasks that must be performed is not known to the analyst, no more than general pattern solutions can be provided. To be able to develop more concrete indicators for HRDD, the analyst must know which groups of employees are at the centre of attention in a transaction. This implies that firms who make use of the HRDD Concept must adapt the pattern solution provided by the Concept to their own M&A transaction. To give an example, assuming that the objective is reinvention, functional competence requires that employees are able to work efficiently with new structures. The question of what kinds of competences are required to be able to do so can only be resolved when one knows the nature of the new structures and about the employee groups that are being considered. In contrast to the other competences, the different components of specialist competence need not be assessed simultaneously in M&A.

[333] Cf. Erpenbeck, John/Rosenstiel, Lutz von. In: Erpenbeck, John/Rosenstiel, Lutz von (Eds.) (2003), pp. XVff. This is due to the task relatedness of specialist competence as pointed out in chapter 1.4.4.

[334] Cf. highlighted indicator in table 3.3.

Competence / Objective	Functional Competence	Process Competence
Synergy Objective	• Work efficiently	• Work efficiently
Financial Return Objective	• Foster competitive advantage of new firm	• Foster competitive advantage of new firm
Resource Access Objective	• Not required	• Not required
Status Objective	• Not required	• Not required
Diversification Objective	• Foster competitive advantage	• Foster competitive advantage
Market Development Objective	• Foster competitive advantage	• Foster competitive advantage
Market Penetration Objective	• Not required	• Not required
Product Development Objective	• Not required	• Not required
Consolidation Objective	• Work efficiently and foster competitive advantage	• Work efficiently and foster competitive advantage
Autonomy Objective	• Not required	• Not required
Reinvention Objective	• **Determine suitability of new structures, work efficiently with them**	• Determine suitability of new processes, work efficiently with these
Linkage Objective	• Not required	• Not required
Preservation Objective	• Not required	• Not required
Renewal Objective	• Perform higher ranked tasks than one's own usual tasks	• Perform higher ranked processes than one's own usual processes
Conservation Objective	• Not required	• Not required
Integration Objective	• Not required	• Not required
Assimilation Objective	• Not required	• Not required
Segregation Objective	• Not required	• Not required
Absorption Objective	• Not required	• Not required
Coexistence Objective	• Not required	• Not required
Creation Objective	• Not required	• Not required
Commutation Objective	• Not required	• Not required
Insulation Objective	• Not required	• Not required
Aggregation Objective	• Work efficiently and foster competitive advantage	• Work efficiently and foster competitive advantage
Independence Objective	• Not required	• Not required
Amalgamation Objective	• Work efficiently and foster competitive advantage	• Work efficiently and foster competitive advantage
Self Containment Objective	• Not required	• Not required
Collaboration Objective	• Not required	• Not required
Impartiality Objective	• Not required	• Not required

Table 3.3: Human Resource Due Diligence Indicators for Specialist Competence

3.1.3.4 Methods Competence

Table 3.4 concentrates on indicators for HRDD for those M&A management objectives for which methods competence is highly important. As for social and systems competence, the indicators for methods competence differ according to the underlying M&A objectives. For instance when the renewal objective is pursued, planning competence can be assessed as competence in setting up a time and resource framework for new more sophisticated tasks.[335] If the reinvention objective is aimed at, planning competence should be assessed as competence in setting up a time and resource framework for the changes that are to be achieved to micro structure.

Competence / Objective	Planning Competence	Problem-solving Competence	Organisation Competence	Decision-making Competence
Synergy Objective	• Plan for attainment of synergies	• Not required	• Not required	• Select functions of the firms' value chains for synergy attainment
Financial Return Objective	• Define new strategy, determine operative measures to implement this strategy	• Not required	• Not required	• Pick strategy from alternatives, choose measures
Resource Access Objective	• Assess which functions to transfer knowledge and skills to	• Not required	• Not required	• Choose functions for knowledge and skill transfer from several alternatives
Status Objective	• Not required	• Not required	• Not required	• Not required
Diversification Objective	• Not required	• Not required	• Not required	• Not required
Market Development Objective	• Define new strategy, determine operative measures to implement it	• Not required	• Not required	• Choose strategy and operative measures from bundle
Market Penetration Objective	• Co-ordinate activities of new firm	• Not required	• Not required	• Select way of co-ordinating future activities
Product Development Objective	• Not required	• Not required	• Not required	• Not required
Consolidation Objective	• Not required	• Solve problems related to new macro structure	• Not required	• Not required
Autonomy Objective	• Not required	• Not required	• Not required	• Not required

335 Cf. highlighted indicator in table 3.4.

Competence / Objective	Planning Competence	Problem-solving Competence	Organisation Competence	Decision-making Competence
Reinvention Objective	• Determine how, when and with what resources to make changes to micro structure	• Determine what new micro structure is supposed to be like	• Redistribute and integrate tasks on micro level	• Decide on a new micro structure based on analysis of alternatives
Linkage Objective	• Plan how, when and with what resource to link micro structures	• Establish adequate linkages, troubleshoot in case linkages do not work	• Not required	• Base decision about linkages to be established on suitability criteria
Preservation Objective	• Not required	• Not required	• Not required	• Not required
Renewal Objective	• **Plan in advance despite more sophisticated new tasks**	• Work towards a set goal without knowing the path towards this goals beforehand	• Split tasks up into subtasks and arrange for their completion	• Consider and weigh alternative courses of action
Conservation Objective	• Not required	• Not required	• Not required	• Not required
Integration Objective	• Not required	• Not required	• Not required	• Not required
Assimilation Objective	• Not required	• Not required	• Not required	• Not required
Segregation Objective	• Not required	• Not required	• Not required	• Not required
Absorption Objective	• Not required	• Not required	• Not required	• Not required
Coexistence Objective	• Not required	• Not required	• Not required	• Not required
Creation Objective	• Not required	• Not required	• Not required	• Not required
Commutation Objective	• Not required	• Not required	• Not required	• Not required
Insulation Objective	• Not required	• Not required	• Not required	• Not required
Aggregation Objective	• Not required	• Not required	• Not required	• Not required
Independence Objective	• Not required	• Not required	• Not required	• Not required
Amalgamation Objective	• Plan for amalgamation to be achieved, cope with new performance criteria	• Find one's way towards amalgamation, cope with new performance criteria	• Distribute and integrate amalgamation-related tasks, cope with new performance criteria	• Select suitable ways of attaining amalgamation, cope with new performance criteria
Self Containment Objective	• Not required	• Not required	• Not required	• Not required

Competence / Objective	Planning Competence	Problem-solving Competence	Organisation Competence	Decision-making Competence
Collaboration Objective	• Not required	• Not required	• Not required	• Not required
Impartiality Objective	• Not required	• Not required	• Not required	• Not required

Table 3.4: Human Resource Due Diligence Indicators for Methods Competence

3.1.3.5 Change Competence

In the following, indicators for change competence are defined for those M&A objectives for which change competence is of high importance (see table 3.5). The indicators for change competence also differ in line with the respective M&A objective. For instance, when the integration objective is aimed for, social change competence is manifested in the integrated employees' competence in dealing with new people and new patterns of behaviour at work.[336] In contrast, when the reinvention objective is pursued, social change competence means competence in getting used to new colleagues, collaborators and superiors.

Competence / Objective	Social Change Competence	Technical Change Competence
Synergy Objective	• Not required	• Not required
Financial Return Objective	• Not required	• Not required
Resource Access Objective	• Not required	• Update knowledge and skills to be transferred
Status Objective	• Not required	• Not required
Diversification Objective	• Not required	• Not required
Market Development Objective	• Not required	• Not required
Market Penetration Objective	• Not required	• Not required
Product Development Objective	• Not required	• Not required
Consolidation Objective	• Not required	• Not required
Autonomy Objective	• Not required	• Not required
Reinvention Objective	• Deal with new colleagues, collaborators or superiors	• Not required
Linkage Objective	• Cope with colleagues, collaborators or superiors met with through linkage	• Not required
Preservation Objective	• Not required	• Not required
Renewal Objective	• Not required	• Deal with new or modified technical requirements
Conservation Objective	• Not required	• Not required

[336] Cf. highlighted indicator in table 3.5.

Objective \ Competence	Social Change Competence	Technical Change Competence
Integration Objective	• **Get along with new people and new patterns of behaviour at work (integrated firm's employees)**	• Not required
Assimilation Objective	• Adapt to new people and new patterns of behaviour (all employees)	• Not required
Segregation Objective	• Not required	• Not required
Absorption Objective	• Not required	• Not required
Coexistence Objective	• Not required	• Not required
Creation Objective	• Not required	• Not required
Commutation Objective	• Not required	• Not required
Insulation Objective	• Not required	• Not required
Aggregation Objective	• Adopt new patterns of behaviour	• Cope with new or modified technical requirements
Independence Objective	• Not required	• Not required
Amalgamation Objective	• Not required	• Get used to new or modified technical requirements
Self Containment Objective	• Not required	• Not required
Collaboration Objective	• Deal with new human resource managers	• Not required
Impartiality Objective	• Not required	• Not required

Table 3.5: Human Resource Due Diligence Indicators for Change Competence

3.2 Evaluation Tools for Human Resource Due Diligence

The following chapters serve to acquire adequate evaluation tools from psychological literature that can be used when applying the Human Resource Due Diligence Concept (chapters 3.2.1 and 3.2.2). Moreover, it demonstrates what tools can be used for which competence groups – task- versus non task-related –, and implications for the HRDD Concept are deduced (chapter 3.2.3).

3.2.1 Possible Evaluation Tools for Human Resource Due Diligence

To determine what types of evaluation tools can be taken into consideration for the Concept, psychological literature has been reviewed to find typical distinction criteria for human resource tools.[337] Five different distinction criteria have been identified. Diagnostic tools can

[337] The following literature sources have been reviewed. Eberle, Walter (1996), p. 223. Eckert, Angelika (2002), p. 23. Huffcutt, Allen I./Arthur, Winfried (1994), p. 185. Ioannis, Tsaousis/Ioannis, Nikolaou, E. (2001), p. 290. Jochmann, Walter (1999), p. 18. Kanning, Uwe Peter/Walter, Manuela (2003), pp. 40f. Klimecki, Rüdiger G./Gmür, Markus (2001), p. 243. Pichler, Martin (2001), pp. 17ff. Pollack, Walter/Pirk, Dieter (2001), pp. 64f. Reilly, Richard R./Chao, Georgia T. (1982), p. 15. Sarges, Werner/Wottowa, Heinrich (Eds.)

be distinguished according to their nature, to their field of application and – in line with indicators for HRDD – according to their measurability, focal point and time horizon. The five different types of tools are described in the following.

(1) As far as their **nature** is concerned, diagnostic tools can be based on document analysis, interrogation or observation.[338] A person's competences can be assessed based on documents that allow inferences about his behaviours. Besides evaluation based on documents, a person's competences can also be appraised based on interrogations about his behaviour. Finally, competences can be estimated by observation of a person's behaviour. Since the HRDD Concept provides a way of appraising competences based on new data, documents cannot serve as evaluation tools for it. The other two types of tools – interrogations and observations – can be used.

(2) Diagnostic tools can also be distinguished according to their **field of application**. Many diagnostic tools are used for recruitment, whereas others are more suitable for assessing already recruited employees. It is assumed that Human Resource Due Diligence is performed to assess already recruited employees, whereas recruiting probably takes place upon completion of HRDD.

(3) Regarding the **measurability** of tools for HRDD, quantitative or qualitative assessments can be made, using diagnostic tools.[339] Given the focus of the Concept on quantitative indicators, evaluation tools selected for the HRDD Concept must allow the use of these quantitative indicators.

(4) Diagnostic tools also differ according to their **focal point**. They can be input-, behavioural- and output-oriented.[340] Given the management objective-oriented perspective of analysis and the competence definition underlying this thesis, the tools selected for the HRDD Concept must show a behavioural focus.

(5) Concerning their **time orientation**, some diagnostic tools are related to the past, some to the present and others to the future. Due to the management objective-oriented perspective of analysis of this thesis, tools for HRDD need to be suitable for employing future-related indicators.

(2001) (entire book). Schmidt, Frank L./Hunter, John E. (1998), p. 265. Schmidt, Frank L./Hunter, John E. In: Kleinmann, Martin/Strauß, Bernd (Eds.) (2000), p. 23. Schuler, Heinz (2004), p. 451. Schuler, Heinz/Funke, Uwe (Ed.) (1991) (entire book). Wottawa, Heinrich /Hossiep, Rüdiger (1987), p. 30 quoted after Neuberger 1980, Jeserich 1981, Block 1982 and Dirks 1982. Rosentiel, Lutz von (2003), p. 156. Few publications in the M&A literature deal with evaluation tools for a HRDD. Exceptions are Aldering, Christoph/Hutten, Christina Freiin von. In: Berens, Wolfgang et al. (Eds.) (2002), pp. 421ff. Corporate Leadership Council (1999), p. 22. Gut-Villa, Cornelia (1997), p. 164. Pack, Heinrich. In: Picot, Gerhard (Ed.) (2002), p. 243. Wucknitz, Uwe D. (2002a), p. 158). Therefore the selection of tools for the HRDD Concept is based on a review of psychological – non-M&A-related – literature.

338 Cf. Klimecki, Rüdiger/Gmür, Markus (2001), p. 234.

339 Cf. chapter 3.1.1.

340 Ditto.

3.2.2 Evaluation Tools Selected for the Human Resource Due Diligence Concept

Seventeen sources in psychological literature have been reviewed to discover the most frequently named diagnostic tools.[341] The following eleven tools have been identified: assessment centres, credentials, CVs, dialogues, feedback, graphology, interviews, questionnaires, reference letters, role plays and tests. These eleven evaluation tools are investigated in the following with regard to the degree to which they fulfil the five suitability criteria in chapter 3.2.1. For a tool to be functional for the HRDD Concept, it must fulfil all five suitability criteria. **Assessment centres** serve to observe a person's behaviour. Assessment centres are employed in recruiting but also in other business situations. They are usually based on predefined evaluation criteria, which is why they allow the use of quantitative indicators. Assessment centres can among other things be based on behavioural indicators and be related to the future.[342] **Credentials** encompass a person's track record including school and further education results. They are usually historical, which is why they are of limited use when applying the HRDD Concept. Moreover, they are primarily used for recruiting diagnostics. However, credentials can be used to generate quantitative data. Still, these data are of an input-oriented and not a behavioural nature. In addition, credential data are related to the past.[343] **Curricula Vitae** can also be used to assess competences. They are a representation of how a person presents herself to a potential employer. They are usually historical, which is why they are of no use for the HRDD Concept. Moreover, their usual field of application is recruiting. Using CVs, quantitative assessments can be made. In addition, CVs are input-oriented and related to the past, which is why they are not suitable for further argumentation.[344] **Dialogues** usually take place one-on-one, often between superiors and their collaborators. They can be subdivided into different types, e.g. developmental dialogue and employee dialogue. All these different types have in common the fact that they serve to interrogate people. They are amongst other things used to assess employees in non-recruiting situations. Dialogues are qualitative in nature – they usually do not involve the use of predefined indicators and scales, but they allow for the use of behavioural indicators, and they are related to the future.[345] **Feedback** reflects one or several persons' perception of another person's behaviour, and can hence be allocated to interrogation tools. Feedback is often used in day-to-day business situations, but not usually in recruiting. A person's behaviour can be described by another person, which is why feedback allows the use of behavioural indicators. Feedback is usually related to the past, but can, under certain circumstances, also be related to the future.[346] **Graphology** is sometimes used in diagnostics to produce assumptions about a person from his style of writing. It can be allocated to documented tools and is used in

---

[341] Cf. chapter 3.2.1.

[342] Cf. Kanning, Uwe Peter/Walter, Manuela (2003), p. 40. Wottawa, Heinrich/Hossiep, Rüdiger (1987), p. 30. Kleinmann, Martin (1997), p. 9.

[343] Cf. Hentze, Joachim/Kammel, Andreas (2001), p. 300.

[344] Cf. Wottawa, Heinrich/Hossiep, Rüdiger (1987), p. 30. Hentze, Joachim/Kammel, Andreas (2001), p. 299.

[345] Cf. Eberle, Walter (1996), p. 223. Pollack, Walter/Pirk, Dieter (2001), p. 70.

[346] Cf. Pichler, Martin (2001), pp. 17 – 20. Schmidt, Frank/Hunter, John. In: Kleinmann, Martin/Strauß, Bernd (Eds.) (2000), p. 23. Hilb, Martin (2002), pp. 79ff. Taubert, Rolf/Piorr, Rüdiger (1999), p. 49.

recruiting. The results of graphology are of a quantitative nature, even though no metric scales can be produce based on graphology. No behavioural data can be generated using this diagnostic tool. Moreover, it is related to the past or to the present, and not to the future as required by the HRDD Concept.[347] Many different types of **interviews** can be distinguished that are often used in diagnostics, ranging from structured to unstructured ones. Interviews can be allocated to interrogation tools. They can, but need not be used for recruiting purposes. Structured interviews allow the use of predefined criteria, whereas unstructured ones do not. The use of behavioural, future-related indicators when conducting interviews is possible.[348] **Questionnaires** can also serve to appraise a person's disposition to act. Different types of surveys can be distinguished that differ according to the manner in which they are carried out, e.g. on paper or online. Questionnaires are interrogation tools. They are usually employed in every day business, and not for recruiting purposes. Questionnaires are of a quantitative nature and can be shaped in such a way as to assess behavioural, future-related indicators, under the assumption that the answers given are honest.[349] Using **references** is a way of basing employee-related decisions on former employers' perceptions of a person's competences. References are usually provided in written form, which means that they are considered as part of documented tools. However, in some cases, they can be given orally, hence belonging to the interrogation tools. References are a typical example for recruiting tools and are therefore unsuitable for the HRDD Concept. References can be allocated to quantitative tools, assuming that in diagnostics, a common language that enables experienced recruiters to assign grades to a verbal description of a person's behaviour is utilised. Written references usually contain a description of a person's past behaviour, whereas oral references can also be future-related.[350] **Role plays** are sometimes used in diagnostics to observe how a person reacts to and is able to cope with certain social settings. This can be done both after and prior to hiring someone. Analysis of role plays can be based both on quantitative and on qualitative indicators. Role plays are clearly of a behavioural, future-related nature, given the possibility of mapping expected future social settings.[351] **Tests** of all kinds are also a way of evaluating competences. Tests can be task- or non-task-related; they can be allocated to interrogation tools, and are amongst other things used for firms' existing employees. Quantitative indicators are normally the basis for tests, and tests can be shaped in a way to allow for behavioural, future-related aspects to be covered.[352]

As can be seen in table 3.6, five evaluation tools – namely assessment centres, structured interviews, questionnaires, role plays and tests – fulfil all five suitability criteria. Hence, they

---

[347] Cf. Schuler, Heinz (2004), p. 451. Klimecki, Rüdiger/Gmür, Markus (2001), p. 237.

[348] Cf. Huffcutt, Allen I./Arthur, Winfried (1994), p. 185. Interviews are usually guided by one party, whereas dialogues are directed by the two or more participating parties.

[349] Cf. Jochmann, Walter (1999), p. 18. Eckert, Angelika (2002). p. 23. Schuler, Heinz/Funke, Uwe (Eds.) (1991) (entire book).

[350] Cf. Hentze, Joachim/Kammel, Andreas (2001), p. 301.

[351] Cf. Klimecki, Rüdiger G./Gmür, Markus (2001), p. 243.

[352] Cf. Sarges, Werner/Wottowa, Heinrich (Eds.) (2001) (entire book). Ioannis, Tsaousis/Ioannis, Nikolaou, E. (2001), p. 90. Schmidt, Frank L./Hunter, John E. (1998), p. 265.

can be used when applying the HRDD Concept. The other six tools fail to meet all the criteria and are therefore not included in the further analysis. However, those tools that fulfil the behavioural and the future relation criterion can serve as a complement to the 5 selected tools. Hence, it can be useful to include dialogues and possibly feedback into HRDD, despite the limited measurability of their underlying indicators.[353]

Selection Criterion / Tool	Interrogation/ Observation	Assessment Tools	Quantitative	Behavioural	Future-Related
Assessment Centres	+	+	+	+	+
Credentials	–	–	+	–	–
Curriculum Vitae	–	–	+	–	–
Dialogues	+	+	–	+	+
Feedback	+	+	–	+	+
Graphology	–	–	+	–	–
Interviews (structured)	+	+	+	+	+
Questionnaires (Surveys)	+	+	+	+	+
References	+	–	+	+	+
Role plays	+	+	+	+	+
Tests	+	+	+	+	+

Table 3.6: Tools for Human Resource Due Diligence according to the reviewed Psychological Literature

Applying these five tools in HRDD requires that the indicators from chapter 3.1.2 are translated into measurable items. In the case of assessment centres, real work situations should be simulated, and in structured interviews, behavioural questions be formulated. Similarly, questionnaires, role plays and tests must also be shaped in line with the underlying indicators. Applying these tools requires that the analyst is familiar with the set of M&A management objectives pursued in a specific transaction. Moreover, he must be informed about which employee groups are at the centre of attention in an M&A.

3.2.3 Applicability of the Human Resource Due Diligence Tools to Competence Groups

This chapter deals with the question of whether the selected five tools for HRDD are suitable for assessing all five competence groups or not. This question can be answered by evaluating the required task-relation of the indicators that can underlie the five tools. **Assessment centres** are suitable for measuring many different types of competences based on several types of assessment settings[354], which can both be task- and non-task-related. All five competence groups can be measured in assessment centres. **Structured interviews** can theoretically also be performed to evaluate all five competence groups. However, given

[353] However, the results gained from using these tools cannot be integrated into the HRDD Concept. They should be used as complements to the Concept.

[354] Cf. Klimecki, Rüdiger G./Gmür, Markus (2001), pp. 241ff.

reliability and validity considerations[355] they are probably of limited use for assessing task-related competences, especially specialist competence. Certain, competences particularly those related to manual labour, can be difficult to appraise based on behavioural interview questions. In contrast, non-task-related competences, especially systems-, social-, and change competence are assessable in structured interviews. **Questionnaires** can be used to evaluate both task and non-task-related competences. Nevertheless, assessing task-related competences demands that the analyst defines very specific task-related indicators for the questionnaire.[356] It should be considered whether the use of the questionnaire outweighs the effort required to create the required indicators. Presumably, other tools are easier to employ and return the same intended result. It is useful to employ **role plays** when non task-related competences such as change, systems, and social competence are at the core. This is because role plays enable one to observe a person's reaction to specific social situations, his perception of the system he lives in and of changes imposed on this system.[357] **Tests** are generally applicable to all five competence groups. Most probably, different tests focus on different competence groups.[358] For instance, work sample tests can be combined with simulations and complex problem-solving tests. In this way, specialist competence can be appraised on the one hand and methods competence on the other hand. Table 3.7 illustrates which tools for HRDD are applicable to which competence groups.

Competence Group / Tool	Social Com-petence	Systems Com-petence	Specialist Com-petence	Methods Com-petence	Change Com-petence
Assessment Centres	+	+	+	+	+
Structured Interviews	+	+	+	+	+
Questionnaires (Surveys)	+	+	+	+	+
Role plays	+	+	–	–	+
Tests*	+	+	+	+	+

Table 3.7: Tools for Human Resource Due Diligence and Competence Groups

* One test is usually suitable for assessing one or two of the five competence groups.

The insights about the applicability of the tools for HRDD to competence groups can be summarised as follows. First, presumably more than one tool must be utilised when performing Human Resource Due Diligence to be able to cover a wide range of human resource requirements, unless if assessment centres are employed. Second, by combining two tools – e.g. task-related tests and role plays – the entire required spectrum of indicators for HRDD can be covered. Third, firms that do HRDD must select and shape concrete tools. This is because the mix of M&A objectives pursued determines the adequacy of the five tools. An

---

355 Cf. Wottawa, Heinrich/Hossiep, Rüdiger (1987), p. 11.
356 Cf. Jochmann, Walter (1999), p. 20.
357 Supposing that the employees who are assessed in a role play can identify with the roles they are to play. Cf. Klimecki, Rüdiger G./Gmür, Markus (2001), p. 243.
358 Cf. Sarges, Werner/Wottowa, Heinrich (Eds.) (2001) (entire book).

adequate tool mix can be established, based on the results of step 1 of the HRDD Concept. Chapter 3.2.4 shows how this can be done.

3.2.4 Example of Evaluation Tools for the Human Resource Due Diligence Concept

In the following, a fictive combination of the M&A management objectives from chapter 2.2 is taken as a point of departure for presenting tools for HRDD. Indicators for the highly relevant competences have been developed in chapter 3.1.3; in the subsequent chapter, adequate tools for these indicators are defined.

In the fictive M&A, synergies are aimed at. At the same time, the transaction parties wish to penetrate their existing markets. Organisational macro structures are supposed to be merged upon completion of the M&A. Structures and processes are to be integrated for the following functions of the value chains: production, logistics and marketing. Employees in the functions that are to be changed are likely to face enlarged, but not expanded task spectra. The transaction parties' corporate cultures are subject to assimilation. No objectives related to leadership styles and national cultures are defined in the transaction in focus. The M&A parties' human resource strategies, human resource policies and practices, as well as human resource organisations are planned to be aligned upon completion of the M&A transaction. The following competences are demanded in the transaction: uncertainty, communication, conflict, motivation, co-operation, innovation, internal, market, socio-cultural, complexity, functional, process, planning, problem-solving, organisation, decision-making, social change, and technical change competence. All tools outlined previously can be employed when doing Human Resource Due Diligence. When applying these tools, it should be considered that e.g. uncertainty competence is relevant in the M&A in focus, due to the reinvention and due to the collaboration objective. Therefore, the indicators used when e.g. assessing a marketing employee's competences, should be tailored to the underlying reason(s) for their relevance.[359]

---

[359] Cf. chapter 2.2.

4 Compilation of the generated Human Resource Due Diligence Information

Step 3 of the HRDD Concept deals with the compilation of HRDD information through use of controlling ratios (see figure 4.1). The summarised HRDD information is supposed to serve as a basis for further management activities.[360] Controlling ratios are numerical representations of processed and condensed data[361] and enable management to understand the results of HRDD in a straight forward manner.[362] In the following, first, possible types of controlling ratios for HRDD are presented (chapter 4.1). Second, types of controlling ratios are selected for the HRDD Concept (chapter 4.2) and third, examples of controlling ratios that can be used when applying the concept are provided (chapter 4.3). Fictive M&A management objectives and results of HRDD are referred to, when presenting these examples. Thus, professionals who aim to put the HRDD Concept into action are familiarised with the general procedure that should be taken in step 3 of the concept. Still, they need to go some steps on their own when using the concept.

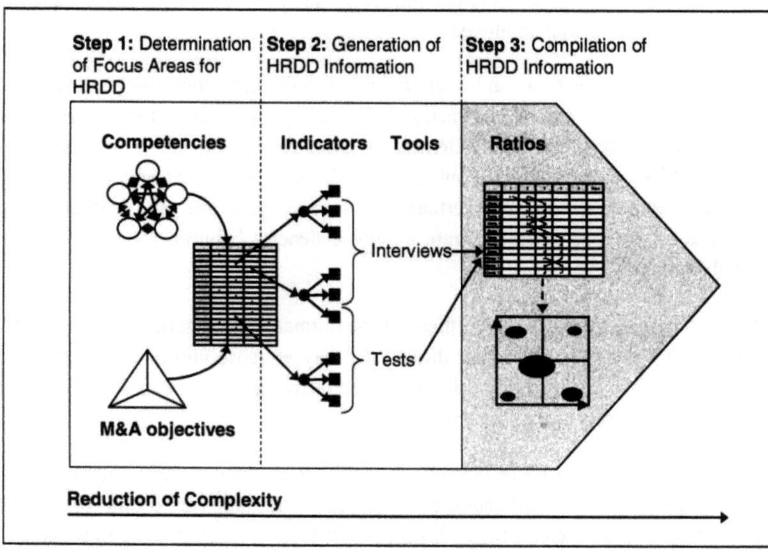

Figure 4.1: Compilation of the Generated Human Resource Due Diligence Information

---

[360] Cf. Weber, Jürgen/Sandt, Joachim (2001), pp. 27ff (instrumental and diagnostic purposes of controlling ratios). Similarly cf. Geiß, Wilfried (1986), p. 242. Controlling ratios co-ordinate human behavior within firms, carry change into firms and make this change visible. Cf. Bühner, Rolf (2000), p. 38. Weber, Manfred (2002), p. 7. Reichmann, Thomas/Lachnit, Laurenz (1976), pp. 705f. Wunderer, Rolf/Jaritz, André (1999), pp. 26f. Based on detected gaps between the status quo and a desired state, management should derive measures and define new objectives. Cf. Schulte, Karl Werner (w. y.), p. 1. Deyhle, Albrecht. In: Risak, Johann/Deyhle, Albrecht (Eds.) (1992), p. 382.

[361] Cf. Gabriel, Roland/Beier, Dirk (2003), p. 100.

[362] Cf. Weber, Manfred (2002), p. 12.

4.1 Possible Types of Controlling Ratios for Human Resource Due Diligence

To determine what types of controlling ratios to consider for the Human Resource Due Diligence Concept, controlling literature has been reviewed to find typical distinction criteria for controlling ratios.[363] Controlling ratios can be distinguished according to five different criteria – nature, level of abstraction, mode, time focus and time horizon.

(1) Controlling ratios can be differentiated according to their **nature**. Ratios can be expressed in absolute numbers, in proportional numbers, in index numbers or in relational numbers.[364] Absolute numbers encompass direct representations of business issues, e.g. production costs or number of employees. Proportional numbers mean a part of an entire whole in relation to this entire whole, e.g. activity rate or equity ratio. Index ratios refer to absolute numbers at one point in time in comparison to another point in time, e.g. growth ratio.[365] Relational numbers describe one business issue in relation to another, e.g. return on equity or return on capital employed.

(2) Different **levels of abstraction** can be referred to when defining controlling ratios. In line with these different levels of abstraction, elementary, advanced, tertiary and fully integrated ratios can be identified.[366] Elementary ratios refer to the individual (employee) level. Advanced ratios can relate to sub units of firms, to groups of employees or to a specific management perspective. Tertiary ratios encompass the organisational level. Fully integrated ratios serve to illustrate interdependencies between ratios on different levels of abstraction.

(3) Ratios can refer to different **modes** – they can be normative or descriptive.[367] Normative ratios deal with a desired state, either directly (if they are absolute) or indirectly (when they are proportional, indexed or relational). Descriptive ratios serve to describe a state without carrying any normative element.

(4) Different **time focuses** can be in place when defining controlling ratios. Ratios can be related to the past, to the present and/or to the future.[368] Past ratios are useful for mapping historical business issues, e.g. a firm's historical production costs. Present ratios refer to current business issues, e.g. current number of employees. Future ratios are suitable for

---

363 The following literature sources have been reviewed. Baetge, Jörg (1998), pp. 26f. Ebert, Günter (1999), p. 3. Weber, Manfred (2002), p. 22. Schulte, Christof (2002), p. 3. Staudt, Erich/Groeters, Ulrich/Hafkesbrink, Joachim/Treichel, Heinz-Reiner (1985), pp. 37ff. Geiß, Wilfried (1986), p. 21.

364 The last three types of ratios can be used to describe cause-effect-relationships between business issues, whereas the first type of ratio relates to direct representations of business issues. Cf. Baetge, Jörg (1998), pp. 26f. Ebert, Günter (1999), p. 3. Schulte, Karl Werner (w. y.), p. 3.

365 Ratios can relate to points in or periods of time. Cf. Dellmann, Klaus. In: Küpper, Hans-Ulrich/Wagenhofer, Alfred (Eds.) (2002), p. 942.

366 Cf. Staudt, Erich/Groeters, Ulrich/Hafkesbrink, Joachim/Treichel, Heinz-Reiner (1985), pp. 37ff.

367 Cf. Geiß, Wilfried (1986), p. 21.

368 Cf. Weber, Manfred (2002), p. 22.

expressing relations concerning future business issues[369], e.g. expected turnover development ratio.

(5) Controlling ratios can be defined for different **time horizons**. They can be short, middle or long term.[370] A short time horizon is assumed to encompass six to twelve months, a mid term time horizon one to three years and a long term time horizon more than three years.[371]

4.2 Types of Controlling Ratios Selected for the Human Resource Due Diligence Concept

In the following, the suitability of the types of ratios for the HRDD Concept is assessed.

(1) With regard to the **nature** of controlling ratios, this thesis focuses on relational ratios. The reason for this lies in the Concept's aim of comparing desired competences to actual ones.[372]

(2) Concerning the **level of abstraction**, the controlling ratios that will be developed in chapter 4.3 refer to all four levels. This is in harmony with the research results aimed at in this thesis. In chapter 1.3.2, it was stated that the HRDD Concept is supposed to serve as a tool for M&A management. To fulfil the predefined function of the Concept, the results of HRDD must not only be interpreted but also carried to higher levels of abstraction, for instance to the employee group and to the organisational level.[373]

(3) The **mode** of the ratios for HRDD is normative. This is due to the fact that the ratios derived for the Human Resource Due Diligence Concept are based on a comparison of desired to actual competences.[374] The M&A management objectives in chapter 2.2 are the basis for deriving desired competences, which form part of the ratios for HRDD.[375] Hence the ratios are of normative nature.

(4) Concerning their **time focus**, the ratios used for the HRDD Concept are related to the future. This is due to the management objective-oriented perspective of analysis of this thesis. Desired and actual competences are also future-related, given the competence definition in chapter 1.4.4.

---

369 Cf. Adelsberger, Heimo H./Stallkamp, Markus. In: Reichmann, Thomas (Ed.) (2003), p. 22.
370 Cf. Geiß, Wilfried (1986), p. 21.
371 Similarly cf. Galpin, Timothy J./Herndon, Mark (2000), pp. 10ff.
372 Cf. chapter 1.5.
373 Cf. chapter 1.5 reduction of complexity.
374 Desired competences are defined in chapter 2.2, actual competences are generated in chapter 3 and in chapter 4, desired and actual competences are compared to each other.
375 Controlling ratios should be intertwined with major management objectives. Cf. Staudt, Erich et al. (1985), p. 28.

(5) Controlling ratios can be defined for different **time horizons**. In chapter 4.3.2.4, both a short as well as a middle term time horizon is referred to. Controlling ratios are derived that enable one to compare the results of HRDD obtained for both these horizons to each other.

4.3 Examples of Controlling Ratios for the Human Resource Due Diligence Concept

In the following, controlling ratios are developed for the Human Resource Due Diligence Concept for four different levels of abstraction. First, elementary (chapter 4.3.1), second advanced (chapter 4.3.2), third tertiary (chapter 4.3.3) and fourth fully integrated ratios are developed (chapter 4.3.4).

The controlling ratios as presented in the subsequent argumentation are developed based on fictive results from HRDD on the one hand.[376] On the other hand, assumed M&A management objectives serve as a basis for arriving at the competences desired. The fictive actual and the assumed desired competences are compared to each other to arrive at controlling ratios.

4.3.1 Elementary Ratios

As already mentioned, elementary ratios refer to the level of individual employees. They are the closest of all ratios to the data generated in HRDD. To arrive at elementary ratios, desired competences are compared to the actual competences generated in HRRD.[377]

To arrive at elementary ratios, in a first step, a fictitious combination of M&A management objectives is used to generate a desired competence profile. The fictitious M&A management objectives are defined for an M&A transaction that comes into existence for the synergy objective.[378] The other M&A management objectives are deduced based on assumed logical interdependencies between the synergy objective and other M&A objectives.[379] It is presumed that structure follows strategy, culture follows structure and human resource management follows culture.[380] Hence, besides the synergy objective, the market penetration, the consolidation, the reinvention, the conservation, the assimilation, the aggregation, the amalgamation and the collaboration objective are pursued. All competences are crucial in the transaction in focus. A desired competence profile is defined for employees active in functions of the value chain where the M&A objectives mentioned show effects.

---

[376] If M&A management aims to develop ratios for HRDD itself, it should rely on its own results, whilst following the procedure as depicted in the following four chapters.

[377] Based on this comparison, the results of HRDD can be interpreted by M&A management.

[378] The synergy objective is used as a basis for the fictitious M&A objective, for it is the most frequently named internal M&A objective, according to M&A literature.

[379] Cf. chapter 1.4.5.

[380] As mentioned in chapter 1.5, there are various other possible interdependencies between the four M&A management dimensions. The interdependencies presumed for the subsequent argumentation are fictive, and serve to illustrate how to develop controlling ratios for the HRDD Concept.

When translating M&A management objectives into competence requirements, it must be determined what stage on the Likert scale the required competences can be associated with. In all future examples, the highly relevant competences are set to stage 4 on the scale, to enhance the transparency of the calculations and argumentation. Setting highly relevant competences to stages on the scale other than 4 would imply more complicated calculations, but would not enhance the illustrative value of the following examples. However, in business practice, it is recommended to use all stages on the scale to reflect differences between human resource requirements. Besides distinguishing between highly important and relatively unimportant competences as is done in this study, professionals should describe each stage on the scale verbally. After having set desired competences to stages on the competence scale, in a second step, fictitious actual competence profiles are established for the examples, as they might have been found as a result of a HRDD. This is done for three employees to whom the M&A management objectives are assumed to apply.

One way of assessing the controlling ratios established is to compare the desired competence profile to the actual profile (see figure 4.2). To derive elementary controlling ratios, the parameter values for actual competences are divided by the parameter values of the desired competences.[381] The relationships between the desired and the actual competences can be expressed as a proportion or in percentages. The formula for calculating elementary ratios is:[382]

$$\text{Competence c ratio}_{\text{employee e}} = \frac{\text{actual parameter value of competence c}}{\text{desired parameter value of competence c}}$$

As can be seen in figure 4.2, using Likert scales the maximum gap between a desired and an actual competence is 0.2. In this case, the employee meets the relevant human resource requirement by 20%. The minimum gap between a desired and an actual competence is 5, meaning that the human resource requirement is met by 500%. The ratios in figure 4.2 can be determined at a given point in time. If the HRDD is repeated at a later point in time, previous ratios can be compared to new ones.[383] Also, ratios for one employee can be compared to the results obtained for other employees.

Based on the ratios obtained from HRDD, M&A management can decide what measures to produce.[384] One possible way for management to proceed is by assigning pattern measures to certain elementary ratios. For instance it can be defined that if an employee fulfils less than 70% of the communication competence requirements in the described transaction, this employee should take part in human resource development measures.

---

[381] For a different approach using weighing factors cf. Baetge, Jörg (1998), p. 36.
[382] Where c = one competence, e = one employee.
[383] Cf. Ebert, Günter (1999), p. 3.
[384] Cf. Dellmann, Klaus. In: Küpper, Hans-Ulrich/Wagenhofer, Alfred (Eds.) (2002), p. 942. For cases where employees show competence ratios higher than 1, firms who apply the HRDD Concept need to decide whether these ratios can compensate for other, rather low competence ratios, or not.

Person	A						B						C					
Parameter Value	1	2	3	4	5	Ratio	1	2	3	4	5	Ratio	1	2	3	4	5	Ratio
Social competence																		
Uncertainty competence	▲			•		0,250				▲•		1,000		▲		•		0,500
Communication competence	▲			•		0,250				▲•		1,000		▲		•		0,500
Conflict competence		▲		•		0,500			▲	•		0,750			▲	•		0,750
Motivation competence		▲		•		0,500				▲•		1,000		▲		•		0,500
Co-operation competence			▲	•		0,750			▲	•		0,750	▲			•		0,250
Systems competence																		
Innovation competence			▲	•		0,750			▲	•		0,750	▲			•		0,250
Internal competence		▲		•		0,500			▲	•		0,750	▲			•		0,250
Market competence			▲	•		0,750			▲	•		0,750			▲	•		0,750
Socio-cultural competence		▲		•		0,500		▲		•		0,500			▲	•		0,750
Complexity competence		▲		•		0,500		▲		•		0,500			▲	•		0,750
Specialist competence																		
Functional competence		▲		•		0,500		▲		•		0,500			▲	•		0,750
Process competence		▲		•		0,500		▲		•		0,500			▲	•		0,750
Methods competence																		
Planning competence			▲	•		0,750		▲		•		0,500			▲	•		0,750
Problem-solving competence			▲	•		0,750		▲		•		0,500			▲	•		0,750
Organisation competence			▲	•		0,750			▲	•		0,750			▲	•		0,750
Decision-making competence			▲	•		0,750			▲	•		0,750			▲	•		0,750
Change competence																		
Social change competence			▲	•		0,750	▲			•		0,250				▲•		1,000
Technical change competence			▲	•		0,750	▲			•		0,250				▲•		1,000

Actual parameter values of competencies ▲
Desired parameter values of competencies •

Figure 4.2: Comparing Desired to Actual Competence Profiles[385]

4.3.2 Advanced Ratios

Advanced ratios relate to a higher level of aggregation than elementary ratios. In this study, employee groups, management dimensions, competence groups and time horizons of M&A management are referred to. Advanced ratios are defined by aggregating several elementary ratios, e.g. by adding the results of HRDD for employee A and for employee B.[386] To add employees' actual competence parameter values would be misleading, since the underlying, desired competences can differ in business practice. The average degree of requirements fulfilled for employee A and B can be determined by calculating the average of employee A's and B's elementary ratios.[387] To give an example, if employee A has an elementary ratio of 0.6 and employee B of 0.8, the average degree of requirements fulfilled for A and B is 0.7. By calculating the standard deviation of the elementary ratios from the mean, differences between

---

385 Competence profiles similar to that from figure 4.2 are used in human resource development. Cf. Henkel, Martin (1994), p. 31.

386 Cf. Dellmann, Klaus. In: Küpper, Hans-Ulrich/Wagenhofer, Alfred (Eds.) (2002), p. 940.

387 Cf. Dellmann, Klaus. In: Küpper, Hans-Ulrich/Wagenhofer, Alfred (Eds.) (2002), p. 941. The assumption underlying the above average is a normal distribution.

employees that might disappear through aggregation can be made visible. In the example, the standard deviation is 0.1.[388] When aggregating individual employees' results, ratios higher than 1 should be transformed into standardised elementary ratios of 1. Maintaining ratios higher than 1 as is done when developing advanced ratios might imply biases in data interpretation.[389]

The same steps as described for employee groups can also be taken for management dimensions, competence groups and time horizons. In the following, advanced ratios are developed for all four aspects. Different employee groups are used to illustrate how different competence requirements for each employee group can be incorporated in HRDD. Different management dimensions have been included to reflect the multidimensional, problem-oriented perspective of analysis of this thesis.[390] Different competence groups are considered to aggregate the results from HRDD to a level of abstraction that facilitates managerial decision making. Different time horizons are relevant to determine the focus areas for HRDD, and are important for M&A management to plan its short and middle term activities.

4.3.2.1 Controlling Ratios per Employee Group

Summarising employee-specific information is useful for supporting management in taking adequate measures upon completion of HRDD. These measures can vary significantly from one employee group to another. For instance, if marketing employees fulfil 90% of the requirements imposed on them, but production employees only 30%, the requirement for directing suitable measures at production employees is higher than it is for marketing employees.

Considering the elementary ratios taken from chapter 4.3.1, employee group specific information can be generated in the following way: Different human resource requirements must be defined for different, clearly delimited employee groups. When interpreting the results of HRDD, the individual employees' competence profiles need to be compared to the competences desired for the employee group they belong to. Elementary ratios must be calculated. Thereafter, advanced ratios for a specific employee group can be determined by adding individual employees' elementary ratios. The formula for calculating advanced ratios per employee group (here managers) is defined as follows[391]:

$$\text{Competence c ratio}_{\text{managers}} = \left(\sum_{m=1}^{M} \frac{\text{actual parameter value of competence c manager m}}{\text{desired parameter value of competence c manager m}} \right) : M$$

M&A management can then be provided with information for all employee groups it is interested in. The HRDD Concept distinguishes solely between employees at lower levels and managers of firm A, B or both/all M&A parties. However, in business practice, many further

388 Presuming that employee A and B are the whole population.
389 This also needs to be taken into account when determining tertiary ratios and the fully integrated ratio.
390 Cf. chapter 1.3.1 perspective of analysis.
391 Where m = one manager, M = total number of managers, c = one competence.

distinctions – e.g. based on functional parts of firms – might need to be made, and hence many more employee groups might need to be identified. In figure 4.3, competence ratios for managers have been calculated.[392] To deal with further employee groups, the business that is at the core in a specific M&A transaction must be known to the person undertaking the HRDD. Since the HRDD Concept is defined in order to provide insights in contents for a general problem[393] (cf. aimed-at research results of this study), obtaining more detailed levels of abstraction is left to professionals.

Person	A						B						C						A and C
Parameter Value	1	2	3	4	5	Ratio	1	2	3	4	5	Ratio	1	2	3	4	5	Ratio	
Social competence																			
Uncertainty competence	▲			•		0,250				▲•		1,000		▲		•		0,500	0,375
Communication competence	▲			•		0,250				▲•		1,000		▲		•		0,500	0,375
Conflict competence		▲		•		0,500			▲	•		0,750			▲	•		0,750	0,625
Motivation competence		▲		•		0,500				▲•		1,000		▲		•		0,500	0,500
Co-operation competence			▲	•		0,750			▲	•		0,750	▲			•		0,250	0,500
Systems competence																			
Innovation competence			▲	•		0,750			▲	•		0,750	▲			•		0,250	0,500
Internal competence		▲		•		0,500			▲	•		0,750	▲			•		0,250	0,375
Market competence			▲	•		0,750			▲	•		0,750			▲	•		0,750	0,750
Socio-cultural competence		▲		•		0,500		▲		•		0,500			▲	•		0,750	0,625
Complexity competence		▲		•		0,500		▲		•		0,500			▲	•		0,750	0,625
Specialist competence																			
Functional competence		▲		•		0,500		▲		•		0,500			▲	•		0,750	0,625
Process competence		▲		•		0,500		▲		•		0,500			▲	•		0,750	0,625
Methods competence																			
Planning competence			▲	•		0,750		▲		•		0,500			▲	•		0,750	0,750
Problem-solving competence			▲	•		0,750		▲		•		0,500			▲	•		0,750	0,750
Organisation competence			▲	•		0,750			▲	•		0,750			▲	•		0,750	0,750
Decision-making competence			▲	•		0,750			▲	•		0,750			▲	•		0,750	0,750
Change competence																			
Social change competence			▲	•		0,750	▲			•		0,250				▲•		1,000	0,875
Technical change competence			▲	•		0,750	▲			•		0,250				▲•		1,000	0,875

Figure 4.3: Controlling Ratio per Employee Group

4.3.2.2 Controlling Ratios per Management Dimension

Advanced controlling ratios can also be tailored to the management dimensions of the HRDD Concept. For most M&A objectives, not all competences are demanded. Certain types of M&A management objectives – e.g. cultural – are linked with certain competence groups – e.g. social competences. It is useful to develop controlling ratios per management dimension, since the measures that are to be derived may differ significantly from one management dimension to another. Advanced ratios per management dimension can be found by decon-

[392] It has been assumed that persons A and C are managers, and person B is an employee at a lower level. Therefore, person B's elementary ratios are not aggregated with person A's and B's.

[393] Cf. chapter 1.3.5 aimed-at research results of this study.

structing the results of HRDD according to the four M&A management dimensions. It can, for instance, be identified which human resource requirements are of cultural origin.[394] By adding the elementary ratios for each culturally relevant competence, a culture-related advanced ratio can be derived (see formula and figure 4.4)[395]:

$$\text{Culture-related competence ratio}_{\text{employee e}} = \left(\sum_{c=1}^{C} \frac{\text{actual parameter value of competence c}}{\text{desired parameter value of competence c}} \right) : C$$

	Person	A						B						C					
	Parameter Value	**1**	**2**	**3**	**4**	**5**	**Ratio**	**1**	**2**	**3**	**4**	**5**	**Ratio**	**1**	**2**	**3**	**4**	**5**	**Ratio**
	Social competence																		
Strategic	Uncertainty competence	▲			•		0,250				▲•		1,000		▲		•		0,500
Cultural	Communication competence	▲			•		0,250				▲•		1,000		▲		•		0,500
Strategic	Conflict competence		▲		•		0,500			▲	•		0,750			▲	•		0,750
Strategic	Motivation competence		▲		•		0,500				▲•		1,000		▲		•		0,500
Cultural	Co-operation competence			▲	•		0,750			▲	•		0,750	▲			•		0,250
	Systems competence																		
Strategic	Innovation competence			▲	•		0,750			▲	•		0,750	▲			•		0,250
Structural	Internal competence		▲		•		0,500			▲	•		0,750	▲			•		0,250
Cultural	Market competence			▲	•		0,750			▲	•		0,750			▲	•		0,750
Strategic	Socio-cultural competence		▲		•		0,500		▲		•		0,500			▲	•		0,750
Structural	Complexity competence		▲		•		0,500		▲		•		0,500			▲	•		0,750
	Specialist competence																		
Structural	Functional competence		▲		•		0,500		▲		•		0,500			▲	•		0,750
Structual	Process competence		▲		•		0,500		▲		•		0,500			▲	•		0,750
	Methods competence																		
Structural	Planning competence			▲	•		0,750		▲		•		0,500			▲	•		0,750
HRM	Problem-solving competence			▲	•		0,750		▲		•		0,500			▲	•		0,750
HRM	Organisation competence			▲	•		0,750			▲	•		0,750			▲	•		0,750
HRM	Decision-making competence			▲	•		0,750			▲	•		0,750			▲	•		0,750
	Change competence																		
Cultural	Social change competence			▲	•		0,750	▲			•		0,250				▲•		1,000
Structural	Technical change competence			▲	•		0,750	▲			•		0,250				▲•		1,000
	Strategic objectives						**0,500**						**0,800**						**0,550**
	Structural objectives						**0,583**						**0,500**						**0,710**
	Cultural objectives						**0,625**						**0,688**						**0,625**
	HRM objectives						**0,750**						**0,666**						**0,750**

Figure 4.4: Controlling Ratios per Management Dimension

The culture-related competence ratio for employee A in figure 4.4 can be combined with the competence ratios for other employees to generate employee group specific information related to the different management dimensions. Cultural and human resource management objectives often imply that social, systems and social change competence are required. At the same time, in the case of strategic and structural M&A management objectives, functional,

[394] As illustrated in chapter 2.2, some competences are relevant due to several M&A objectives, pursued in different management dimensions. If this is the case, it must be determined which of the objectives is most relevant. Accordingly, the elementary ratios in focus can be allocated to management dimensions.

[395] Where c = one culturally relevant competence, C = total number of culturally relevant competences, e = one employee.

methods and technical change competence are often needed.[396] These tendencies can be useful to consider when mapping the results of HRDD graphically (see figure 4.5). The degree to which employees fulfil strategic and structural requirements is illustrated on the y-axis. Moreover, the degree to which they fulfil cultural and human resource management requirements is shown on the x-axis.[397] The sizes of the ovals represent the number of employees that fall into the five categories of strategy enhancers/efficiency managers, all-rounders, culture shapers, question marks and change delayers. Based on the human resource portfolio in figure 4.5, M&A management can produce employee group specific measures tailored to the human resource requirements shown on the y- and on the x-axis.

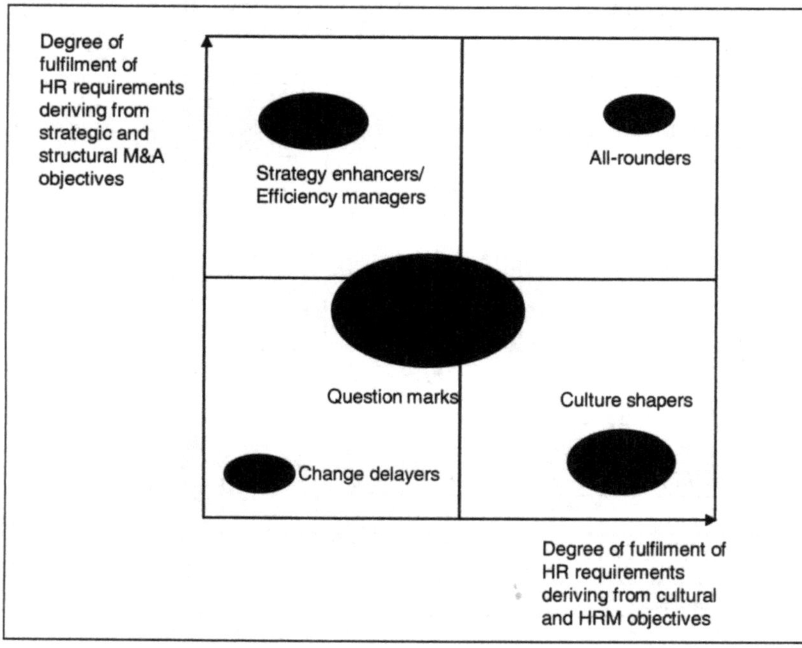

Figure 4.5: Controlling Ratios in line with M&A Management Dimensions[398]

---

[396] Cf. chapter 2.2.

[397] Showing two management dimensions on the y- and two on the x-axis does not, however, mean ignoring the fact that the four management dimensions are analytically independent of each other (cf. chapter 1.4.5). The distinction into human resource requirements deriving from strategic and structural M&A objectives and those deriving from cultural and human resource management objectives helps management classify all measures following HRDD according to employee- and competence groups.

[398] Similarly cf. Papmehl, André (1990), pp. 55ff.

4.3.2.3 Controlling Ratios per Competence Group

The results of HRDD can also be aggregated according to competence groups. The five competence groups presented in chapter 1.4.4 differ according to their degree of task-relatedness. Social, systems and change competence are associated with a low degree, methods competence a middle degree, and functional competence with a high degree of task relatedness. M&A management measures taken for task-related competence gaps are probably different from non task-related ones. Hence, it makes sense to calculate controlling ratios according to competence groups so that M&A management is provided with directly usable information. Advanced ratios per competence group can be identified by aggregating HRDD results (see figure 4.6), with the following formula[399]:

$$\text{Social competence ratio}_{\text{employee e}} = \left(\sum_{s=1}^{S} \frac{\text{actual parameter value of competence s}}{\text{desired parameter value of competence s}} \right) : S$$

Person	A						B						C					
Parameter Value	1	2	3	4	5	Ratio	1	2	3	4	5	Ratio	1	2	3	4	5	Ratio
Social competence																		
Uncertainty competence	▲			•		0,250				▲•		1,000		▲		•		0,500
Communication competence	▲			•		0,250				▲•		1,000		▲		•		0,500
Conflict competence		▲		•		0,500			▲	•		0,750			▲	•		0,750
Motivation competence		▲		•		0,500				▲•		1,000		▲		•		0,500
Co-operation competence			▲	•		0,750			▲	•		0,750	▲			•		0,250
Subtotal social competence						**0,450**						**0,900**						**0,500**
Systems competence																		
Innovation competence			▲	•		0,750			▲	•		0,750	▲			•		0,250
Internal competence		▲		•		0,500			▲	•		0,750	▲			•		0,250
Market competence			▲	•		0,750			▲	•		0,750			▲	•		0,750
Socio-cultural competence		▲		•		0,500		▲		•		0,500			▲	•		0,750
Complexity competence		▲		•		0,500		▲		•		0,500			▲	•		0,750
Subtotal systems competence						**0,600**						**0,650**						**0,550**
Specialist competence																		
Functional competence		▲		•		0,500		▲		•		0,500			▲	•		0,750
Process competence		▲		•		0,500		▲		•		0,500			▲	•		0,750
Subtotal specialist competence						**0,500**						**0,500**						**0,750**
Methods competence																		
Planning competence			▲	•		0,750		▲		•		0,500			▲	•		0,750
Problem-solving competence			▲	•		0,750		▲		•		0,500			▲	•		0,750
Organisation competence			▲	•		0,750			▲	•		0,750			▲	•		0,750
Decision-making competence			▲	•		0,750			▲	•		0,750			▲	•		0,750
Subtotal methods competence						**0,750**						**0,625**						**0,750**
Change competence																		
Social change competence			▲	•		0,750	▲			•		0,250				▲•		1,000
Technical change competence			▲	•		0,750	▲			•		0,250				▲•		1,000
Subtotal change competence						**0,750**						**0,250**						**1,000**

Figure 4.6: Controlling Ratios per Competence Groups

399 Where s = one social competence, S = total number of social competences (here: 5), e = one employee.

Like the management dimension ratio, the social competence ratio can also be further aggregated (e.g. according to employee groups). Aggregated information related to competence groups can be illustrated graphically by a competence group portfolio (see figure 4.7). Non task-related human resource requirements have been plotted on the y-axis, and task-related human resource requirements have been shown on the x-axis. The competence group portfolio provides information that can be directly translated into different types of M&A management measures. An experienced user of the HRDD Concept can develop pattern measures depending on the controlling ratios obtained per competence group.

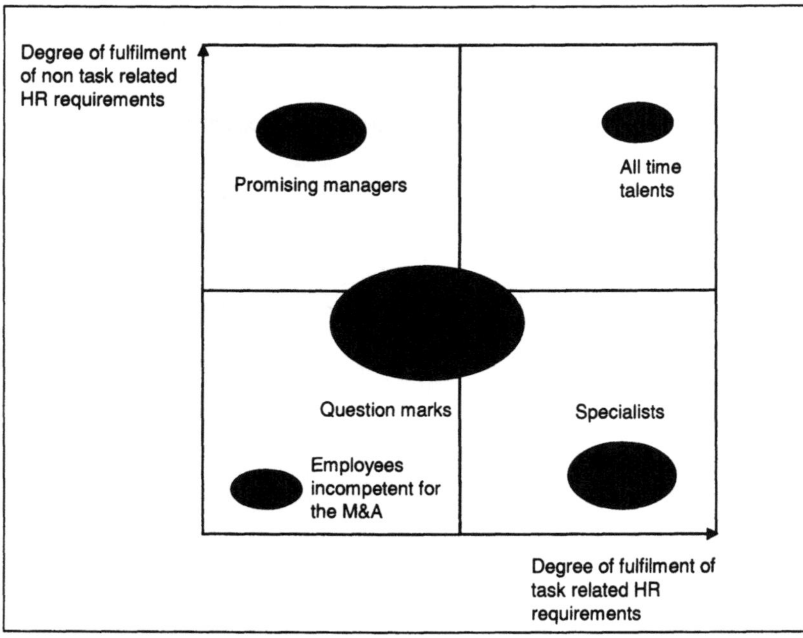

Figure 4.7: Controlling Ratios in line with Competence Groups

4.3.2.4 Controlling Ratios per Time Horizon of Merger & Acquisition Management

The competences in figure 2.2 can differ according to the urgency with which they are required. Some are required within the first six to twelve months following the agreement of an M&A transaction, whereas others are demanded within one to three years.[400] To determine what types of measures must be taken at short and at middle term notice, advanced controlling ratios can be developed in line with the time horizon of M&A management. The degree to

[400] For a short-term view cf. Ashkenas, Ronald N./Francis, Suzanne C. (2000), pp. 110f. For a middle-term view cf. Träm, Michael (2002), pp. 13ff. It is assumed that long term human resource requirements are of no relevance for M&A management, which is why they are excluded from the subsequent argumentation.

which employees are likely to fulfil short and middle term requirements can be calculated and measures can be worked out based on the results obtained. In figure 4.8, short and middle term perspectives have been allocated to each competence respectively. Based on the distinction into short and middle term human resource requirements, all elementary ratios for middle term requirements can be summed up. The formula for calculating the described ratio is[401]:

$$\text{Middle term ratio}_{\text{employee e}} = \left(\sum_{mt=1}^{MT} \frac{\text{actual parameter value of competence s}}{\text{desired parameter value of competence s}} \right) : MT$$

	Person			A						B						C			
	Parameter Value	**1**	**2**	**3**	**4**	**5**	**Ratio**	**1**	**2**	**3**	**4**	**5**	**Ratio**	**1**	**2**	**3**	**4**	**5**	**Ratio**
	Social competence																		
Middle term	Uncertainty competence	▲			•		0,250				▲•		1,000		▲		•		0,500
Middle term	Communication competence	▲			•		0,250				▲•		1,000		▲		•		0,500
Middle term	Conflict competence		▲		•		0,500			▲	•		0,750			▲	•		0,750
Middle term	Motivation competence		▲		•		0,500				▲•		1,000		▲		•		0,500
Middle term	Co-operation competence			▲	•		0,750			▲	•		0,750	▲			•		0,250
	Systems competence																		
Middle term	Innovation competence			▲	•		0,750			▲	•		0,750	▲			•		0,250
Short term	Internal competence		▲		•		0,500			▲	•		0,750	▲			•		0,250
Middle term	Market competence			▲	•		0,750			▲	•		0,750			▲	•		0,750
Middle term	Socio-cultural competence		▲		•		0,500		▲		•		0,500			▲	•		0,750
Short term	Complexity competence		▲		•		0,500		▲		•		0,500			▲	•		0,750
	Specialist competence																		
Short term	Functional competence		▲		•		0,500		▲		•		0,500			▲	•		0,750
Short term	Process competence		▲		•		0,500		▲		•		0,500			▲	•		0,750
	Methods competence																		
Short term	Planning competence			▲	•		0,750		▲		•		0,500			▲	•		0,750
Short term	Problem-solving competence			▲	•		0,750		▲		•		0,500			▲	•		0,750
Short term	Organisation competence			▲	•		0,750			▲	•		0,750			▲	•		0,750
Short term	Decision-making competence			▲	•		0,750			▲	•		0,750			▲	•		0,750
	Change competence																		
Middle term	Social change competence			▲	•		0,750	▲			•		0,250				▲•		1,000
Short term	Technical change competence			▲	•		0,750	▲			•		0,250				▲•		1,000
	Middle term objectives						**0,555**						**0,750**						**0,583**
	Short term objectives						**0,638**						**0,555**						**0,722**

Figure 4.8: Controlling Ratios per Time Horizon of M&A Management

As for the other advanced ratios, the results obtained for individual employees can be carried to the organisational level. To illustrate employee group specific results of HRDD, controlling ratios per time horizon of M&A management can be mapped in a portfolio. As can be seen from figure 4.9, this portfolio plots the degree to which short term requirements are fulfilled, on the y-axis, and the degree to which middle term requirements are fulfilled on the x-axis. The size of each employee group is illustrated by the size of the ovals. The information

[401] Where mt = one middle term relevant competence, MT = total number of middle term relevant competences, e = one employee.

presented in the short and middle term portfolio can be used as a basis for managerial decision-making, with respect to short and middle term M&A management measures.

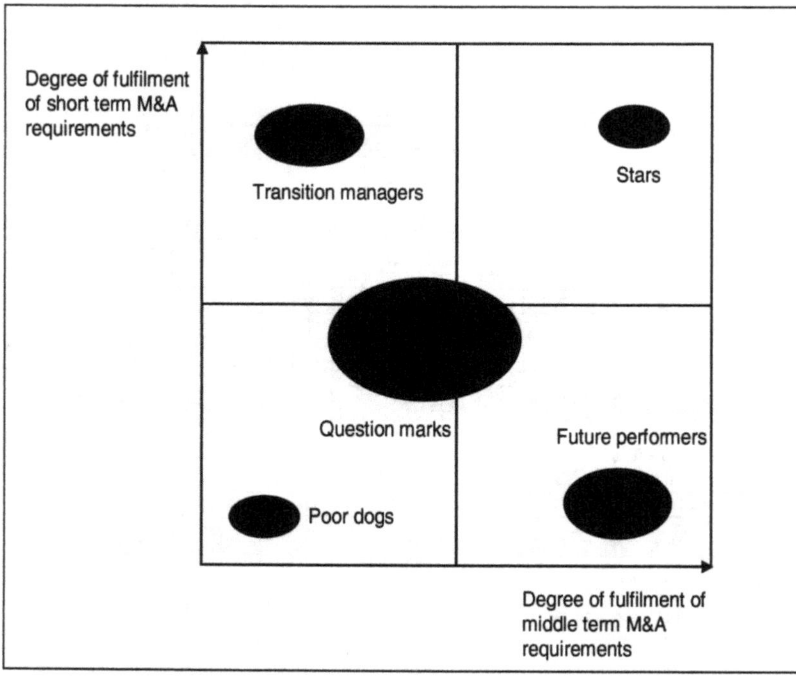

Figure 4.9: Controlling Ratios in line with Time Horizon of M&A Management

4.3.3 Tertiary Ratios

Tertiary ratios relate to firms as a whole. For the Concept, tertiary ratios can be developed by aggregating advanced ratios to the organisational level. Three types of tertiary ratios have been developed based on the advanced ratios from chapter 4.3.2 – one related to management dimensions, one related to competence groups and one related to time horizons. The formulas for calculating these ratios are as follows[402]:

$$\text{Culture-related competence ratio} = \frac{\sum_{e=1}^{E} \text{Culture related competence ratio}_{\text{employee } e}}{E}$$

[402] Where e = one employee assessed in HRDD, E = total number of employees assessed in HRDD.

$$\text{Social competence ratio} = \frac{\sum_{e=1}^{E} \text{Social competence ratio}_{\text{employee } e}}{E}$$

$$\text{Middle term ratio} = \frac{\sum_{e=1}^{E} \text{Middle term ratio}_{\text{employee } e}}{E}$$

4.3.4 Fully Integrated Ratios

Fully integrated ratios are created by summarizing elementary, advanced and tertiary ratios. For step 3 of the HRDD Concept – as for most ratio systems – there is one single fully integrated ratio.[403] This ratio expresses the degree to which employees are expected to fulfil M&A induced requirements. A rationale for calculating this ratio can be to give management an impression of the overall results of HRDD before turning to a more detailed analysis. To arrive at this tertiary ratio, the results of Human Resource Due Diligence must be aggregated for all employee groups, for all management dimensions, for all competence groups or for all time horizons. This can e.g. be done by summing up all ratios related to employee groups and dividing them by the number of employee groups. The same can be done for all other types of advanced ratios (management dimensions, competence groups and time horizons) – the result generated should always be the same. This is because the same individual HRDD results are used as a departure point for defining the controlling ratios. Another possibility is to aggregate all tertiary ratios related to management dimensions and to divide them by the four management dimensions. Hence, a possible formula for calculating the fully integrated ratio is:

Fully integrated ratio = α strategy-related- + β structure-related- + χ culture-related- + δ human resource management-related competence ratio[404]

Figure 4.10 illustrates how the four levels of controlling ratios are interrelated with each other. In general, the relationships between the ratios of a ratio hierarchy can be illustrated in three different ways: they can be established by logical deduction, they can be defined based on subjective perceptions or they can be defined empirically.[405] Given the deductive research strategy of this thesis, the first option has been chosen.

---

403 Cf. Brown, Mark G. (1997), p. 8.

404 α, β, χ and δ enable firms who apply the HRDD Concept to give all four management dimensions the same (then each of the four variables should be 0.25) or different weights.

405 Cf. Dellmann, Klaus. In: Küpper, Hans-Ulrich/Wagenhofer, Alfred (Eds.) (2002), p. 942.

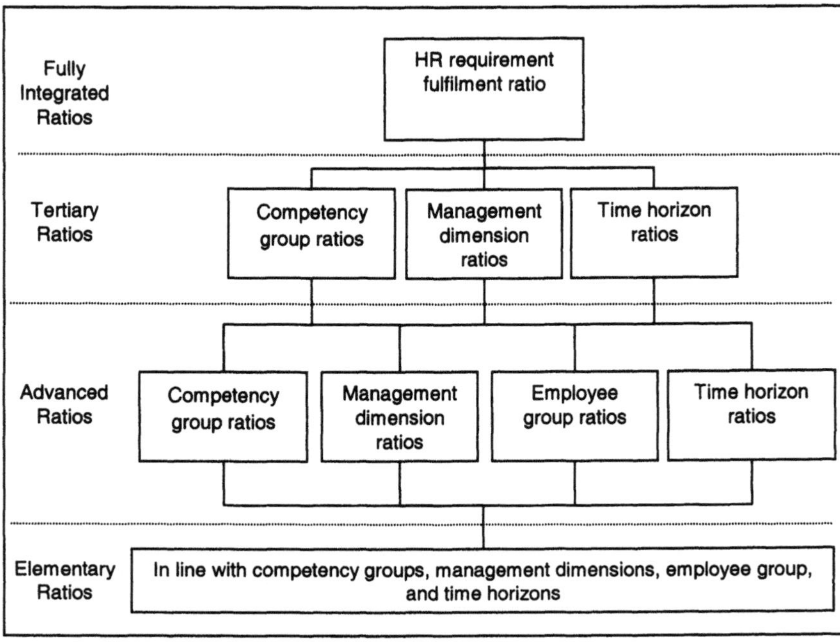

Figure 4.10: Linking Human Resource Due Diligence Controlling Ratios

According to Brown, management controlling ratio systems should not consist of more than 20 ratios[406], implying that management information from the application of the HRDD Concept should not contain elementary ratios. Instead, elementary ratios should be available and be referred to when M&A management wants to impose measures on individuals. In respect of potential changes to M&A management objectives, the ratio system in figure 4.10 can easily be updated to adapt to new circumstances.[407] New ratios can also be added to the ratio system, if M&A management requires different information at an early rather than a later stage of the M&A transaction.[408] Moreover, the ratio system allows for existing ratios to be recalculated, e.g. if the whole population underlying an employee group ratio changes.[409]

406 Cf. Brown, Mark G. (1997), p. 4. 59% of German firms use less than 5 ratios for human resource issues, 30 % between 5 and 10 ratios, and 11 % more than 10 ratios. Cf. Weber, Jürgen/Sandt, Joachim (2001), p. 13.

407 If M&A management objectives change over time, HRDD needs to be repeated. New controlling ratios must be determined to reflect the new relevance of the competences. Cf. Baetge, Jörg (1998), p. 41. The results from HRDD in t1 can be compared to results from HRDD in t2. Cf. Brown, Mark G. (1997), p. 9. Schäffer/Weber call this feed-forward control. Cf. Schäffer, Utz/Weber, Jürgen (2002), p. 9. Schäffer calls it anticipative learning. Cf. Schäffer, Utz (2001), p. 34.

408 Cf. Lichtsteiner, René A. In: Klimecki, Rüdiger/Remer, Andreas (Eds.) (1997), p. 330. For instance, it can be necessary adding time horizon ratios to a system that did not include this type of advanced ratio before, at all.

409 To evaluate the use of the ratio system developed, its performance can be measured. Cf. Gleich, Ronald. In: Gleich, Ronald/Seidenschwarz, Werner (1997), p. 363.

5 Complement of the Human Resource Due Diligence Concept with Insights from an Expert Enquiry

In line with step four of the research strategy of this study, chapter 5 presents the results of the expert survey[410] carried out to complement the theoretical part of this thesis with empirical-singular insights about HRDD practice. First, the research strategy underlying the expert survey is introduced (chapter 5.1). Second, the results from the expert enquiry are elaborated on (chapter 5.2), and finally, implications for the HRDD Concept are illustrated (chapter 5.3).

5.1 Research Strategy for the Expert Enquiry

The aim of this chapter is six-fold, namely to define the method used for data collection, to demonstrate the nature of the survey, to describe the underlying sample, to explain the process of data collection, to present data treatment, and to discuss the quality of the survey.

(1) As pointed out in chapter 1.3.3, step four of the research strategy aims to complement the Human Resource Due Diligence Concept with empirical insights. The insights that are to be generated can be found by using a questionnaire-based, a case-study-based or an expert-interview-based approach.[411] Questionnaires allow the researcher to refer to a large sample size, whereas case studies limit the possible sample size to between four and six firms.[412] Interviews allow one to generate deeper insights than questionnaires do for two reasons. First, they allow one to work with a medium sample size, and second, the interviewer can steer the course of the investigation.[413] Case studies would probably have enabled the researcher to gain even deeper insights about singular HRDD than interviews. However, case studies are not consistent with the aim expressed in step four of the research strategy: to engender as many different, new ideas for the HRDD Concept as possible. Explorative interviews have been conducted to complement the HRDD Concept with empirical insights.[414]

(2) According to Müller-Böling/Klandt, the **nature of a survey** can be determined using eight distinction criteria – directness of approach, degree of standardisation, number of participants, use of media, frequency, objective of survey, importance of linguistic elements, and the possibility that interviewees may distort their answers.[415] In the case of a direct approach, the unit of analysis is equal to the interviewed person(s), whereas in the case of an indirect approach, interviewees are asked about their experiences with a unit of

---

410 The terms "survey" and "enquiry" are used interchangeably in the subsequent argumentation.

411 Cf. Schnell, Rainer/Hill, Paul B./Esser, Elke (1999), pp. 297, 335. Yin, Robert K. (2003), p. 23.

412 Cf. Yin, Robert K. (2003), p. 47.

413 Cf. Bortz, Jürgen/Döring, Nicola (2002), p. 253.

414 Cf. Bortz, Jürgen/Döring, Nicola (2002), pp. 386f. The reason for carrying out explorative interviews was the practical research goal of this study and the aim of step four of the research strategy that is to complement the theoretical HRDD Concept.

415 Cf. Müller-Böling, Detlef/Klandt, Heinz (1996), pp. 27 – 32.

analysis. Twenty-two company representatives and eight consultants were asked to describe their experiences with practical HRDD. Hence, the unit of analysis was not identical with the interviewees. Thus, the survey was of an indirect nature.[416] The degree of standardisation of a survey depends on the number of questions posed, and the order in which they are posed. The interviews conducted for the purpose of this thesis were semi-standardised as they were based on an interview guide tailored to the experiences of the interviewees (with a non-fixed order and with a slightly varying number of questions). The reason for choosing a semi-structured approach was the exploratory nature of the interviews, and their underlying aim of detecting facts and causes related to practical HRDD.[417] Adaptations were made to the order in which the questions were posed depending on the interviewee's answers, meaning that appropriate follow-up questions were posed. Certain interviewees were not given all the questions from the interview guide, since their experience did not enable them to answer all questions. However, there was no room for questions outside the spectrum of the predefined interview guide.[418] The interviews took place at the time when the HRDD Concept was being created. As far as the number of participants is concerned, both one-to-one interviews and interviews with two participants were conducted. This appeared useful in order to generate a maximum of insights. All interviews were conducted viva voce, with 87% of all interviews being held in person.[419] The remaining 13 % of the interviews were conducted over the telephone.[420] All expert interviews were conducted once, only. Hence the expert survey can be classified as cross-sectional. This is in line with its objective of completing the HRDD Concept with empirical-singular insights. Given the objective of the survey, t was not necessary to generate longitudinal insights. The objective of the survey was to determine the experiences of the interviewees with respect to practical HRDD. Hence, the interviews were conducted in order to obtain information about the interviewees' experiences with practical HRDD.[421] The survey was based on linguistic elements. Thus, possible problems related to linguistic elements had to be considered.[422] All interviews were carried out in the German language. The interviewer did not intend to conceal his real objective of investigation. As can be seen from the enclosed contact letter, interviewees were given concise and honest information about the purpose of the survey. Therefore the survey can be classified as open.

[416] A risk with indirect surveys can be that experts' answers reflect their opinions rather than social reality. Cf. Bortz, Jürgen/Döring, Nicola (2002), p. 251. Most of the questions were posed in an open manner, in order to prevent this bias from appearing.

[417] Cf. Müller-Böling, Detlef/Klandt, Heinz (1996), p. 29.

[418] Cf. Lamnek, Siegfried (1995), p. 91.

[419] Twenty-six persons were interviewed in person.

[420] Four telephone interviews were carried out (due to the impossibility of arranging a personal appointment) despite their disadvantages. Cf. Müller-Böring, Detlef/Klandt, Heinz (1996), p. 43. Schnell, Rainer/Hill, Paul B./Esser, Elke (1999), pp. 330ff. Given the expert knowledge of the interviewees, the opportunity of questioning them was considered more important than optimum interview conditions. Moreover, the focus of this thesis on factual questions made telephone interviews almost as valuable as personal ones. Cf. Bortz, Jürgen/Döring, Nicola (2002), pp. 241f.

[421] Cf. chapter 1.3.3.

[422] Cf. Witt, Frank H. (1995), pp. 319f quoted after Wittgenstein, Ludwig.

(3) The expert survey included **thirty interviews**, of which twenty-two were with company representatives and eight with consultants. Two possible ways of finding interviewees for an exploratory survey are random and conscious selection, respectively.[423] In this study, the interviewees were consciously selected. The main reason for this is that few firms seem to have carried out Human Resource Due Diligence in their M&A transactions so far. The preliminary interviews with consultants[424] demonstrated that these firms are known to consultants and/or know each other. To start with, firms and prospective interview partners that were known to have experience with HRDD in M&A transactions were contacted. New interviewees were identified by recommendation of the first interviewees. Sometimes interviewees knew that a certain person had experience with HRDD, and sometimes that a specific firm had done HRDD, before.[425] Had firms been contacted randomly, this might have implied a high number of rejections, for only firms with HRDD experience could be included into the survey. Another reason for consciously selecting the interviewees was that, in order to achieve step four of the research strategy, it was not necessary to ensure a statistically representative sample size and sample composition.[426] Given the multidimensional perspective of analysis of this study, a maximum of expert interviews was aimed for to generate new insights for the HRDD Concept. After having carried out more than twenty interviews, the snowball effect became weaker. When nearly thirty interviews had been carried out, hardly any new company representatives and consultants could be identified that had not yet been included into the survey. Moreover, the insights generated from the interviews became increasingly similar, which allowed for the assumption that, if even more interviews were carried out, the number of new insights for the HRDD Concept would be minor. These two observations marked the end of the exploratory survey upon completion of thirty interviews.

(4) **Data collection** in the expert survey took place as follows. The actual interviews were carried out during a period of five months from the beginning of April 2003 to the end of August 2003. The interviews took between forty-five minutes, and two and a half hours, depending on the interviewees' experience of the topic and their style of answering. All interviews, except one where the interviewee did not agree to have the conversation taped, were recorded on micro-cassettes. Besides recording the conversations, notes were taken by the interviewer. Prior to data treatment, all 30 interviews were first transcribed. Second, the transcribed information was cross checked with the notes taken during the interviews. Third, interviewees were given the opportunity to review the transcribed text, and small amendments and additions were made to the transcripts if applicable. Certain

---

423 Cf. Schnell, Rainer/Hill, Paul B./Esser, Elke (1999), p. 277.

424 Cf. chapter 1.1.

425 This procedure is called the snowball procedure (translation by the author, original: "Schneeball-Verfahren"). Cf. Schnell, Rainer/Hill, Paul B./Esser, Elke (1999), p. 280.

426 Therefore, questioning different professionals might have implied different results and hence different implications for the theoretical HRDD Concept. If a statistically representative sample size and composition had been aimed for, firms might have been selected according to their annual M&A volume or human resource intensity.

interviewees did not want their own or their firm's name and evidence about their/its experience with Human Resource Due Diligence to appear in any official documentation.

(5) For **data treatment and data interpretation**, the procedure suggested by Mayring has been used.[427] He suggests using a three step approach upon completion of the data collection. First, the collected data are summarised to their most important contents. Second, unclear text passages (e.g. terms or phrases) are clarified, e.g. by taking additional information into account. Third, the condensed and clarified text is analysed as regards contents. Categories for analysing the contents of the text are developed. These categories can be defined according to three different principles – according to topics and contents, according to types of characteristics[428] or according to ordinal values associated with types of characteristics. Step one of Mayring's procedure consisted of entering the most important interview data into an interview synopsis table. In step two, the data were grouped in another table, according to six content groups. In step three, actual data interpretation took place. The grouped interview data were allocated to types of characteristics. These types of characteristics were defined based on the three elements of the HRDD Concept.[429] The frequency of appearance of each type of characteristic was determined. Data interpretation was carried out manually, meaning that no language software was employed as a support tool. There are three reasons for this. First, the relatively small amount of data, which can be traced back to the fact that the majority of the interviewees gave brief answers. Second, the semi-structured nature of the interview guide, which allowed for a question-wise approach to data interpretation. Third, the nature of the majority of the questions posed in the survey, which was aimed at getting to know about facts (and not opinions), namely the interviews experience with HRDD. Data interpretation was conducted independently for consultants and company representatives. The reason for analysing both groups of interviews individually was that the interviewees differed in the nature and frequency of their experience with HRDD.[430] Apart from the distinction of the interviewees into consultants and company representatives, no further distinction was made, since this would not have been in line with the purpose of the expert survey.[431] Further distinctions might have been made according to the interviewees' industry experience, the positions in the firm(s) they worked for and their exposure to M&A transactions, and the interviewees' style of responding to the interview questions.[432]

[427] Cf. Mayring, Philipp (1989), pp. 190ff. According to Mayring, qualitative content analysis is a method for processing large text material in a structured manner to enhance inter-subjective comparability.

[428] Translation by the author, original: "Merkmalsausprägungen". Cf. Bortz, Jürgen/Döring, Nicola (2002), p. 332.

[429] Cf. chapter 1.5.

[430] Still, all answers, no matter whether they had been given by an interviewee with HRDD experience from 1 or from 50 M&A transactions, were given the same weight in data interpretation.

[431] Given the aim of the expert survey, which was to gather as many new ideas as possible to complement the Concept, further differences are viewed as a way of enhancing the variety of the interview answers.

[432] Still, the design of practical HRDD may differ from one industry to another. Moreover, the interviewees' answers may have been influenced by their different positions. Cf. Bortz, Jürgen/Döring, Nicola (2002),

(6) The **quality of a survey** can be described by its reliability, validity and objectivity.[433] Reliability describes the degree to which a re-measurement can produce the same results as the first measurement.[434] Validity can be subdivided into construct, internal and external validity.[435] Construct validity relates to the fact that correct operational measures must be established for the concepts being studied, so that the investigation studies the concepts to be studied, and no other. Internal validity means that causal relationships should be identifiable between the concepts that are studied. External validity describes the need for finding a domain to which a study's findings can be generalised.[436] Objectivity means the degree to which the results of an empirical investigation are independent of the person conducting the investigation. For this thesis, construct validity, reliability and objectivity are considered as relevant to describe the quality of the survey. Internal validity is not considered as important, given the exploratory nature of the study, and external validity is not relevant since the interview results are not supposed to be generalised. In the expert interviews, construct validity mainly depended on whether the questions posed were understood correctly by the interviewees, so that their answers referred to what was sought for.[437] Four measures were taken to ensure construct validity for the interviews. First, test interviews[438] were held with both professionals and researchers in order to check the quality of the interview guide. This included two test interviews with professionals (human resource managers), and four reviews with researchers to determine whether the questions posed were unambiguous and logical. The test interviews with professionals led to some amendments to the wording of the formerly too academic interview questions. Moreover, the review with researchers helped to improve the logical structure of the interview guide. The final interview guide contained twenty-two open questions[439] – in line with the exploratory nature of the survey – to limit the influence of the interviewer on his interviewees. Second, the interview guide was sent to the interviewees in advance so that they were able to familiarise themselves with the questions. The interview guide included a short introduction that served to explain the purpose of the survey to them. Third, questions were reformulated during the actual interviews to ensure that they were understood in the intended way. Fourth, interviewees were given the opportunity to check the interview transcripts to make sure that their answers had been transcribed correctly.[440]

---

pp. 248f. Some interviewees provided long answers and others rather brief ones. For the open questions from the interview guide, multiple answers were allowed for, whereas for the closed ones, singular answers had to be given. Those interviewees who tended to provide long answers often named many items for the multiple-answer-questions, whereas those who tended to answer briefly named fewer items. In data interpretation, all answers have been considered.

433 Cf. Prim, Rolf/Tilmann, Heribert (2000), p. 8. Bortz, Jürgen/Döring, Nicola (2002), pp. 326ff.

434 Cf. Müller-Böling, Detlef/Klandt, Heinz (1996), p. 19.

435 Cf. Schnell, Rainer/Hill, Paul B./Esser, Elke (1999), pp. 145 – 151.

436 Cf. Yin, Robert K. (2003), p. 37.

437 Validity can be reached amongst other by maximising the information provided to interviewees. Cf. Müller-Böling, Detlef/Klandt, Heinz (1996), p. 34.

438 Even though pretests are common for structured surveys mostly, it seemed to be useful to perform one. Cf. Schnell, Rainer/Hill, Paul B./Esser, Elke (1999), p. 324

439 Except for questions 2, 6 and 10, all questions were open.

440 Cf. Müller-Böling, Detlef/Klandt, Heinz (1996), p. 18.

Still, the backgrounds of the interviewees may have limited the construct validity of the interviews. Interviewees for indirect surveys should be selected based on the criteria of expertise and objectivity.[441] The expertise of the interviewees in this survey is undoubted, but their objectivity is not. Consultants in particular but also some of the company representatives are involved economically with practical HRDD. Their responses may have been biased due to this fact. Hence, what has been measured in the survey may be different from practical HRDD in some cases. Reliability means that the results of a study should not be influenced by situational factors. Three measures were taken to enhance the reliability of the expert interviews. First, the procedures followed in the investigation were accurately documented, with respect to data collection, treatment of data, and data interpretation. Second, the interviews were transcribed. However, the accuracy of interviewees' responses may have suffered from the fact that the interviews had to be carried out in a retrospective manner. Bad memory on the part of the interviewees may have limited the accuracy and variety of their answers. Third, even though this thesis is in English, the interviews were carried out in German. Despite this, the repeatability of the survey had to be ensured. Therefore, for one group of interview questions, data interpretation has been complemented with translation tables showing which German synonyms have been translated into which English expressions.[442] To enhance the objectivity of this survey, it was intended to keep the number of interpretative elements in data interpretation to a minimum, by adhering to the interviewees' answers.[443] Still, interviewer effects – e.g. the interviewer's young age – may have limited the reliability and the objectivity of the survey. Supposing that a different – e.g. older – person carried out the same interviews as those conducted for this thesis, slightly varying results might be obtained.[444]

5.2 Insights from the Expert Enquiry

In the following, the results of the expert enquiry are presented separately for both groups of interviewees and then compared to each other. First, the insights of the expert enquiry related to step 1 (chapter 5.2.1), second those related to step 2 (chapter 5.2.2), and third those related to step 3 of the HRDD Concept (chapter 5.2.3) are presented, and it is appraised in how far they are consistent with and/or even complement the HRDD Concept.

5.2.1 Determination of Focus Areas for Human Resource Due Diligence

To generate insights concerning step 1 of the HRDD Concept – determination of focus areas for Human Resource Due Diligence –, first possible focus areas for HRDD (current and future) are elaborated on (chapters 5.2.1.1 to 5.2.1.3) and second, it is illustrated, what factors may influence the relevance of these focus areas (chapters 5.2.1.4 to 5.2.1.6).

---

[441] Cf. Marten, Kai-Uwe/Köhler, Annette G. (1999), p. 340.
[442] Cf. Schnell, Rainer/Hill, Paul B./Esser, Elke (1999), pp. 330ff.
[443] Still, there are limitations to objectivity. For details see Bortz, Jürgen/Döring, Nicola (2002), p. 194.
[444] Cf. Bortz, Jürgen/Döring, Nicola (2002), pp. 246f.

5.2.1.1 Possible Focus Areas according to Company Representatives

According to the company representatives questioned, forty-eight different aspects are currently subject to Human Resource Due Diligence in the context of Mergers & Acquisitions. Given the large number of different aspects named by company representatives, elaborating on each individual issue would lead one into too much detail, and would impair transparency. Therefore, to reduce complication, the aspects mentioned by the company representatives have been grouped by topics. Jaeger's HRDD checklist served as point of departure for generating these topics.[445] Twelve topics have been identified – basic data, qualifications, contracts, pension agreements, motivations, culture, human resource risks, organisation structure, competences, tariff agreements, employee potential, and human resource policies and practices. After a brief description of the interview results, these results are interpreted. Looking more closely into the twelve topics indicated that two distinction criteria can be identified for describing possible focus areas of HRDD. These are the level of abstraction and the time horizon of focus areas for HRDD. Accordingly, the answers given by the company representatives can be allocated to the nine fields in the matrix in figure 5.1.

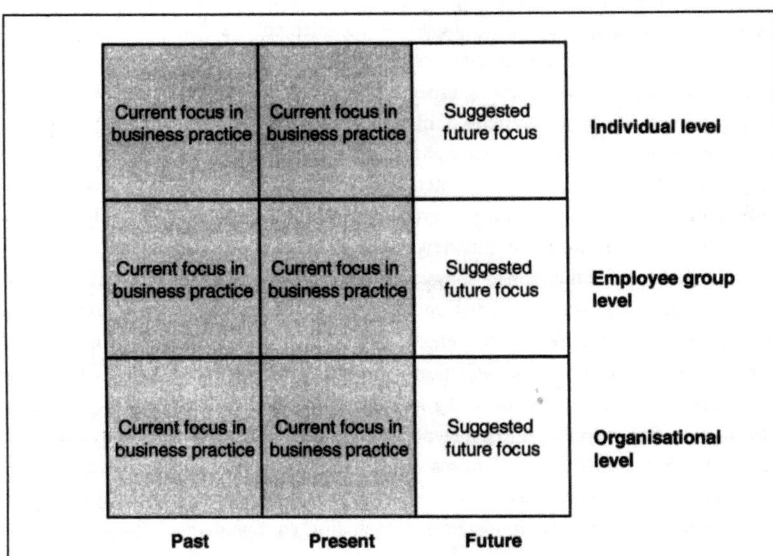

Figure 5.1: Focus areas of Human Resource Due Diligence according to Company Representatives

---

445 Jaeger, Michael (2001), p. 47. The reason for selecting Jaeger's list was that a first review of the interview answers showed that the contents of his list were closest to these answers.

In many cases, the interviewees mentioned multiple topics that should be subject to HRDD. Also, they often mentioned several human resource aspects per topic. To determine the frequency of appearance of each topic in the interviews with company representatives, each topic has been counted once only, even though some interviewees mentioned it several times.[446] Still, the frequency of appearance of each topic in the interviews has hardly been accounted for in data interpretation, since the objective underlying the expert enquiry favours a focus on contents instead of frequencies.[447] The following topics were named most often in the interviews: employee basic data, qualifications, pension agreements, human resource policies and practices (especially compensation and benefits), organisation structure, culture, and contracts. Human resource risks, employee potential, motivation, and competences appeared least repeatedly. Hence the current focus of practical HRDD seems to be on past, and present, organisational, and individual topics. Future-related individual topics – as employee competences – are currently neglected in HRDD.

After determining the current focus of HRDD, the individual aspects mentioned per topic have been reviewed in detail to find whether the focus areas of the HRDD Concept had been supported in the interviews. Also, it was necessary to establish whether company representatives suggested aspects that would be suitable to complement the Concept. Given the focus of the Concept on competences, only those aspects which accord with this focus can serve to support or complement it. The following aspects were **supported** in the interviews with company representatives: Strategic- (systems-), market-, specialist-, social- including leadership-, creativity (innovation-), and flexibility (change competence), which all also can be found in the HRDD Concept.[448] The fact that four interviewees named certain competences, which can also be found in the Concept, underlines the relevance of these competences in M&A transactions in general. However, from the interview responses, it cannot be determined whether the evaluations carried out for the named competences were in practice based on future-related indicators or on past- and present-related ones. Some professionals may have used the term competences presuming a different competence definition than the one applied in this study. No matter if a different competence definition is applicable or not, the generally low frequency of the appearance of competences in the interviews emphasises the practical relevance of the research gap. Entrepreneurial competence could theoretically complement the HRDD Concept as it is not included in the Concept yet. However – given the competence group and competence definitions used in this thesis – entrepreneurial competence is partly reflected in systems, and partly in methods competence.[449] Including entrepreneurial competence in the Concept would yield intersections with other competences, which would harm the transparency of the Concept. The relatively broad competence group and competence definitions the Concept is based on obviously make it very difficult to complement it. Two implications can be deduced from this fact. First, professionals who apply the Concept must be familiar with

[446] This was to neutralise potential effects of the interviewees' different answering styles. Cf. chapter 5.1.
[447] Cf. introduction of chapter 5.1.
[448] Cf. chapter 2.1.2.
[449] Ditto.

the competence and competence group definitions underlying it. In particular, understanding the behavioural competence definition used in the HRDD Concept could represent a challenge in this respect.[450] Second, professionals need to be prepared to apply the Concept without making major adaptations to it. This might require them to forget about their own competence definitions, e.g. those previously used in human resource development. The other eleven topics are **not suitable to complement** the Concept. Basic data are ruled out as they relate to the organisational level. Qualifications are not considered given that they lack future orientation. Contracts are inconsistent with the HRDD Concept as they relate to the present. Pension agreements are often defined on an organisational level. Even if referring to individual employees, pension agreements are not suitable for describing M&A induced human resource requirements. Motivations encompass the individual level, and the future, but are not consistent with the management objective-oriented perspective of analysis taken in this thesis.[451] The same applies to human resource risks, and employee potential.[452] Tariff agreements, and human resource policies and practices are related to the present, and to the organisational level. The same applies to organisation structure, and culture. To conclude, many topics, especially the frequently-named ones, do not correspond with the future-related, individual, management objective-oriented focus of the HRDD Concept. Some of the topics that are not in line with the Concept – namely human resource policies and practices, organisation structure, and culture – should be subject to the analyses preceding HRDD. This fact illustrates once again that the perspective from which the Concept has been defined is new and therefore does not correspond with current HRDD practice. Moreover, the Concept apparently only covers a small section of all the human resource information which professionals possibly want to generate in an M&A transaction. However, even if the eleven topics mentioned above are not suitable to complement with the Concept, professionals can assess these in addition to applying the Concept, supposing that they find a way of linking the Concept and other assessments with each other.

Apart from being questioned about the actual focus areas of HRDD in past M&A, company representatives were also asked what they thought future HRDD should be focused on. They named eight different topics that should be included in future Human Resource Due Diligences. These were culture, qualifications, competences, employee potential, motivations, human resource policies and practices, management tools, and organisation structure.[453] Apart from management tools, the professionals named topics that they had already referred to when describing the current focus of HRDD. For these topics, the same interpretation as given in the previous paragraph is applicable, which means that all topics apart from competences were **not suitable to complement** the Concept. Management tools are not suitable to complement it, since they are related to the organisational level, and to the present. Competences

[450] This is because some professionals possibly use competence definitions of their own, which are related to the past and to the present rather than to the future.
[451] Cf. chapter 1.3.1.
[452] Ditto.
[453] The most frequently named topics are mentioned first.

were amongst the most frequently named topics, which future HRDD should focus on, and serve to **support** the Concept. The substance of two individual competences was supported in the interviews, namely socio-cultural, and co-operation competence. Company representatives – as well as academics – seem to be starting to recognise the usefulness of a management objective-oriented perspective in HRDD. Regarding the other named topics, two observations have been made. First, there still seems to be a serious need to evaluate culture in the context of M&A transactions, despite the fact that cultural assessments have already been tackled extensively in M&A literature[454]. Second, the company representatives interviewed identified a general need to assess future-related topics, such as motivations, competences, and employee potential, more intensely in the future. This observation underlines the usefulness of the future-related perspective of this study.

5.2.1.2 Possible Focus Areas according to Consultants

According to the enquired consultants, twenty-seven different aspects are currently subject to Human Resource Due Diligence in the context of M&A. The aspects mentioned by the consultants were also grouped by topics. As for company representatives, the starting point was Jaeger's HRDD checklist. Nine topics were identified in the interviews, namely basic data, qualifications, contracts, pension agreements, culture, organisation structure, competences, tariff agreements, and human resource policies and practices.

The results from interviews with consultants can be interpreted using the same matrix as applied for the results from interviews with company representatives (see figure 5.2). Human resource policies and practices, qualifications, basic data, contracts, and culture were the most frequently mentioned topics in the interviews with consultants. Pensions, tariff agreements, competences, and organisation structure appeared least frequently. This is similar to the responses by the company representatives, in terms of the most frequent topics. However, the interview results obtained from consultants differed slightly from those from company representatives, when it comes to the least mentioned topics. The consultants named organisational topics (pensions, tariff agreements, and organisation structure), and one individual topic (competences) the least, whilst company representatives mentioned individual topics the least. The differences between the interview results can possibly be explained by the different experiences of both groups of interviewees with practical HRDD. Perhaps firms tend to hire M&A consultants for HRDD, and lawyers for assessing pensions and tariff agreements. This would explain why two topics were mentioned so seldom by the interviewed consultants. The different answering styles of the interviewees, alluded to in chapter 5.1, are also a possible explanation for the discrepancies between the two groups of interviewees.

---

[454] To name a few examples cf. Althauser, Ulrich/Tonscheidt-Göstl, Dagmar (1999), p. 40. Fischer, Heinz/Steffens-Duch, Silvia (2001), p. 49. Stahl, Günter K. (2001), p. 61. Cartwright, Sue/Cooper, Cary L. (1996), p. 10. Nahavandi, Afsaneh/Malekzadeh, Ali R. (1988), p. 82. Buono, Anthony F./Bowditch, James L. (1989), p. 143. Not all of the named authors use the term cultural due diligence.

After determining the current focus of HRDD, the topics mentioned by the consultants have been looked into in detail. This was to support and/or complement the HRDD Concept. The following items were **supported** in the interviews with consultants – specialist, learning (change), strategic (systems), leadership (motivation), change, planning, and social competence.[455] The appearance of these competences in the interviews with consultants stresses their relevance in M&A transactions. Nevertheless, consultants may have based their competence evaluations on criteria which correspond or do not correspond with the management objective-oriented perspective of analysis of this study. Non-corresponding criteria would mean that the interview answers provided by consultants do not support the Concept. Only two out of the eight interviewees said they had already included competences into HRDD, a fact which once again highlights the practical relevance of the research gap. No topics named in the interviews with consultants can complement the HRDD Concept. This is even though business competence, as mentioned by one consultant, represents a competence which yet is not integral to the Concept. The competence group and competence definitions in chapters 1.4.4 and 2.1.1 do not allow one to add a competence that is already represented in several others, to the Concept.[456] The following items were **not suitable to complement** the Human Resource Due Diligence Concept – basic data, qualifications, contracts, pension agreements, culture, organisation structure, tariff agreements, and human resource policies and practices. The same interpretations as given for company representatives in chapter 5.2.1.1 also apply to the results from interviews with consultants.

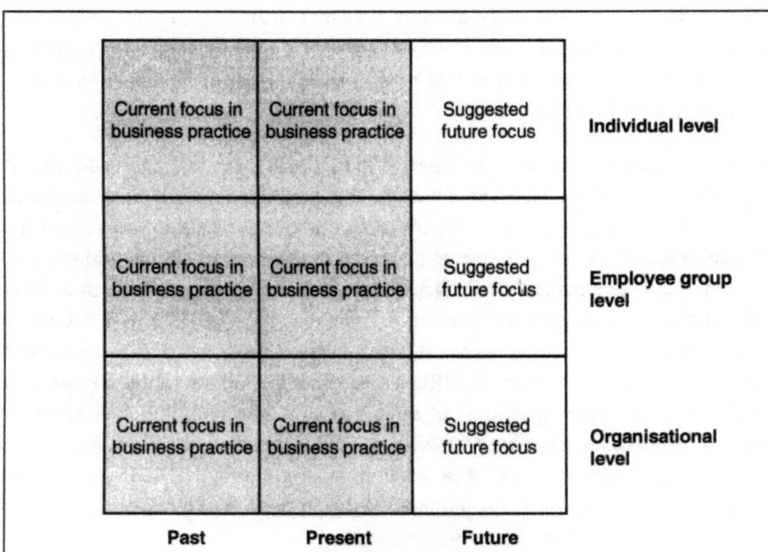

Figure 5.2: Focus areas of Human Resource Due Diligence according to Consultants

[455] Cf. chapter 2.1.2.
[456] Business competence is already reflected in methods and systems competence. Cf. chapter 2.1.1.

Apart from being asked about the current focus areas of HRDD in past M&A transactions, the consultants were also asked what they thought future HRDD should be focused on. They argued that culture, competences, qualifications, and human resource policies and practices[457] should be focused on more intensely in future HRDD. As mentioned in the previous paragraph, culture, qualifications, and human resource policies and practices are **not suitable to complement** the HRDD Concept. The fact that three consultants proposed concentrating more on competences in future HRDD accentuates the research gap that it is intended to close in this study and the human resource requirements definition underlying it.[458] Moreover, the three consultants **supported** the importance of two competences in M&A, which also form part of the Concept: socio-cultural, and co-operation competence. Like the company representatives, the consultants interviewed also pointed to the importance of cultural assessments in the context of M&A transactions. The other two topics which future HRDD should concentrate on, according to consultants, are not related to the future. This illustrates again that professionals who apply the HRDD Concept may possibly need to cover additional topics to generate all relevant human resource information.

5.2.1.3 Summary of Possible Focus Areas

Consultants and company representatives supported certain focus areas of the HRDD Concept, namely strategic (systems), market, specialist, social (including leadership and motivation), creativity (innovation), flexibility (change), learning (change), and planning competence can also be found in the HRDD Concept.[459] None of the additional competences named by both parties can be added to the Concept, since intersections with already existing competences would be the consequence.

The interviews illustrated how diverse practical HRDD has been so far. As illustrated in figures 5.1 and 5.2, the HRDD Concept only deals with a small fraction of what professionals want to know about employees in M&A transactions. In addition, the expert survey has shown that there seems to be a significant gap between the current and the desirable future focus areas of Human Resource Due Diligence. Some of the interview results were contradictory. For instance, some professionals within the same group of interviewees found that HRDD should concentrate on culture in the future, whereas others stated that culture was already assessed extensively in current HRDD. These contradictions could only have been investigated further by working with a larger sample size. This would, however, not have been in line with the research strategy of this study. The contradictions manifested in the expert survey lead to the assumption that some firms who perform HRDD in their M&A transactions, are (already) closer to the proposed Concept, than others. This indicates that the Concept will be easier for some firms to apply than others.

---

[457] The most frequently named topics are mentioned first.
[458] Cf. chapters 1.1 and 1.4.4.
[459] Cf. chapter 2.1.2.

When comparing the results from interviews with both groups of interviewees to each other, it can be found that the results from interviews with company representatives showed slightly different current and future focus areas respectively. Company representatives picked the current relevance of qualifications, a topic hardly named by consultants. At the same time, consultants stated that current HRDD concentrated on cultural assessments, a topic hardly mentioned by company representatives. Both groups of interviewees highlighted the current focus on basic data in HRDD. Coming to the potential level, the top answer given by company representatives was that HRDD should focus more on culture. The suggestions made by consultants were more diverse. They proposed focussing more on culture, but also on competences, and human resource policies and practices.

5.2.1.4 Factors influencing Focus Areas according to Company Representatives

The company representatives asked named twenty-eight different factors that can have an impact on the focus of Human Resource Due Diligence.[460] The factors named by the enquired professionals have been assigned to two answer groups – answers being in line with the M&A management definition of this thesis, and such that are not.

(1) Those answers that are consistent with the M&A management definition of this study can be subdivided according to the four M&A management dimensions in chapter 1.4.5. The following strategic factors were named by the company representatives: M&A objectives, the time relatedness of M&A objectives (short or middle term), and the degree of similarity of the M&A parties' businesses. Regarding structural factors, the focus of HRDD can be determined by differences in the operating systems of the transaction parties, the M&A parties' organisational structures, and the sizes of the transaction parties, according to the interviewees. In the cultural management dimension, the company representatives argued that the focus of HRDD depended on the corporate and national cultures of the transaction parties, as well as the firms' historical developments. When it comes to human resource management factors mentioned by the professionals asked, human resource policies and practices, and the degree of development of the M&A parties' human resource management were said to influence the focus of HRDD.[461]

[460] Some of these factors were named once by company representatives, whereas others were mentioned more than once. However, all factors were treated the same. Hence they only had to be mentioned once to be included in data interpretation.

[461] For the frequency of each answer, cf. figure 5.3.

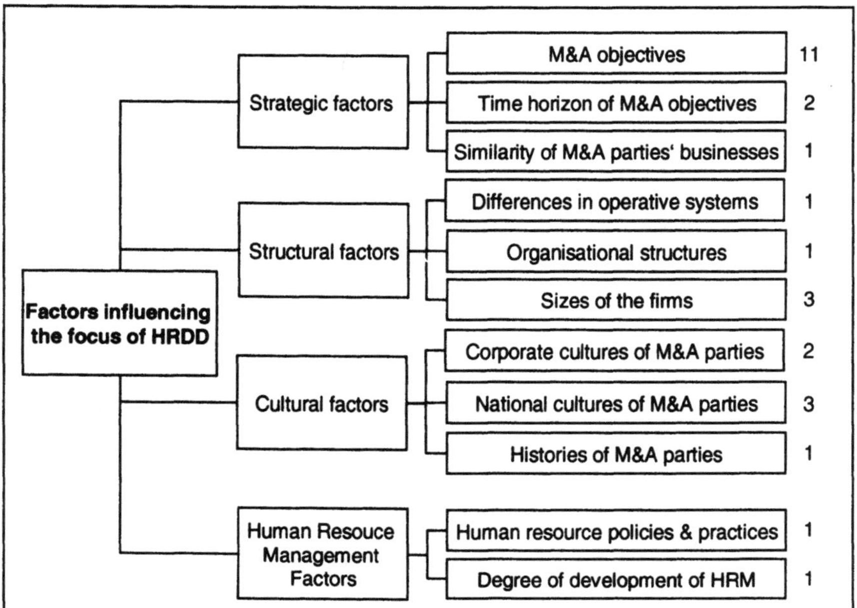

*Some interviewees mentioned several factors influencing the focus of HRDD, whereas others only named one or even none. Therefore, the number of answers is not identical to the number of interviews.

Figure 5.3: Factors influencing the Focus of Human Resource Due Diligence according to Company Representatives

(2) Besides naming factors that are consistent with the M&A management definition of this study, the company representatives also came up with seventeen factors that do not fall into the management dimensions of the Concept. These factors are not elaborated on individually for this would lead one too far into detail, and would impair the transparency of the argumentation. To reduce complication, the factors mentioned by company representatives have been classified into types of factors. The different components of the new St. Gallen management framework – especially the environmental spheres, and the stakeholder groups – have been taken as a point of departure for identifying the following types of factors: firm-related, industry-related, employee-related, and deal-related factors.[462] Four firm-related, one industry-related, eight employee-related, and four deal-related factors that may have an impact on the focus of HRDD were mentioned by the interviewees, in this context.

[462] Cf. Rüegg-Stürm, Johannes (2003), p. 89.

The following paragraphs serve to evaluate whether the results from the interviews with company representatives support and/or complement the Concept.

(1) Regarding the strategic factors named by some interviewees, M&A objectives shape the focus of HRDD according to the HRDD Concept, thus this interview response **supports** the Concept.[463] The same applies to the time relation of M&A objectives.[464] The degree of similarity of the M&A parties' businesses is not reflected in the M&A objectives of the HRDD Concept, but can form part of the analyses preceding HRDD in order to arrive at M&A objectives. To be able to arrive at strategic M&A objectives which serve as a basis for the Concept, M&A management needs to know whether the M&A parties' businesses overlap or not. As far as differences in operating systems used by the transaction parties are concerned, the analyses preceding HRDD need to cover these, but the HRDD Concept does not. The same holds true for the firms' organisational structures, and their sizes. All three structural factors – macro and micro structure as well as task spectra – may have an impact on the structural M&A objectives. The HRDD Concept takes national-, and corporate culture into account when generating human resource requirements.[465] Thus, these two factors mentioned by some professionals **support** the Concept. However, the historical development of the M&A parties' corporate cultures is not considered in the Concept, but should be the subject of the analyses preceding the application of the Concept. Human resource policies and practices have an impact on the focus of HRDD. This is supported not only by some interviewees, but is also an assumption of the HRDD Concept.[466] Thus, this answer provided by some of the company representatives **supports** the HRDD Concept. One company representative suggested that the degree of development of the M&A parties' human resource management was a factor that determined the focus of HRDD. The professional's suggestion is **not suitable to complement** the Concept, since it is not consistent with the management objective-oriented perspective of analysis it is based on.

(2) Most of the seventeen factors (that do not fall into the management dimensions of the extended trilogy) represent characteristics of the firms involved in an M&A transaction, of the industry in which the transaction takes place, the transaction as such, and the M&A parties' employees.[467] Few factors relate to the expected consequences of an M&A transaction from an employee and deal perspective. None of the factors mentioned by the interviewees supports or complements the HRDD Concept. Those factors which describe characteristics have no impact on the focus of HRDD. For instance, the M&A experience of the transaction parties does not influence the importance of the human resource

---

[463] Cf. chapter 2.2.
[464] Cf. chapter 2.2 where a distinction has been made between long and middle term human resource requirements.
[465] Ditto.
[466] Ditto.
[467] Firm-related factors, industry-related factors, deal-related factors and employee-related factors.

requirements of the HRDD Concept.[468] It is, however, useful to consider the firm, industry-, deal- and employee-related characteristics named by the company representatives in the analyses preceding the HRDD. For instance, the number of employees affected by an M&A transaction must be known to be able to assess on which employee groups M&A induced human resource requirements are imposed. Knowledge about the industry in which an M&A transaction takes place is important in order to generate strategic-, and human resource management objectives.[469] Those factors, which relate to the expected consequences of M&A transactions, are **not suitable to complement** the Concept, as they do not explain the relevance of the particular human resource requirements. Instead, firms' preparedness to carry out a HRDD can be estimated based on these factors. For instance, the expected human resource costs incurred by a transaction can be crucial for a firm's decision to carry out a HRDD. As can be seen from the above argumentation, the professionals interviewed named many factors, which according to them have an impact on the focus of HRDD. Still, according to the Concept, the design of HRDD should be adapted to the underlying M&A context. Therefore, all factors that do not have an impact on the management objectives of an M&A transaction can be ignored for the Concept. Nevertheless, all characteristics mentioned by the interviewees should be considered in the analyses which are carried out prior to actual HRDD. Those factors encompassing expectations are also productive of insights, as they explain the current design of HRDD in practice.

5.2.1.5 Factors influencing Focus Areas according to Consultants

The consultants interviewed generated seventeen different factors that may have an impact on the focus of a Human Resource Due Diligence. These different factors are assigned to the same two answer groups as those used for presenting the results from interviews with company representatives, namely strategic, structural, cultural, and human resource management factors.

(1) The following strategic factors were mentioned by the enquired consultants – competitive position of the transaction parties (prior to the M&A transaction), M&A objectives, degree of maturity of the firms, and the firms' markets. For structural factors, the focus of HRDD can be influenced by the size of the transaction parties' (businesses), and by their organisational structures. In the cultural management dimension, the histories of the M&A parties, the degree of cultural integration, and the national cultures of the firms involved in

---

[468] Only under the presumption that employees who have M&A experience have more ability to cope with M&A induced requirements, can this factor be useful in considering when to apply the HRDD Concept. From a behavioral learning perspective, it is assumed that a high M&A experience of the transaction parties enhances the probability of a successful transaction. Haleblian, Jerayr/Finkelstein, Sydney (1999), p. 29.

[469] For example professional services Cf. Hitt, Michael A./Bierman, Leonard/Shimizu, Katsuhiko/Kochhar, Rahul (2001), pp. 13ff or knowledge intensive firms cf. Sattelberger, Thomas (Ed.) (1999) (entire book). Siegert, Theo. In: Bühler, Wolfgang/Siegert, Theo (Eds.) (1999), p. 37.

an M&A were viewed as important. Human resource strategy was also said to be an important human resource management factor influencing the focus of HRDD.

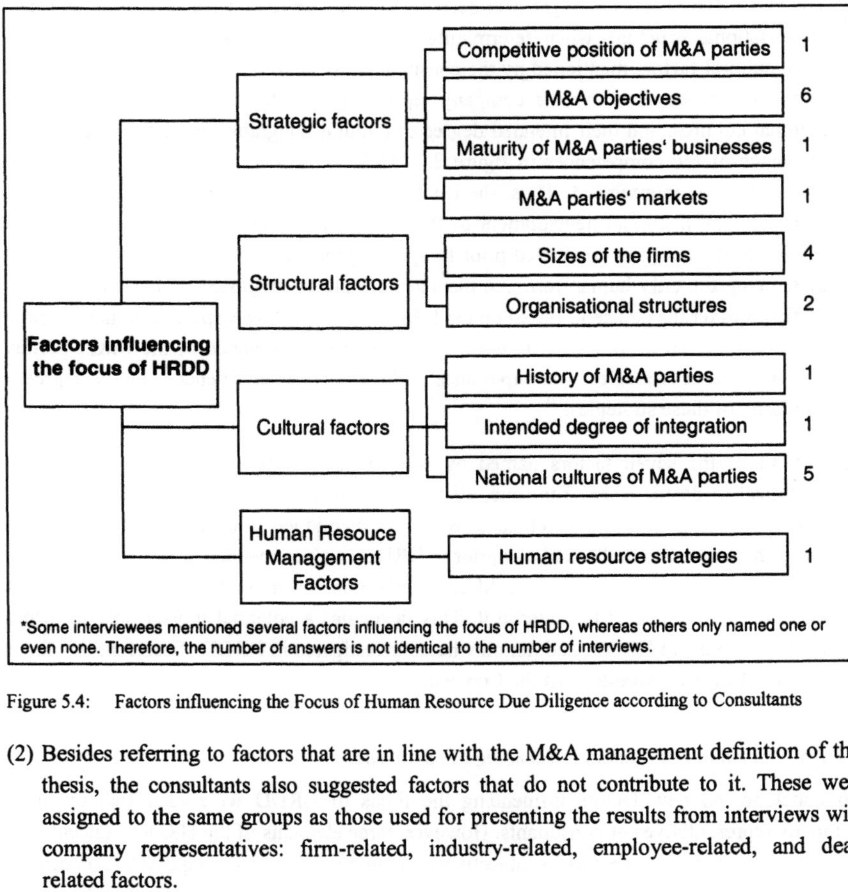

Figure 5.4: Factors influencing the Focus of Human Resource Due Diligence according to Consultants

(2) Besides referring to factors that are in line with the M&A management definition of this thesis, the consultants also suggested factors that do not contribute to it. These were assigned to the same groups as those used for presenting the results from interviews with company representatives: firm-related, industry-related, employee-related, and deal-related factors.

The following insights can be produced by the analyses of the interviews with consultants.

(1) The competitive positions of the transaction parties prior to the M&A transaction are not part of the Human Resource Due Diligence Concept, since they do not represent M&A objectives. Nonetheless, these positions can be subject to the analyses preceding HRDD to determine strategic M&A objectives. (Strategic) M&A objectives are integral to the Concept.[470] Therefore, the second strategic factor named by the consultants interviewed **supports** the HRDD Concept. The degree of maturity of the transaction parties' (busi-

[470] Cf. chapter 2.2.

nesses) may have an impact on strategic M&A objectives, and should therefore be included in the analyses preceding the HRDD. The same applies to the M&A parties' markets. The pre-HRDD analyses might also account for the transaction parties' sizes, and their organisational structures when determining structural M&A management objectives. The three cultural factors mentioned by the consultants asked are fully in accordance with the three factors suggested by the company representatives. Moreover, the M&A parties' national cultures, and their intended degree of cultural integration have an impact on the relevance of the competences in figure 2.2. This was also mentioned by the company representatives interviewed. Thus, these factors **support** the suggestions of the HRDD Concept. The historical development of the M&A parties' corporate cultures should be subject to the analyses conducted prior to applying the Concept. Human resource strategies, being the only human resource management factor suggested by the professionals, partly **support** the Concept. Based on the HRDD Concept, M&A specific human resource requirements can be produced based on the intended coexistence of the M&A parties' human resource strategies. The importance of these requirements depends on the degree of similarity of these strategies.[471]

(2) Not all of the seven factors named by consultants that fall outside the Concept are discussed in detail. Apart from one, all factors named by the consultants refer to firm, industry, deal, and employee characteristics. As mentioned in chapter 5.2.1.4, assessing these characteristics in the analyses prior to HRDD is recommended. The remaining factor relates to the expectations of an M&A transaction, or more precisely to the human resource risks expected to underlie it. This factor has a potential impact only on firms' likeliness to do an HRDD, and not on what is investigated in HRDD. Therefore this factor is **not suitable to complement** the Concept.

5.2.1.6 Summary of Factors influencing Focus Areas

To conclude, no new factors influencing the focus of HRDD were identified by either company representatives or consultants. However, three elements of the HRDD Concept were entirely supported – strategic M&A objectives, the time horizon of strategic M&A objectives, and the intended degree of (cultural) integration after closing the transaction. According to the Concept as well as to the professionals, these three elements also have an impact on the focus of HRDD. Moreover, five elements of the Concept were partly supported. The professionals argued that organisational structures, corporate cultures, national cultures, human resource policies and practices, and human resource strategies had an impact on the focus of HRDD. According to the HRDD Concept, M&A objectives must be defined in relation to these five factors for human resource requirements to ensue. The interviewees did not, however, define any objectives relating to the five factors. This fact illustrates that professionals currently seem to be very concerned about assessing the M&A parties' specifics (which should take

---

[471] Cf. chapter 2.2.

place prior to HRDD according to the Concept) but hardly about defining M&A objectives based on these specifics. This finding underlines the practical relevance of the HRDD Concept, as it enables professionals to take a future-related perspective. Those strategic, structural, cultural, and human resource management factors, which are not M&A objectives, should be subject to the analyses preceding HRDD. Those factors which do not fall into the M&A management dimensions can either usefully be evaluated before the actual HRDD (characteristics), or they are not suitable to complement the Concept (expectations). In general, the answers provided by the interviewees were similar in contents but sometimes differed in relative frequency.

5.2.2 Generation of Human Resource Due Diligence Information

As to step 2 of the Concept – generation of Human Resource Due Diligence Information –, the interviewees were asked about the measurability of human resource aspects and about the information base for HRDD. The measurability of human resource aspects was covered to engender insights for the development of indicators for HRDD, whereas the information base for HRDD was addressed to get generate insights about suitable tools for HRDD.

5.2.2.1 Insights from Interviews with Company Representatives

Regarding the measurability of human resource aspects, the interviewees were asked which human resource aspects were easy, and which were difficult to generate. When it comes to the information base for HRDD, they were asked what human resource aspects could be evaluated based on historical data, and which should be assessed based on new data.

(1) Concerning the measurability of human resource aspects, the company representatives interviewed considered information about the following aspects to be easy to assess: human resource policies and practices, organisational structure, basic data, qualifications, quantitative, measurable, and historical data. Regarding aspects that are difficult to assess, the company representatives mentioned: qualifications, motivations, culture, competences, employee potential, human resource policies and practices, and non-measurable aspects.[472] As can be seen from the interview answers, some of the interviewees named concrete aspects that were easy and difficult to assess, whereas others described characteristics of aspects that are easy and difficult to assess.

[472] For the frequency of each answer, cf. figure 5.5.

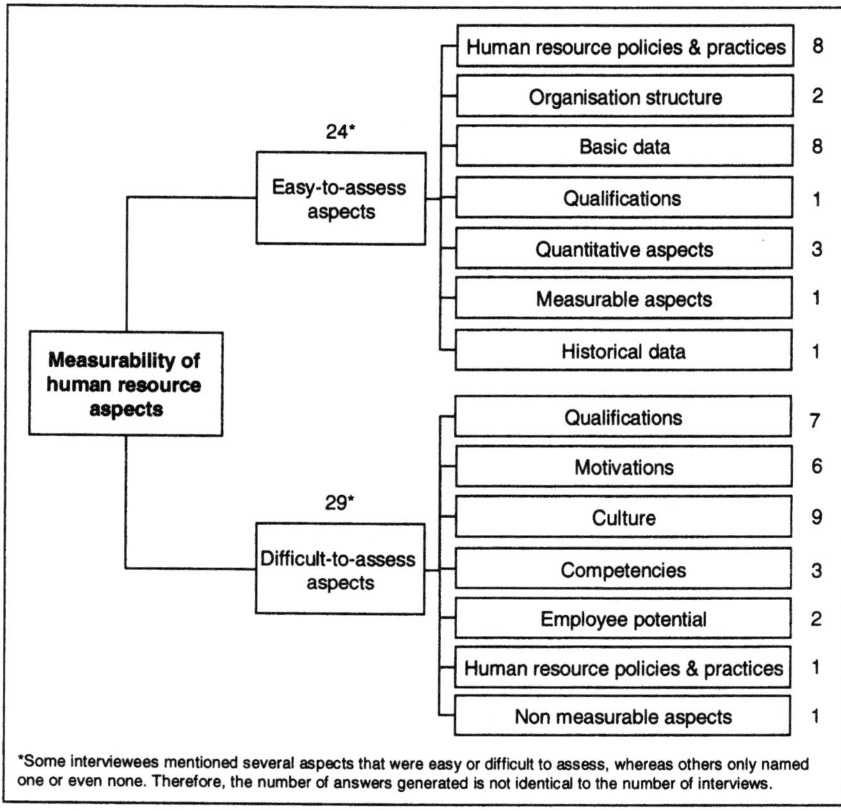

Figure 5.5: Measurability of Human Resource Due Diligence Focus Areas according to Company Representatives

(2) As regards the information base for HRDD, according to the company representatives interviewed, the following HRDD aspects can be evaluated based on historical data: basic data, qualifications, pension agreements, motivations, tariff agreements, and human resource policies and practices.[473] To assess these aspects, data room information can be utilised. New data have to be collected to appraise basic data, qualifications, pension agreements, motivations, culture, competences, employee potential, and human resource policies and practices.[474] Possible tools for collecting new data are interviews, and feed-back from superiors, and colleagues. The answers of the company representatives that are related to the information base for HRDD are summarized in figure 5.6.

[473] For the frequency of each answer, cf. figure 5.6.

[474] For the frequency of each answer, cf. figure 5.6.

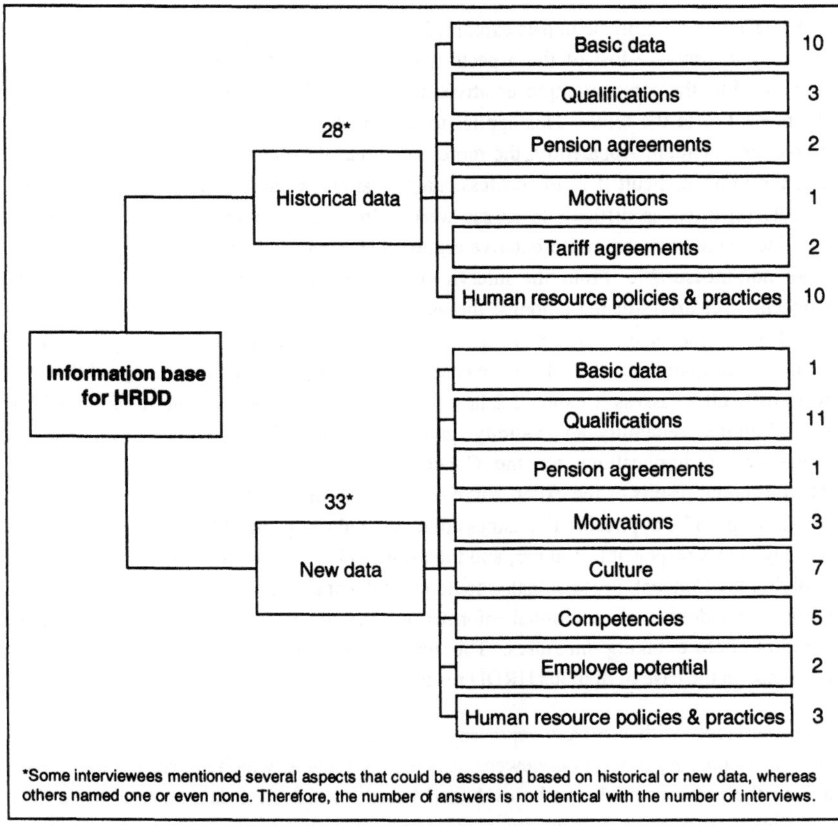

Figure 5.6: Information Base for Human Resource Due Diligence according to Company Representatives

When translating the results from interviews with company representatives into implications for the HRDD Concept, the following has been found.

(1) The majority of the company representatives considered aspects which are related to the organisational level, and to the past or to the present to be easy to assess. This is true of human resource policies and practices, basic data, and organisation structure. One company representative mentioned explicitly that historical data were easy to assess in HRDD. Qualifications are the only aspect related to the individual level (and to the past/present), which was considered as easy to assess by the professionals interviewed. Besides their time orientation, aspects that are easy to assess show two other characteristics, according to four of the interviewees – they are quantitative, and measurable. All aspects that are easy to assess mentioned by the company representatives are **not suitable to complement** the HRDD Concept. At the same time, they are the aspects currently concentrated on in practical HRDD, according to company representatives. The current focus

of HRDD may possibly be in part explained by the fact that the aspects which are in focus are easy to assess. Most of the aspects which are difficult to assess were consistently mentioned by the company representatives asked, and relate to the individual level, and to the present or to the future. This applies to qualifications, motivations, competences, and employee potential. Apparently, the more individual the aspects that should be assessed are, the more difficult it is for professionals to appraise them. The only organisational aspects regarded as difficult to assess were culture, and human resource policies and practices. One company representative argued that aspects which were difficult to assess were non-measurable. From the interviewed professionals' point of view, the HRDD Concept is clearly situated amongst the aspects that are difficult to measure, since it is based on competences.[475] The Concept is based on the assumption that competences can be measured quantitatively, whilst the enquired company representatives argued that they were difficult to assess. Chapter 3.2 has already pointed to the fact that tools for HRDD are of limited reliability and validity, given the future-related nature of competences. However, no implications for the Concept have yet been deduced from this fact. Therefore, the results of the expert survey serve to **complement** the HRDD Concept. For the Concept to be applicable in business practice, indicators and tools for HRDD must be employed in a responsible manner, and their downsides must be well understood by those applying the Concept. Professionals should critically appraise the results of HRDD, and, if there is any doubt, use additional information other than that acquired by applying the Concept, before taking measures. The interests of individual employees should be respected in the case of dubious HRDD results.

(2) The interviews with company representatives also dealt with the information base for HRDD. According to the interviewees, it is mostly aspects, which are related to the past, and to the present which can be evaluated based on historical data such as basic data, qualifications, pension agreements, tariff agreements, and human resource policies and practices. Apart from qualifications, all these data are related to the organisational level. Motivations relate not only to the individual level but also to the future. All aspects related to the past and to the present that can be assessed by the use of historical data, are currently under consideration in practical HRDD.[476] It seems as if professionals are currently putting an accent on the named aspects because no new data need to be generated to assess them. Presuming that new data are generated, future-related individual aspects can be evaluated, such as qualifications, motivations, competences, and employee potential. Moreover, organisational aspects can also be appraised by the use of new data, e.g. culture, human resource policies and practices, pension agreements, and basic data. The HRDD Concept is based on new data.[477] Hence the results of interviews with company representatives **support** the assumption underlying the Concept that new data

[475] Cf. chapter 1.4.4.
[476] Cf. chapter 5.2.1.
[477] Cf. chapter 3.

need to be generated when evaluating competences in HRDD. The other human resource aspects do not form part of the Concept[478], and thus they are not further discussed.

A general observation from the interviews with company representatives is that the interviewees contradicted each other to some extent. For instance, some interviewees argued that human resource policies and practices were easy to assess, whereas others found them difficult to evaluate. Also, some of the professionals found that motivations could only be appraised based on new data, whereas others opted for referring to historical data. The contradictions may be due to two facts. First, they can be explained by the different interests of the professionals in the HRDD data. Second, they may be due to the differing attitudes of the interviewees to future-related human resource data – some are possibly sceptical whilst others are in favour of future-related data. Since no contradictions were found for competences, the contradictions have no impact on further argumentation in this study.

5.2.2.2 Insights from Interviews with Consultants

As for company representatives, the results from the expert interviews with consultants are presented as far as the measurability of human resource aspects, and the information base for HRDD are concerned.

(1) The consultants asked considered the following human resource aspects to be easy to assess: basic data, contracts, human resource policies and practices, pension agreements, and quantitative aspects. With regard to aspects that are difficult to assess, the consultants mentioned qualifications, culture, organisational structure, motivations, and competences.[479] Figure 5.7 summarizes the answers given by consultants.

[478] Cf. chapter 2.1.

[479] For the frequency of each answer, cf. figure 5.7.

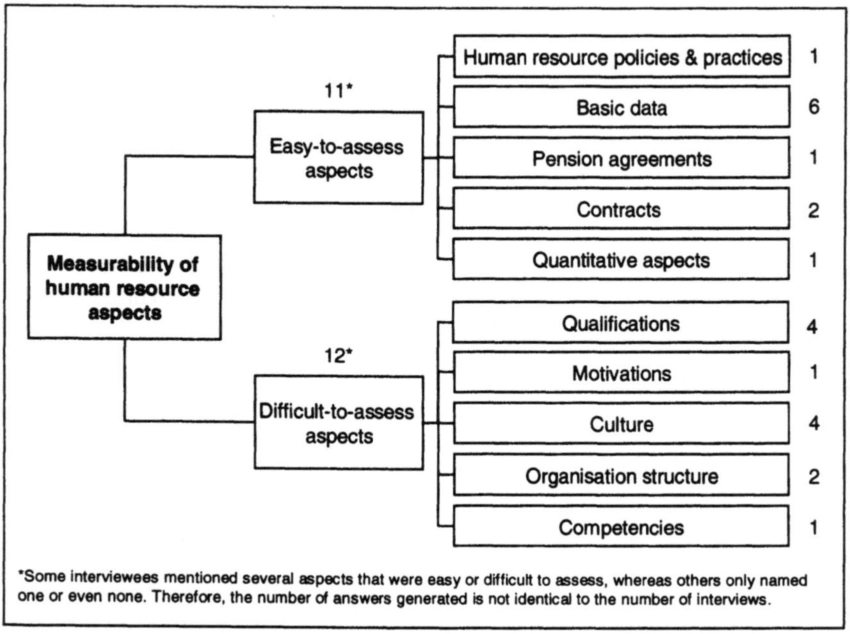

Figure 5.7: Measurability of Human Resource Due Diligence Focus Areas according to Consultants

(2) According to the interviewed consultants, the following human resource aspects can be evaluated based on historical data: basic data, contracts, pension agreements, organisation structure, tariff agreements, and human resource policies and practices.[480] Appraising the following aspects requires the collection of new data – basic data, qualifications, motivations, culture, competences, employee potential, and human resource policies and practices.[481] Interviews are a possible tool for assessing the above-named aspects.

---

[480] For the frequency of each answer, cf. figure 5.8.
[481] For the frequency of each answer, cf. figure 5.8.

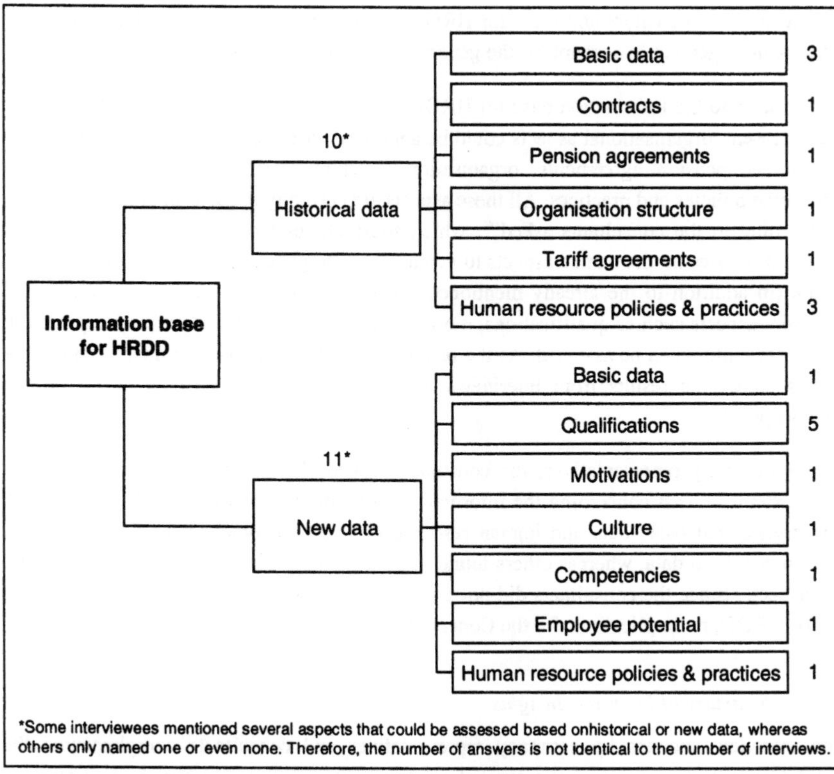

Figure 5.8: Information Base for Human Resource Due Diligence according to Consultants

When interpreting the results from interviews with consultants with regard to the indicators and tools for Human Resource Due Diligence, the following can be found.

(1) Concerning the measurability of the results from HRDD, there are strong similarities between the answers provided by the consultants, and those of the company representatives asked. All consultants found that organisational, past- and present data were easy to assess. This includes basic data, contracts, human resource policies and practices, pension agreements. As for company representatives, one consultant declared that in general, quantitative aspects were easy to assess. The aspects named by the consultants are those currently concentrated on in practical HRDD. This underlines the assumption that aspects that are easy to assess are consciously at the centre of attention in current practical HRDD. Nearly all of the aspects that were identified by consultants as difficult to assess, apart from culture and organisation structure, are related to the individual level, and to the future. Hence, the consultants asked also situated the competences of the HRDD Concept amongst the aspects that are difficult to assess. Accordingly, the results from interviews with the second group of interviewees are also suitable for **complementing** the HRDD

Concept. The indicators and tools for HRDD in chapter 3 must be applied cautiously by M&A management to account for the general difficulty of assessing competences.

(2) In relation to the information base for HRDD, the consultants asked found that only past, and present, organisational aspects could be appraised based on historical data: basic data, contracts, pension agreements, organisation structure, tariff agreements, and human resource policies and practices. All these aspects are currently in focus in practical HRDD, according to the consultants asked[482], which substantiates the assumption that practical HRDD focuses on the named aspects to avoid having to generate new data. Based on new data (in addition to the already mentioned aspects) in particular individual, future, and present aspects such as qualifications, motivations, competences, and employee potential, but also culture can be assessed. As the results from interviews with company representatives show, the results from interviews with consultants also **support** step 2 of the Concept.

Like the company representatives, the consultants asked also contradicted each other to a certain extent, at least concerning the information base for Human Resource Due Diligence. Some argued that basic data and human resource policies and practices could be assessed based on historical data, whereas others found that new data needed to be generated to assess these aspects. Since the consultants did not contradict each other concerning the information base for HRDD, no implications for the Concept need to be assumed.

5.2.2.3 *Summary of Interview Insights*

Some interview answers by company representatives and consultants complemented the HRDD Concept. By stressing the limited measurability of competences, both groups of interviewees pointed to the necessity of remembering the limitations of the indicators and tools for HRDD in chapter 3 in practical HRDD. The interviews also supported the necessity of generating new data when deploying the Human Resource Due Diligence Concept.

5.2.3 Compilation of the generated Human Resource Due Diligence Information

Step 3 of the HRDD Concept deals with the compilation of the generated HRDD information. To gain new insights related to step 3 of the Concept, the experts were asked to name indicators for the usefulness of a HRDD. These indicators were supposed to provide insights for a useful compilation of the generated HRDD information.

[482] Cf. chapter 5.2.1.2.

5.2.3.1 Insights from Interviews with Company Representatives

The answers provided by company representatives were diverse. They identified fourteen different indicators to assess the usefulness of a Human Resource Due Diligence. These answers can be assigned to two different answer groups: results-related and process-related indicators. Presuming results-related indicators are used, HRDD usefulness is measured based on the achievement of certain results. If based on process-related indicators, HRDD is useful, if the management processes following HRDD can be undertaken in the desired manner.

(1) The company representatives interviewed mentioned the following results-related indicators – employee satisfaction, employees' identification with the new firm, M&A success, prevention of human resource risks, retention of key employees, integration costs, purchase price, fairness of downsizing, and to what extent the most important human resource issues in an M&A are resolved.

(2) The following process-related indicators were named by the enquired company representatives – facilitation of M&A integration processes, employees' attitude towards the transaction, identification of key employees, enhanced decision-making processes, and attitude of the workers' council towards the M&A transaction.

Results-related indicators are **suitable to complement** the HRDD Concept. The HRDD Concept is a tool which serves to support further M&A management measures. The impact of HRDD on the success of an M&A transaction or other results-related indicators is not at the core of this thesis.[483] Therefore, the suggestions made by company representatives in the first answer group are of no relevance for the further course of the analysis. However, it might have been important to consider them, if the perspective of analysis of this study had been more results-oriented. Some indicators identified in the second answer group **support** the perspective taken by the HRDD Concept. The identification of key employees, and improved decision-making processes as a result of this, are what the application of the Concept aims to bring about.[484] As a result of improved decision-making processes, the M&A integration processes can be facilitated. The other two process-related indicators do not play a part in the Concept. Influencing the workers' council's or employees' attitude towards a particular transaction is not what the Concept is meant for. None of the indicators suggested by the company representatives can be identified as a complement to the Concept. The results from interviews with company representatives illustrate that business practice currently seems to be more concerned with the results than with the processes that can be engendered when carrying out a HRDD. According to the Concept, in contrast, the usefulness of HRDD can be seen from the processes following a HRDD. On the one hand, the discrepancy detected underlines the originality of the Concept for business practice. On the other hand, it indicates the potential relevance of results-oriented research in further studies, as company representatives seem to be very concerned with results-related indicators.

---

[483] Cf. chapter 1.3.1.
[484] Cf. chapter 1.1.

5.2.3.2 Insights from Interviews with Consultants

Eight different indicators of the usefulness of HRDD were identified by the consultants asked. These have been allocated to the same answer groups as those identified for the interviews with company representatives. Apart from one[485], all the answers provided by the consultants were identical to some of the answers provided by company representatives.

(1) In the first answer group, the consultants mentioned four results-related indicators: employees' identification with the new firm, retention of key employees, integration costs, and fairness of the solutions found in the case of downsizing of a firm.

(2) The following process-related indicators were assigned to the second answer group: ease of M&A integration (processes), identification of human resource risks, identification of key employees, and enhanced decision-making processes.

The suggestions made by the consultants interviewed in answer group one are **not suitable to complement** the assumptions of the HRDD Concept, and are therefore not included in further argumentation, on the same basis as that outlined for company representatives. Some answers provided in the second answer group **support** the perspective taken when creating the Concept, namely facilitation of M&A integration, identification of key employees, and enhanced decision-making processes.[486] None of the suggestions made by consultants can be used to complement the HRDD Concept. In comparison to the company representatives asked, the consultants named relatively more process-related indicators: half of the indicators suggested were process-related. This may be due to the different involvement of consultants with practical HRDD. Firms may possibly hire consultants to enhance the quality of the processes following HRDD especially if appointed in early M&A phases rather than to engender immediate results.

5.2.3.3 Summary of Interview Insights

Three answers generated both from the interviews with company representatives and consultants support the Concept. In the perspective of analysis of this study, it has been presumed implicitly that HRDD is useful, if immediate measures can be generated based on its results. This view is supported by the interviewees. Still, none of the professionals addressed the desired nature of HRDD results, for them to be useful for further M&A management measures. According to the HRDD Concept, for HRDD information to serve as an immediate basis for further management activities, the HRDD results must be compiled, a fact which none of the interviewees recognised. Hence, the use of HRDD as a management

---

485 The consultants argued that the usefulness of HRDD could be seen from the detection of human resource risks – a process-related factor –, whereas the company representatives named the prevention of human resource risks – a results-related indicator.

486 Cf. chapter 1.3.1.

tool seems to be new to professionals, which emphasises the practical relevance of step 3 of the HRDD Concept.

5.3 Final Remarks on the Expert Enquiry

Concerning step 1 of the HRDD Concept, the consultants and company representatives supported certain competences which are integral to it, namely strategic (systems), market, specialist, social (motivation), creativity (innovation), flexibility (change), learning (change), and planning competence.[487] Apart from that, the expert survey has illustrated that current practical HRDD is diverse, but hardly takes the importance of employee competences into account. Moreover, a number of professionals supported the object of analysis of this study by stating that M&A-specific competences should be considered more in future HRDD. As to factors influencing the focus of HRDD, the professionals supported certain factors which are part of the Concept, namely strategic M&A objectives, the time horizon of strategic M&A objectives, the intended degree of (cultural) integration after closing the transaction, organisational structures, corporate culture, national culture, human resource policies and practices, and human resource strategies. As to step 2 of the HRDD Concept, both company representatives and consultants mentioned the necessity of keeping the limitations of the indicators and tools, which are integral to the Concept, in mind in practical HRDD. The interviews also supported the generation of new HRDD data, when applying the Concept. Referring to step 3 of the Concept, the importance of compiling HRDD information as an immediate basis for measures to be taken by management, has been supported. Figure 5.9 shows the empirically complemented HRDD Concept.

[487] Cf. chapter 2.1.2.

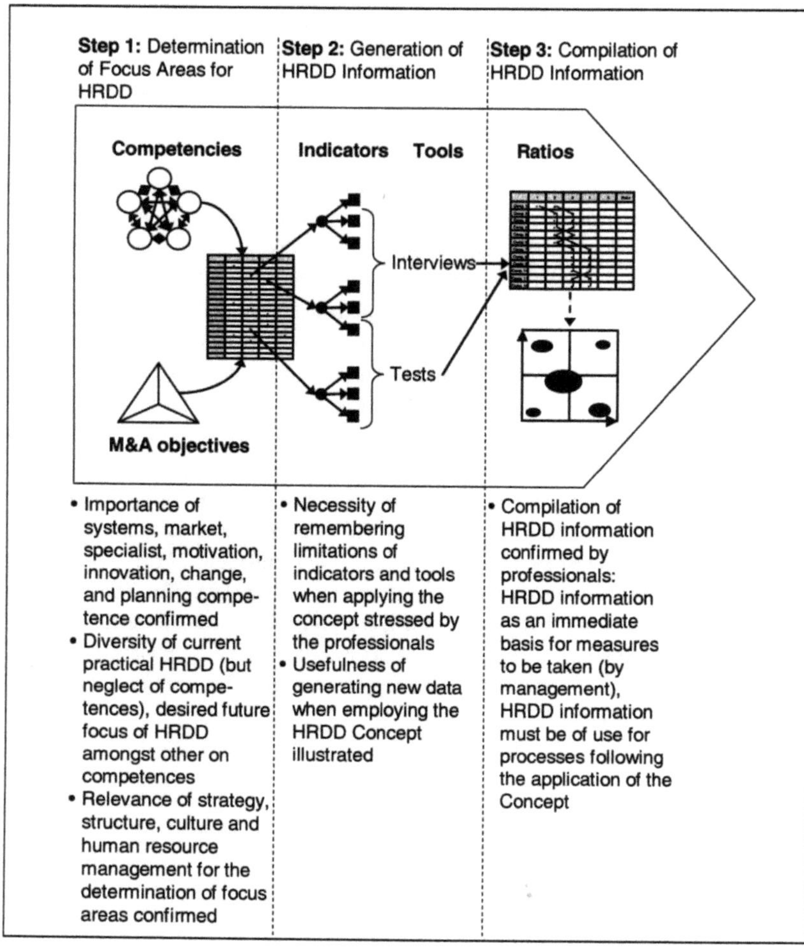

Figure 5.9: Empirically Complemented Human Resource Due Diligence Concept

Given the similarity of the results from the interviews with company representatives and consultants for the majority of the interview answers[488], it would perhaps not have been necessary to interpret the data from both groups of interviewees separately. Still, the few differences between the answers by both groups of professionals have enhanced the diversity of the insights generated about practical HRDD.

[488] For all groups of questions, the same answer groups have been used for both groups of interviewees, which shows the similarity of their answers.

6 Illustration of the Application of the Human Resource Due Diligence Concept based on Case Studies

This chapter deals with the application of the empirically complemented Human Resource Due Diligence Concept to business practice.[489] Two polar case studies were conducted to illustrate this application. In the first case study, the merger between Deutsche Genossenschaftsbank and GZ-Bank in 2001 is elaborated on from a HRDD perspective. In this transaction, HRDD was carried out upon completion of the merger. In the second case study, the planned acquisition of Company X by Beiersdorf in 2001 is the subject of analysis. Here, HRDD was carried out prior to the acquisition. The transaction did not come about for financial reasons. There are four reasons for choosing these two transactions. First, neither DZ Bank nor Beiersdorf participated in the expert enquiry. Second, both firms were prepared to provide the information required to carry out the case studies. Third, the transactions analysed took place in human resource intense industries – presumably a good prerequisite for illustrating the application of the HRDD Concept to business practice. Fourth, the two cases are of a polar nature: one case covers a pre-completion example of the application of HRDD in business practice, whereas the other represents a post-completion example. In the following, the research strategy underlying the case studies is outlined (chapter 6.1). Thereafter, the results of each case study are presented individually (chapter 6.2 and 6.3). Finally, overall insights from both cases are derived (chapter 6.4).

6.1 Research Strategy for the Case Studies

As already mentioned, the objective of the case studies is to illustrate the application of the empirically complemented HRDD Concept to business practice.[490] Thus the case studies are of an illustrative nature. Besides being of an illustrative nature, case studies can also be of an exploratory, causal or descriptive nature.[491] Illustrative cases appeared to be the most suitable for achieving the objective underlying the case studies. In the following paragraphs, the research strategy chosen for carrying out the cases is presented with regard to the

(1) components of the case study design,

(2) type of case study design,

(3) quality of the case study design and

(4) treatment and interpretation of case data.

---

[489] Cf. step 5 of the research strategy from chapter 1.3.3.

[490] Besides case studies, one could also have carried out archival or historic analyses. Given the practical research goal of this study and the necessity of dealing with contemporary events, the two empirical methods mentioned would not have been suitable for step 5 of the research strategy. Cf. Yin, Robert K (2003), p. 5.

[491] For details please refer to the related literature cf. Yin, Robert K. (2003), pp. 23ff.

(1) According to Yin, each case design consists of **five main components**, namely the case objective, the unit of analysis, the assumptions underlying the case study, the relationship between the case data and the assumptions, and the criteria for interpreting the case results.[492] The objective of the case studies has already been presented. The unit of analysis for the case studies is firms that already have been involved in a Human Resource Due Diligence in the context of their M&A activities. The assumption underlying the case studies is that the application of the HRDD Concept to business practice can be illustrated by applying it to case studies. The data to be generated in the case studies helps demonstrate that this assumption holds true. If the results of the case studies enable one to compare actual HRDD to desired HRDD, the illustrative case studies are suitable for demonstrating how to apply the HRDD Concept to business practice.

(2) A **multiple type of design** is used for the case studies. For each firm, a past M&A transaction (no longer ago than 3 years) is analysed, in which a HRDD was carried out. The reason for choosing to carry out two case studies is a two-tail approach to selecting the case study candidates.[493] Using a two-tail approach, the selection of the two case study firms is made based on at least one fundamental difference between them. For this thesis, one of the cases refers to a transaction in which HRDD had been carried out, but that, in the end, did not come about. In the other case, the underlying transaction was carried out. Moreover, the case design underlying this study can be described as holistic, as the cases refer to firms as a whole, and not to specific parts of them.[494]

(3) The **quality of a case study design** can be described in terms of its validity (external validity, internal validity, and construct validity) and reliability.[495] External validity means that the case studies must be comparable to each other. In order to enhance external validity, case studies should be carried out in a similar manner.[496] However, given the two-tail approach used in this thesis, external validity is unimportant. Internal validity means the necessity of establishing causal relationships in explanatory and causal studies. It is irrelevant for this thesis, since the case studies are of an illustrative nature. Four measures were taken to attain construct validity.[497] First, as many different sources of information as possible were used for data collection – three different sources of information, in line with the data triangulation requirement.[498] Second, the chains of evidence detected when writing the case reports were documented, so that other persons should be able to re-do

---

492 Cf. Yin, Robert K. (2003), p. 21.

493 Cf. Yin, Robert K. (2003), pp. 39ff. The opposite of a multiple is a single case study design. Given the aim of step five of the research strategy to illustrate the application of the empirically complemented HRDD Concept to business practice, a multiple design was useful choosing.

494 Cf. Yin, Robert K. (2003), p. 42.

495 Cf. Bortz, Jürgen/Döring, Nicola (2002), pp. 195 – 202, Yin, Robert K. (2003), p. 34.

496 Cf. Müller-Böling, Detlef/Klandt, Heinz (1996), p. 82.

497 Cf. Yin, Robert K. (2003), p. 34.

498 In the interviews with company representatives, external and internal documents were used.

the data interpretation.[499] Third, a draft case study report was sent to the firms, which included the description of practical HRDD, but not its evaluation, so that the information could be double-checked. Fourth, the case study firms had not participated in the expert survey, which means that they were not biased by previous empirical steps.[500] Besides the general case-related measures, the same measures as for the expert survey were taken to enhance the construct validity of the interviews with company representatives. First, test interviews with academics were conducted, second, the interview guide was sent to the interviewees in advance, third, interview questions were amended and updated, and fourth, the interviewees were given the chance to check their interview transcripts. The reliability of the cases was enhanced by accurately documenting the procedures used for the case studies, and by transcribing the interviews.

(4) Data collection is referred to in the case protocols. For **the treatment and interpretation of case data,** the procedure suggested by Mayring was also used for the case studies. In step one of this procedure, the most important interview, internal and external data were summarised. In step two, the data were grouped in a table, according to nine content groups. In step three, the grouped interview data were allocated to types of characteristics. These types of characteristics were developed based on the three steps of the HRDD Concept.

6.2 First Case Study

In the first case study, the merger between DG Bank (Deutsche Genossenschaftsbank) and GZ-Bank (Genossenschaftszentralbank) into DZ Bank (Deutsche Zentral-Genossenschafts-bank) has been analysed. In the following, the firms and the main characteristics of the merger and the HRDD conducted are first introduced. Second, the strategic-, structural-, cultural-, and human resource management objectives of the transaction are described. Third, the HRDD Concept is applied to the DZ Bank transaction. Fourth, the first case study concludes with a final remark.

6.2.1 Introduction to the Parties and the Transaction

In September 2001, a long planned merger was agreed on between DG Bank and GZ-Bank, and DZ Bank was formed. At the time of the transaction, DG Bank had approximately 4,500 employees and a reported net income of Euro 423 million in 2000. GZ-Bank had around 1,500 employees and a reported net income of Euro 62 million in 2000. Since the end of 2001, both banks make up DZ Bank, which had about 4,000 employees[501] and a net income of

[499] A comparison of the information across all three sources was carried out. The subsequent argumentation is based on at least two out of the three types of sources, unless specifically quoted.

[500] Cf. Schnell, Rainer/Hill, Paul B./Esser, Elke (1999), p. 331. The interviewees could have tended to agree with the interviewer, if they had participated in previous empirical steps ("Akquieszenz").

[501] All employee numbers mentioned in this paragraph refer to the corporate centre.

Euro 351 million in 2002. DZ Bank fulfils three functions. First, it serves as a central bank for its associated co-op banks. Second, it serves as a management holding for its 1,204 associated co-op banks. Third, it operates as an independent commercial bank with a special focus on the financing of small and medium enterprises.[502]

Prior to the completion of the DZ Bank transaction, no Human Resource Due Diligence was carried out. This was because the rationales for the merger to occur were regarded as so important that human resource aspects were considered to be relatively less important. Common types of due diligence including financial, tax, and legal due diligence were carried out before the transaction was closed. Upon completion of the merger, staffing for the new firm had to be decided on. Therefore, a post-closing Human Resource Due Diligence was carried out. According to the expert survey conducted prior to the case studies, different reasons can drive firms to perform a Human Resource Due Diligence. In the case of the DZ Bank transaction, Human Resource Due Diligence was carried out due to specifics of the M&A context, which will be elaborated on in chapter 6.2.2.

The post-closing Human Resource Due Diligence consisted of two steps. In the first step, all managers down to level three in the hierarchy were asked to determine which of their collaborators they thought were suitable for DZ Bank. All employees who had been declared suitable for the new firm (high performers) became part of a firm-wide internal staffing process. Low performers (employees who had been declared unsuitable) were transferred to a predefined social plan. In the second step, human resource management policies and practices were investigated regarding the necessity of making immediate post-merger adaptations to them. According to the expert survey, the focus areas of Human Resource Due Diligence can be classified according to the level of abstraction, and its time horizon. The Human Resource Due Diligence conducted in the DZ Bank transaction was primarily related to the future, and covered both the organisational and the individual level.[503]

No universal, predetermined criteria were employed when evaluating the suitability of employees. Hence, a qualitative approach was used. When determining employees' suitability for the new firm, managers relied both on past experience with, and on future behavioural expectations related to their collaborators. Managers used their own criteria as a decision-making aid, especially the criterion of trust deriving from past experience with their collaborators. These criteria were future-related and behavioural, and past-related and output-oriented.[504] No new tools for generating information about collaborators were deployed.[505]

---

[502] Its tasks are to provide liquidity, to support payment transactions (translation by the author, original: "Zahlungsverkehr"), to develop e-banking solutions and to manage the development of new products. Cf. DZ Bank Deutsche Zentral-Genossenschaftsbank AG (Ed.) (2003), p. 11.

[503] Cf. chapter 5.2.1.1 to 5.2.1.3.

[504] Cf. chapter 3.1.

[505] Cf. chapter 3.2.

The outcomes of Human Resource Due Diligence were not documented, but were only used to support the firm-wide internal staffing process, and post M&A adaptations to human resource policies and practices. The results of staffing-related Human Resource Due Diligence were transferred to the organisational level. By distinguishing between high performers and low performers, a (simplified) human resource portfolio was set up. [506] Low performers were transferred to the social plan whilst high performers were retained. The staffing process was a one time event, which implies that no controlling ratios were developed for M&A management. The results of human resource policy and practice-related HRDD were not stored or processed any further.

6.2.2 Merger Management Objectives underlying the Transaction

Merger Management Objectives encompass the strategic, structural, cultural, and human resource management objectives of the DZ Bank transaction, and are described in the following.[507]

6.2.2.1 Strategic Objectives underlying the Merger

The underlying strategic objectives of an M&A transaction can be described by taking an internal or an external perspective.[508] The main internal strategic objective in the DZ Bank transaction was the production of synergies. This objective was relevant at the time of the transaction for two reasons. First, for political reasons, arising from the intention of the association of German co-op banks (Bundesverband der Volks- und Raiffeisenbanken) to unite. Second, because of the economic circumstances the German banks in general, and especially the DG Bank, were facing at the time of the merger. The underlying external strategic objective was to generate competitive advantage over the savings banks both in terms of products and in terms of refinancing. As far as products are concerned, DZ Bank endeavoured to become a universal bank and show a broader product portfolio than all other German banks. As far as refinancing is concerned, a united central bank was meant to provide more secure dispositions than several central banks.

6.2.2.2 Structural Objectives underlying the Merger

As illustrated in chapter 2.2.2, the structural management objectives of an M&A transaction can be described on three different levels of abstraction. First, objectives related to macro structure, second, objectives related to structures and processes, and third, objectives related to job descriptions. Specifics of the DZ Bank transaction related to macro structure can be described as follows. Prior to the transaction, DG Bank had a divisional organisation. It held

---

506 Cf. chapter 4.3.

507 The following approximates were made use of to determine the M&A management objectives: human resource development for human resource polices, and organisation charts for micro structure.

508 Cf. chapter 2.2.1.

shares in its associated co-op banks, and served as a management holding for them. GZ-Bank also had a divisional organisation, and operated as a management holding for its associated co-op banks. Hence, both banks' macro structures were largely similar. After the merger, both firms became part of an entirely integrated divisional organisation, thus DZ Bank is a management holding for its associated co-op banks.[509] As far as micro structure is concerned, before the transaction, DG Bank and GZ-Bank had sixty and twenty-eight departments on the first level below the management board, respectively. Both DG Bank's and GZ-Bank's processes resulted from the nature of the described organisational structures. All structures (and indirectly all processes) were reinvented upon completion of the merger. Out of two micro organisations, an entirely new one was created. In 2004, DZ Bank had seventeen departments on the first level below the management board. Processes still followed from the organisational structures. The DZ Bank transaction implied changes to job descriptions for almost all positions. The only exceptions were pure settlement tasks, to which no major changes occurred, meaning that only a few positions at low levels in the hierarchy were unaffected. All other job descriptions changed in line with the new organisational structures.

6.2.2.3 *Cultural Objectives underlying the Merger*

The management of firms involved in M&A often sets itself cultural objectives. First, objectives related to national cultures implying human resource requirements, second, objectives related to corporate cultures, and third, objectives related to leadership styles. No objectives related to national cultures were of any relevance in the DZ Bank case, since two German firms were subject to the merger. Both the DG Bank and the GZ-Bank originated from Frankfurt, which is why no regional specifics had to be considered either.[510] In terms of corporate culture, the following attributes characterised the DG Bank culture prior to the M&A – bureaucratic, project-oriented, analytical, and inefficient at putting plans into action. The GZ-Bank culture was characterised by the following attributes: dynamic, direct, efficient at putting plans into action, and rather weak in a conceptual sense.[511] As can be seen from the attributes, there were some major differences between the DG and the GZ-Bank culture. Both firms were supposed to culturally assimilate upon completion of the M&A in order to acquire the best of both cultures for DZ Bank. Integration workshops were carried out upon completion of the transaction in order to enhance cultural assimilation. Officially, however, no new values for DZ Bank were communicated directly after the merger. Instead, new values emerged from management activities during the first years after the merger, and employees had to adjust to these new values. The DZ Bank culture is characterised by a focus on speed management, and a combination of analytical depth, and the ability to put plans into action.

---

[509] Cf. DZ Bank Deutsche Zentral-Genossenschaftsbank AG (Ed.) (2003), p. 11.

[510] Regional differences might also have played a role in the transaction (e.g. in the case of an M&A between a Bavarian firm and a firm from Hamburg).

[511] The description of both firms' corporate culture originates from a former GZ-Bank employee – the DZ Bank contact person and responsible for HRDD. This fact may have influenced the nature of the perceived differences between both firms' corporate cultures. Possibly fewer or more cultural differences existed between the transaction parties "in reality" than are illustrated in this thesis.

Neither DG Bank nor GZ-Bank had official/documented leadership principles before the merger. DZ Bank does not prescribe its managers any officially desired leadership behaviour either, thus no documented leadership guidelines exist.

6.2.2.4 Human Resource Management Objectives underlying the Merger

Human resource requirements can also ensue from objectives of M&A management, which are related to human resource strategy, human resource policies and practices, and the organisation of human resource management. In the forefront of the transaction, the human resource strategy of DG Bank was characterised by a tendency to large human resource investments, whilst GZ-Bank's human resource strategy aimed at cost-efficiency. Upon completion of the merger, the economic situation of the transaction parties forced them to cut down on all human resource investments that were not urgent. In the DZ Bank/GZ-Bank transaction, there were two main differences between the human resource management policies and practices of the firms. First, DG Bank's compensation and benefits were generally higher than GZ-Bank's, and contained exemptions and separate treatment for certain employees. GZ-Bank generally abstained from exemptions and separate treatment. GZ-Bank's compensation and benefits system was more easily structured than that of DG Bank. After the merger, both firms' compensation and benefits systems were maintained in the short term, and aligned in the middle term. GZ-Bank's human resource development was more task-related than DG Bank's prior to the merger. At GZ-Bank, human resource development measures had to be of direct use for employees' every day work in order to be accepted. Post completion, human resource development was suspended for approximately two years, given the financial situation of the new firm. DG Bank's human resource management department consisted of about a hundred human resource managers, whereas GZ-Bank's human resource management consisted of some twenty-five human resource managers. After the merger, an entirely new human resource management department was created containing eighty-four human resource managers, of which nineteen come from the former DG Bank, fifty-five from the former GZ-Bank, with ten new ones.

6.2.3 Application of the Human Resource Due Diligence Concept to the Merger

In the following, it is first described what the determination of focus areas should have been like in the DZ Bank merger if applying the Concept. Second, the generation of HRDD information is elaborated on, and third, the compilation of HRDD results is referred to. Apart from illustrating the application of the HRDD Concept in the DZ Bank merger based on its underlying M&A objectives, actual HRDD is turned to in contrast to the desired to show the advantages of applying the Concept.

6.2.3.1 Determination of Focus Areas for Human Resource Due Diligence

Table 6.1 contains a summary of the competence requirements that resulted from the strategic management objectives underlying the DZ Bank transaction. Also, the actual focus areas of HRDD are shown in comparison to the desired ones.[512]

Strategic Objectives / Competence	Synergy Objective	Market Development Objective	Market Penetration Objective	Actual Focus Areas of HRDD
Uncertainty Competence				
Communication Competence				
Conflict Competence				
Motivation Competence	•			
Co-operation Competence				
Innovation Competence	•	•		
Internal Competence	•			
Market Competence		•		
Socio-cultural Competence				
Complexity Competence				
Functional Competence	•	•		
Process Competence	•	•		
Planning Competence	•	•	•	
Problem-solving Competence				
Organisation Competence				
Decision-making Competence	•	•	•	
Social Change Competence				•
Technical Change Competence				•

Table 6.1: Competences and DZ Bank's Strategic Merger Management Objectives

Table 6.1 shows that Human Resource Due Diligence in the DZ Bank transaction focused on social change-, and technical change competence. According to the Concept, motivation, innovation, internal, market, functional, process, planning, and decision-making competence are crucial to support synergies, market development and market penetration.[513] By overlooking these, DZ Bank disregarded competences that were important for the realisation of the strategic objectives underlying the merger. For instance, combining the transaction parties' value chains without knowing about employees' innovation competence could have implied that synergies would be realised less effectively than desired. Undetected market competence

[512] The desired competences are illustrated in columns two to four and the actual in column five.
[513] The reasons for the substance of these competences can be derived from the argumentation in chapter 2.2.1.

shortcomings could have meant that the new firm intended tapping new customer groups without knowing about their needs.[514] If the competences in table 6.1 had been considered in HRDD, adequate measures could have been taken to make the best possible use of them. Aiming for the strategic objectives underlying the DZ Bank merger without having focused on these competences meant relying on a reactive instead of a proactive M&A management approach.[515]

Table 6.2 summarises the human resource requirements that resulted from the structural management objectives underlying DZ Bank transaction.

Structural Objectives / Competence	Consolidation Objective	Reinvention Objective	Renewal Objective	Actual Focus Areas of HRDD
Uncertainty Competence		•		
Communication Competence	•	•		
Conflict Competence				
Motivation Competence	•	•		
Co-operation Competence	•	•		
Innovation Competence		•		
Internal Competence				
Market Competence				
Socio-cultural Competence				
Complexity Competence	•	•		
Functional Competence	•	•	•	
Process Competence	•	•	•	
Planning Competence		•	•	
Problem-solving Competence	•	•	•	
Organisation Competence		•	•	
Decision-making Competence		•	•	
Social Change Competence		•		•
Technical Change Competence			•	•

Table 6.2: Competences and DZ Bank's Structural Merger Management Objectives

As already mentioned, future-related individual HRDD in the DZ Bank transaction concentrated on social change and technical change competence. Hence, DZ Bank took two competences into consideration that were important for the reinvention and the renewal objectives to be achieved. Anyhow, the structural objectives of the merger implied more than just these two human resource requirements. According to the HRDD Concept, it would have been recommendable to evaluate uncertainty, communication, motivation, co-operation,

[514] Ditto.
[515] Cf. chapter 1.4.5.

innovation, complexity, functional, process, planning, problem-solving, organisation, and decision-making competence.[516] DZ Bank ignored competences that were vital to achieving the structural objectives of the merger. By disregarding communication competence, for instance, consolidation could have been difficult to accomplish, since it is based on well-functioning information flows between employees at all levels. An unnoticed lack of complexity competence could have given rise to inefficiencies, due to employees' lack of competence in managing complexity.[517] As mentioned for the strategic objectives of the merger, the inclusion of the disregarded competences into HRDD would have enabled DZ Bank to take proactive M&A management measures based on the results obtained.

Besides strategic, and structural M&A objectives, M&A management also had cultural objectives to consider after the decision to unite DG and GZ-Bank. The human resource requirements resulting from these objectives are summarised in table 6.3. As mentioned in chapter 6.2.2.3, only M&A objectives related to corporate culture were relevant in the DZ Bank transaction. Objectives related to national culture did not have to be considered, as the transaction took place between two German firms, between which no regional differences existed. Moreover, no leadership objectives were pursued in the DZ Bank transaction, at least not consciously. For a summary of the human resource requirements that ensued from the assimilation objective underlying the DZ Bank transaction, see table 6.3.

Cultural Objectives / Competence	Assimilation Objective	Actual Focus Areas of HRDD
Uncertainty Competence		
Communication Competence	•	
Conflict Competence	•	
Motivation Competence	•	
Co-operation Competence		
Innovation Competence		
Internal Competence		
Market Competence		
Socio-cultural Competence		
Complexity Competence		
Functional Competence		
Process Competence		
Planning Competence		
Problem-solving Competence		
Organisation Competence		
Decision-making Competence		
Social Change Competence	•	•
Technical Change Competence		•

Table 6.3: Competences and DZ Bank's Cultural Merger Management Objectives

516 The reasons for the relevance of these competences can be found in chapter 2.2.2. All named competences were of importance for all of both firms' employees, except for those required due to the renewal objective. For employees working with pure settlement tasks, no changes to task spectra resulted from the merger.

517 Cf. chapter 2.2.2.

Due to the assimilation objective, communication, conflict, motivation, and social change competence were required.[518] In HRDD, however, social change, and technical change competence were in focus. This means that DZ Bank succeeded in taking competences into account that were crucial for the assimilation objective to be attained. Still, it did not consider the other three competences in table 6.3. Assessing conflict competence would, however, have been useful to prevent unresolved disagreements about cultural norms and values endangering the success of assimilation. Limited motivation competence could have hampered the implementation of the cultural changes they wished to introduce.[519] If DZ Bank had considered all the competences suggested by the HRDD Concept, it would have been able to actively encourage its employees to support assimilation.[520] The assessment of technical change competence, as done in the merger, would not have been necessary from the point of view of the Concept.

In the fourth M&A management dimension, objectives related to human resource strategy, human resource policies and practices, and human resource organisation were formulated. The human resource requirements that resulted from these objectives are listed in table 6.4.

HRM Objectives / Competence	Aggregation Objective	Amalgamation Objective	Collaboration Objective	Actual Focus Areas of HRDD
Uncertainty Competence		•	•	
Communication Competence	•	•		
Conflict Competence	•	•		
Motivation Competence	•	•	•	
Co-operation Competence	•	•		
Innovation Competence	•	•		
Internal Competence				
Market Competence		•		
Socio-cultural Competence		•		
Complexity Competence				
Functional Competence	•	•		
Process Competence	•	•		
Planning Competence		•		
Problem-solving Competence		•		
Organisation Competence		•		
Decision-making Competence		•		
Social change Competence	•		•	•
Technical Change Competence	•	•		•

Table 6.4: Competences and DZ Bank's Human Resource Management Objectives in the Merger

518 The reasons for the importance of these competences are elaborated on in chapter 2.2.3.
519 Cf. chapter 2.2.3.
520 Cf. chapter 1.3.1 object of analysis.

According to the HRDD Concept, apart from change competence, it would have been crucial to evaluate uncertainty, communication, conflict, motivation, co-operation, innovation, market, socio-cultural, functional, process, planning, problem-solving, organisation, and decision-making competence.[521] By not realising the relevance of these competences, DZ Bank overlooked their importance for the achievement of its human resource management objectives. For instance, insufficient specialist competence could have hampered the amalgamation of performance appraisal systems. If employees from one firm are able to carry out certain functional tasks, but those from the other are not, it can be difficult to use the same performance criteria for both. Also, overlooking insufficient uncertainty competence could have resulted in the collaboration of the transaction parties' human resource management departments frustrating employees.[522] Extending HRDD by the competences in table 6.4 would have been useful for encouraging the attainment of the human resource management objectives of the merger.

To conclude, the following competences should have been assessed in the DZ Bank transaction (in addition to change competence), to account for all of its M&A management objectives: uncertainty, communication, conflict, motivation, co-operation, innovation, internal, market, socio-cultural, complexity, functional, process, planning, problem-solving, organisation, and decision-making competence. There are multiple reasons for the relevance of these competences, in line with the underlying objectives of the merger.[523] DZ Bank succeeded in considering two vital human resource requirements that resulted from its merger objectives. However, it has not been considered that there can be several reasons for the importance of these two human resource requirements. Besides, many crucial human resource requirements were overlooked in the DZ Bank case.

Besides assessing social change, and technical change competence, HRDD in the DZ Bank transaction was focused on human resource management policies and practices. The rationale for analysing the latter was to determine whether, and if so what kinds of, post-merger adaptations to undertake with respect to human resource policies and practices. As outlined in chapter 5.2.1, the HRDD Concept refers to individual, future-related human resource aspects. Human resource policies and practices can be allocated to the organisational level, and to the future, and are therefore not integral to the Concept[524], but should be subject to analyses preceding HRDD.

6.2.3.2 Generation of Human Resource Due Diligence Information

In the DZ Bank transaction, qualitative indicators were employed, based on future-related, behavioural, and past-related, output-oriented data. No (new) tools for generating HRDD

---

[521] The reasons for the relevance of these competences have been elaborated on in chapter 2.2.4.
[522] Cf. chapter 2.2.4.
[523] Ditto.
[524] Cf. chapter 5.2.1.

information were utilised, but instead, managers' experience with their collaborators served as a substitute for tools for HRDD. Had the HRDD Concept been applied, quantitative, behavioural, future-related indicators would have been used. For certain competences, several indicators would have been necessary to employ, for instance for innovation competence. One indicator would have been required for the achievement of strategic objectives, another indicator for its significance for the attainment of structural objectives. The same applies to all competences that are relevant for several reasons (see table 6.5). All the tools in chapter 3.2 could have been applied in the DZ Bank transaction (see table 6.5). One might have used task-related tools for certain employee groups and non task-related tools for all key employees. Upon generation of the HRDD information, DZ Bank should have critically reflected on this information, to ensure that the limitations of the indicators and tools underlying it were taken into account.[525]

Competence	Underlying M&A objective	Indicators	Tools
Uncertainty Competence	Reinvention objective	• Cope with uncertainty deriving from new micro structure	Assessment centres, structured interviews, questionnaires, role plays and tests
	Amalgamation objective	• Accept uncertainty deriving from new compensation systems and performance criteria	Ditto.
	Collaboration objective	• Deal with uncertainty about where and how to proceed in the new firm	Ditto.
Communication Competence	Consolidation objective	• Deal with increased number of communication partners	Ditto.
	Reinvention objective	• Work with more communication partners, communicate more intensely	Ditto.
	Assimilation objective	• Establish information flows and relationships with other firm's employees	Ditto.
	Aggregation objective	• Communicate more effectively	Ditto.
	Amalgamation objective	• Get used to e.g. a higher communication density	Ditto.
Conflict Competence	Assimilation objective	• Deal with different patterns of behaviour	Ditto.
	Aggregation objective	• Deal constructively with conflicts caused by new behavioural requirements	Ditto.

[525] Cf. chapter 5.2.2.

Competence	**Underlying M&A objective**	**Indicators**	**Tools**
	Amalgamation objective	• Negotiate constructively in the case of conflicts due to new behavioural requirements	Ditto.
Motivation Competence	Synergy objective	• Enthuse collaborators for M&A despite downsi-zing	Ditto.
	Consolidation objective	• Help collaborators cope with organisational chan-ges (e. g. new roles, sta-tes)	Ditto.
	Reinvention objective	• Compensate for missing leadership through struc-tures and processes	Ditto.
	Assimilation objective	• Support collaborators in dealing with new patterns of behaviour	Ditto.
	Aggregation objective	• Help collaborators get along with new behavi-oural requirements	Ditto.
	Amalgamation objective	• Enhance commitment of collaborators despite changes to policies and practices	Ditto.
	Collaboration objective	• Support collaborators in dealing with unpre-dictable changes	Ditto.
Co-operation Competence	Consolidation objective	• Make joint macro structure work	Ditto.
	Reinvention objective	• Enhance efficiency of new structures and pro-cesses	Ditto.
	Aggregation objective	• Cope with new patterns of co-operation	Ditto.
	Amalgamation objective	• Change co-operation ha-bits, e.g. introduce joint decision-making	Ditto.
Innovation Competence	Synergy objective	• Foster synergies e. g. through process innova-tions	Ditto.
	Market development objective	• Find new applications for existing products	Ditto.
	Reinvention objective	• Make process innovations	Ditto.
	Aggregation objective	• Find a way of aggre-gating human resource strategies (process in-novation)	Ditto.
	Amalgamation objective	• Show a generally higher degree of innovation	Ditto.
Internal Competence	Synergy objective	• Realise synergies in a responsible way	Ditto.

Competence	Underlying M&A objective	Indicators	Tools
Market Competence	Market development objective	• Develop new products & applications, tap new customers	Ditto.
	Amalgamation objective	• Be more market-oriented than before	Ditto.
Socio-cultural Competence	Amalgamation objective	• Be able to cope with people from different national cultures	Ditto.
Complexity Competence	Consolidation objective	• Create macro structure that reduces complexity, deal with every day complexity	Ditto.
	Reinvention objective	• Cope with complexity caused by new micro structure	Ditto.
Functional Competence	Synergy objective	• Work efficiently	Assessment centres, structured interviews, questionnaires and tests
	Market development objective	• Foster competitive advantage	Ditto.
	Consolidation objective	• Work efficiently and foster competitive advantage	Ditto.
	Reinvention objective	• Determine suitability of new structures, work efficiently with them	Ditto.
	Renewal objective	• Perform higher ranked tasks than one's own usual tasks	Ditto.
	Aggregation objective	• Work efficiently and foster competitive advantage	Ditto.
	Amalgamation objective	• Work efficiently and foster competitive advantage	Ditto.
Process Competence	Synergy objective	• Work efficiently	Ditto.
	Market development objective	• Foster competitive advantage	Ditto.
	Consolidation objective	• Work efficiently and foster competitive advantage	Ditto.
	Reinvention objective	• Determine suitability of new processes, work efficiently with these	Ditto.
	Renewal objective	• Perform higher ranked processes than one's own usual processes	Ditto.
	Aggregation objective	• Work efficiently and foster competitive advantage	Ditto.

Competence	Underlying M&A objective	Indicators	Tools
	Amalgamation objective	• Work efficiently and foster competitive advantage	Ditto.
Planning Competence	Synergy objective	• Plan for attainment of synergies	Ditto.
	Market development objective	• Define new strategy, determine operative measures to implement it	Ditto.
	Market penetration objective	• Co-ordinate activities of new firm	Ditto.
	Reinvention objective	• Determine how, when and with what resources to make changes to micro structure	Ditto.
	Renewal objective	• Plan in advance despite more sophisticated new tasks	Ditto.
	Amalgamation objective	• Plan for amalgamation to be achieved, cope with new performance criteria	Ditto.
Problem-solving Competence	Consolidation objective	• Solve problems related to new macro structure	Ditto.
	Reinvention objective	• Determine what new micro structure is supposed to be like	Ditto.
	Renewal objective	• Work towards a set goal without knowing the path towards this goals beforehand	Ditto.
	Amalgamation objective	• Find one's way towards amalgamation, cope with new performance criteria	Ditto.
Organisation Competence	Reinvention objective	• Redistribute and integrate tasks on micro level	Ditto.
	Renewal objective	• Split tasks up into sub-tasks and arrange for their completion	Ditto.
	Amalgamation objective	• Distribute and integrate amalgamation-related tasks, cope with new performance criteria	Ditto.
Decision-making Competence	Synergy objective	• Select functions of the firms' value chains for synergy attainment	Ditto.
	Market development objective	• Choose strategy and operative measures from bundle	Ditto.
	Market penetration objective	• Select way of co-ordinating future activities	Ditto.

Competence	Underlying M&A objective	Indicators	Tools
	Reinvention objective	• Decide on a new micro structure based on analysis of alternatives	Ditto.
	Renewal objective	• Consider and weigh alternative courses of action	Ditto.
	Amalgamation objective	• Select suitable ways of attaining amalgamation, cope with new performance criteria	Ditto.
Social Change Competence	Reinvention objective	• Deal with new colleagues, collaborators or superiors	Assessment centres, structured interviews, questionnaires, role plays and tests
	Assimilation objective	• Adapt to new people and new patterns of behaviour (all employees)	Ditto.
	Aggregation objective	• Adopt new patterns of behaviour	Ditto.
	Collaboration objective	• Deal with new human resource managers	Ditto.
Technical Change Competence	Renewal objective	• Deal with new or modified technical requirements	Ditto.
	Aggregation objective	• Cope with new or modified technical requirements	Ditto.
	Amalgamation objective	• Get used to new or modified technical requirements	Ditto.

Table 6.5: Generation of Human Resource Due Diligence Information in the DZ Bank Merger

By using qualitative indicators, DZ Bank prevented the results of HRDD from being of further use to M&A management, as they would have been if they had employed quantitative indicators.[526] Behavioural, future-related, and output-oriented, past-related data were used in the DZ Bank case. However, the behavioural, future-related data were merely created by extrapolation of historical performance data, which is inconsistent with the propositions of the Concept. A consequence could have been that managers wrongly extrapolated their collaborators' past behaviour, and hence identified false high performers. It would have been necessary to collect new data, based on the tools for HRDD, to be able to estimate whether employees were able to meet merger-induced human resource requirements. Hence, from the Concept's point of view, DZ Bank did not succeed in taking a real future-related, behavioural perspective. As pointed out in chapter 5.2.2, considering additional, output-oriented, past-

[526] This argument is underlined by the fact that, according to the HRDD representative at DZ Bank, the results from HRDD were neither documented nor further utilized.

related data can be useful to complement the data collected for the HRDD Concept. However, in the DZ Bank merger, no new data were recorded to complement the historical data.

6.2.3.3 Compilation of the generated Human Resource Due Diligence Information

The data obtained in Human Resource Due Diligence were not condensed to be used for future management activities. The data from individual HRDD were not even stored, whereas the data from organisational HRDD were. The results of individual HRDD served as a basis for the staffing decisions made. According to the propositions of the HRDD Concept, DZ Bank should have developed elementary ratios based on the results of HRDD (see figure 6.1). Moreover, these elementary ratios should have been translated into advanced ratios. It would have been possible to define ratios for different management dimensions, competence groups, and employee groups. These ratios could have served as a basis for all M&A management activities following Human Resource Due Diligence.[527] By not utilising the results from HRDD for measures other than immediate staffing, DZ Bank disregarded the additional use of HRDD data for M&A management. Measures other than immediate staffing may therefore have been inconsistent with the results of Human Resource Due Diligence, and accordingly with the objectives underlying the merger.

[527] Cf. chapter 4.3.

Person	A						B						C					
Parameter Value	1	2	3	4	5	Ratio	1	2	3	4	5	Ratio	1	2	3	4	5	Ratio
Social competence																		
Uncertainty competence	▲			•		0,250				▲•		1,000		▲		•		0,500
Communication competence	▲			•		0,250				▲•		1,000		▲		•		0,500
Conflict competence		▲		•		0,500			▲	•		0,750			▲	•		0,750
Motivation competence		▲		•		0,500				▲•		1,000		▲		•		0,500
Co-operation competence			▲	•		0,750			▲	•		0,750	▲			•		0,250
Systems competence																		
Innovation competence			▲	•		0,750			▲	•		0,750	▲			•		0,250
Internal competence		▲		•		0,500			▲	•		0,750	▲			•		0,250
Market competence			▲	•		0,750			▲	•		0,750			▲	•		0,750
Socio-cultural competence		▲		•		0,500		▲		•		0,500			▲	•		0,750
Complexity competence		▲		•		0,500		▲		•		0,500			▲	•		0,750
Specialist competence																		
Functional competence		▲		•		0,500		▲		•		0,500			▲	•		0,750
Process competence		▲		•		0,500		▲		•		0,500			▲	•		0,750
Methods competence																		
Planning competence			▲	•		0,750		▲		•		0,500			▲	•		0,750
Problem-solving competence			▲	•		0,750		▲		•		0,500			▲	•		0,750
Organisation competence			▲	•		0,750			▲	•		0,750			▲	•		0,750
Decision-making competence			▲	•		0,750			▲	•		0,750			▲	•		0,750
Change competence																		
Social change competence			▲	•		0,750	▲			•		0,250				▲•		1,000
Technical change competence			▲	•		0,750	▲			•		0,250				▲•		1,000

Actual parameter values of competencies ▲
Desired parameter values of competencies •

Figure 6.1: Compilation of the Generated Human Resource Due Diligence Information in the DZ Bank Merger

6.2.4 Final Remark about the Merger

The DZ Bank case study demonstrates that important aspects were neglected in HRDD. The design of HRDD would have been completely different if the HRDD Concept had been applied in the merger. Designing HRDD in the way suggested by the Concept would have enabled the firm to better manage the implications of its M&A objectives on employees at an early M&A stage.[528] DZ Bank would also have benefited from the HRDD results for human resource management measures following the M&A. The case study also illustrates, that the HRDD Concept is not concrete enough to allow for a Human Resource Due Diligence to be carried out immediately. Professionals must define what competences are required for which employee groups for the Concept to be applicable.[529] When applying the Concept, qualitative competence indicators can be useful as a complement to the indicators for HRDD outlined in chapter 3.1, to see whether they are in line with each other.

528 Cf. chapter 1.3.3.
529 Cf. chapter 1.3.2 practical research goal.

6.3 Second Case Study

The second case study refers to the planned acquisition of Company X by Beiersdorf AG. The same four steps as for the first case study are taken to present the results of the Beiersdorf case – introduction to the parties and the planned transaction (chapter 6.3.1), acquisition management objectives underlying the planned transaction (chapter 6.3.2), application of the HRDD concept to the planned transaction (chapter 6.3.3) and final remark about the planned transaction (chapter (6.3.4).

6.3.1 Introduction to the Parties and the Planned Transaction

In 2001, Beiersdorf AG planned to acquire Company X, at the time an affiliated company of a large US pharmaceutical holding company. At the time when the transaction was envisaged, Beiersdorf AG had 16,600 employees and an EBIT of 389 million Euros in 2000. Company X had 4,000 employees and an undisclosed EBIT[530] in 2000. Since the end of 2001, Company X has belonged to Procter and Gamble. The transaction with Beiersdorf failed to come about, since Company X was sold in a public bidding process, and Procter and Gamble's bid was higher than Beiersdorf's.

The main reason for Beiersdorf to conduct a Human Resource Due Diligence prior to the planned transaction was to anticipate human resource costs that might have been incurred had the acquisition taken place. According to the expert survey conducted prior to the case studies, different types of reasons can drive firms to carrying out a Human Resource Due Diligence. The reason for carrying out a Human Resource Due Diligence in the Beiersdorf AG and Company X transaction is not consistent with the management objective-oriented perspective taken in this thesis, but rather with a cost perspective.

Human Resource Due Diligence in the Beiersdorf/Company X transaction focused on 15 different aspects, and their cost implications, namely corporate culture, labour relationships, performance management, training and development, compensation and benefits, employee details (headcount etc.), key employees, retention plans, potential employee perceptions of acquisition, diversity, pensions, legal aspects, outsourcing of human resource management services, organisational structures and staffing, human resource information systems and employee communication. Of the fifteen aspects, the following four can be identified as core, given their frequency of appearance in Human Resource Due Diligence documentation, and their perceived relevance according to the contact person at Beiersdorf, who was responsible for HRDD. These are corporate culture, labour relationships, compensation and benefits, and legal aspects. According to the expert survey conducted prior to the case studies, the possible focus areas of HRDD can be classified according to two different criteria – the level of

[530] The firm was a carve-out from the above mentioned pharmaceutical holding company, which explains the undisclosed EBIT, which was undisclosed for confidentiality reasons.

abstraction, and the time horizon.[531] Thus, the focus areas of Human Resource Due Diligence in the Beiersdorf and Company X case can be matched with the following fields in the matrix (see figure 6.2). Corporate culture assessment, performance management, training and development, diversity management, and compensation and benefits data, as assessed by Beiersdorf, can be allocated to the organisational level, and to the present. The same applies to retention plans, employee details, labour relationships, outsourcing of human resource management services, organisational structure and staffing, human resource information systems, and employee communication. The analysis of key employees is related to the present, and to the individual level. Legal aspects and pensions relate to the present and past, and to the organisational and individual level. Analysis of potential employee perceptions of the acquisition can be associated with the organisational level, a future-related perspective.

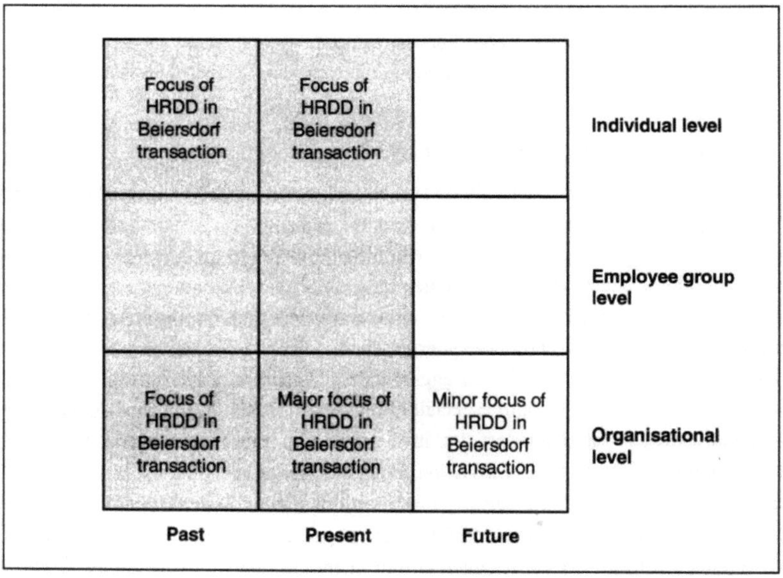

Figure 6.2: Focus Areas of Human Resource Due Diligence in the Beiersdorf Acquisition

No new tools were utilised to measure the human resource aspects, instead existing data were reviewed. Predefined criteria were employed when evaluating the existing data, meaning that quantitative indicators were employed. The criteria used for assessing key employees were input-oriented, behavioural, and output-oriented. The following three tools for Human Resource Due Diligence were employed prior to the planned transaction. First, public information was analysed, such as Internet data and newspaper articles. Second, data room information was assessed over several weeks. Based on this review, a request list was sent to

[531] Cf. chapter 5.2.1.

the due diligence organisers in order to acquire information on those relevant human resource aspects not covered by the data room information.[532] Third, information generated by the management presentation was reviewed.

The results of Human Resource Due Diligence were documented, but documentation was destroyed for confidentiality reasons, upon completion of the public bidding process for Company X. The results of HRDD were summarised by estimating the human resource costs that it was expected to incur. No controlling ratios were defined to support M&A management, primarily because the transaction finally did not come about. M&A management had, however, not envisaged using HRDD information for controlling purposes.

6.3.2 Acquisition Management Objectives underlying the Planned Transaction[533]

The strategic, structural, cultural, and human resource management objectives of the Beiersdorf/Company X transaction are discussed in the following.

6.3.2.1 Strategic Objectives underlying the Planned Acquisition

As presented in chapter 2.2.1, the underlying strategic objectives of an M&A transaction can be described by taking an internal and an external perspective. At the time when the transaction was envisaged, both parties were multinational corporations involved in the fabrication of similar products at the same stage of the value chain. However, their knowledge of the fabrication of certain products differed significantly. The underlying internal strategic objectives for Beiersdorf were to produce synergies, and to benefit from a knowledge transfer. The aim was to produce synergies by an aggregation of the firms' value chains in certain areas. Knowledge transfer was the aim especially in those fields where Company X possessed a knowledge advantage over Beiersdorf, i.e. in the fabrication and development of haircare products. At the time of the planned transaction, Beiersdorf had a low market share on the US market in general, especially on the haircare market with its brand Nivea Haircare. Company X occupied market segments that Beiersdorf had not yet gained access to, for instance the hair coloration segment. Thus, Beiersdorf's main aim in intending to acquire Company X was to benefit from Company X's strong standing in certain market segments of the US market. Hence the underlying external strategic objective in the Beiersdorf transaction was to penetrate and to extend existing markets.

---

[532] Data were generated by a project team consisting of lawyers, consultants and Beiersdorf company representatives.

[533] The M&A management objectives were identified based on the following indicators named by the interviewees: organisation charts for micro structure, values for corporate culture.

6.3.2.2 *Structural Objectives underlying the Planned Acquisition*

Structural M&A management objectives can be described on three different levels. Management objectives related to macro structure, structures and processes, and job descriptions can be produced.[534] At the time of the planned transaction, Company X was a subsidiary and a separate legal entity of a large US pharmaceutical holding company. Beiersdorf had a divisional organisation at the time of the planned acquisition. Its divisions were not separate legal entities. After completing the acquisition, Beiersdorf had planned to integrate Company X as a subsidiary and a new business division. Prior to the planned acquisition, Beiersdorf and Company X had rather similar structures and processes. Both organisations showed a similar degree of complexity, and followed the principle "process follows structure"[535]. It was intended to integrate Beiersdorf and Company X in certain areas. Examples of such areas were distribution, human resource management, finance, and IT, i.e. support functions and support processes. In those areas in which the firms were supposed to be merged, layoffs were expected to produce synergies. For instance, Beiersdorf would no longer have utilised a distribution network of its own in the United States. Other, core business areas such as marketing and research & development were not supposed to be changed upon completion of the acquisition. Finally, modifications and extensions were to be expected for those areas in which the acquisition produced changes to macro, and micro structure would take place.

6.3.2.3 *Cultural Objectives underlying the Planned Acquisition*

The cultural management objectives of the planned transaction can be described on three levels. First, management objectives related to national cultures, second to corporate cultures, and third to leadership styles can be analysed.[536] Beiersdorf is a firm of German origin, and Company X is a US firm. At the time of the planned transaction, co-operation was intended at certain levels of the organisation. A main difference between the Beiersdorf and the Company X culture at the time of the planned acquisition was Company X's rather short term orientation, and Beiersdorf's rather long term orientation. Beiersdorf did not intend to change Company X's culture, and was not planning to actively govern cultural coexistence in the new firm. Instead, both firms' employees were supposed to try and find ways of working together for themselves. Hence, the cultural coexistence objective was one of assimilation, indicating a best-of-both approach. Managers in particular would have been required to find patterns of working together in a constructive manner, despite cultural barriers. On an operative level, a clash of cultures was expected to emerge in few areas. The firms' predominant leadership styles prior to the planned acquisition were very different. Neither firm had documented leadership principles.[537] Whereas the leadership style at Company X was characterised by command and control, and thus authoritative, the leadership style at Beiersdorf was co-

---

[534] Cf. chapter 2.2.2.

[535] This means that they set up their organizational structures prior to defining new processes. Cf. chapter 2.2.2.

[536] Cf. chapter 2.2.3.

[537] In contrast to the first case, in the Beiersdorf case, the transaction parties' managers' previous actual leadership style has been taken as an indicator of the leadership style intended by M&A management.

operative, with a strong focus on joint problem-solving. It was planned to allow the leadership practices of Company X and Beiersdorf to coexist next to each other in the new firm. This means that Beiersdorf managers would have co-operated with "old" collaborators in the same way as before. Also, Company X's managers would have worked with "old" collaborators in the same way as before. Hence, in the short term, two leadership styles would have been maintained, and in the middle term, one would have expected a new leadership style to emerge.

6.3.2.4 Human Resource Management Objectives underlying the Planned Acquisition

Besides strategic, structural, and cultural management objectives that have an impact on human resource requirements, human resource management objectives are also integral to the Human Resource Due Diligence Concept. Human resource management objectives encompass the coexistence of human resource strategies, human resource policies and practices, and human resource organisation.[538] The human resource strategies of Beiersdorf and Company X were different at the time of the planned acquisition, with respect to the envisaged coexistence of human resource management strategies. Company X's human resource management strategy was characterised by strong influence from the parent company. Subsidiaries of Company X in other countries than the United States received detailed guidelines on how to manage their human resources. Employees were highly valued in Company X, and talented employees were promoted accordingly. At the same time, Company X was hire-and-fire-oriented. Beiersdorf's human resource strategy was (and still is) characterised by the guiding role of the parent company, and the co-operative relationship of the parent company's human resource management with general managers in the subsidiaries. Moreover, Beiersdorf's human resource management is development-oriented in comparison to that of Company X. If the M&A had occurred, the two firms would have combined their human resource management strategies in terms of a best-of-both-approach. Company X's human resource strategy was planned to be retained for Company X dominated subsidiaries of the new firm. The Beiersdorf human resource strategy would have dominated in all other parts of the new firm. Human resource management policies and practices had not been analysed entirely at the time of the planned transaction. Solely those policies and practices that were important at short notice (cost drivers) – had been evaluated, such as compensation and benefits. Company X's compensation and benefits practices were different from those at Beiersdorf, both with respect to the level, and to the composition of remuneration. It was planned to organise coexistence in such a way as to retain the respective best solution at a subsidiary. Thus, for the US market, this would have meant that Company X's practices would have been kept, whereas in Europe, the dominance of Beiersdorf's practices was expected. Before the planned acquisition, Beiersdorf had a central human resource department in Hamburg, and human resource officers in its subsidiaries. Company X's human resource management was centralised in New York, but as with Beiersdorf, general managers in the subsidiaries were responsible for

---

[538] Cf. chapter 2.2.4.

certain human resource management tasks. Upon completion of the transaction, human resource management for the whole of Beiersdorf (including Company X) was expected to be centralised in Hamburg, meaning that human resource managers from the corporate centre human resources from Company X would have moved from the US to Germany. Both human resource management departments would have coexisted in the short term. In the middle term, the human resource management department would possibly have been reorganised, depending on the development of co-operation between the departments, and the human resource management requirements of the joint firm.[539] The reason for aiming for coexistence of both human resource management departments was to gain knowledge about the nature of the former human resource management at Company X, and to co-operatively develop a joint one.

6.3.3 Application of the Human Resource Due Diligence Concept to the Planned Acquisition

In the following, it is first illustrated what the determination of focus areas should have been like in the Beiersdorf acquisition if applying the Concept. Second, the generation of HRDD information is focused on, and third, the compilation of HRDD results is related to. Apart from illustrating the application of the HRDD Concept in the DZ Bank merger based on its underlying M&A objectives, actual HRDD is turned to in contrast to the desired to show the advantages of applying the Concept.

6.3.3.1 Determination of Focus Areas for Human Resource Due Diligence

Table 6.6 resumes the human resource requirements that resulted from the strategic management objectives underlying the Beiersdorf transaction. Moreover, the actual focus areas of HRDD are shown in comparison to the desired ones.[540]

[539] Hence, Beiersdorf wanted self-organisation to determine the development of the new firm's human resource management department. Cf. Müller-Stewens, Günter/Frankenberger, Sebastian (2004), p. 38.

[540] The desired competences are illustrated in columns one to four, whilst the actual competences are shown in column five.

Strategic Objectives / Competence	Synergy Objective	Resource Access Objective	Market Develop-ment Objective	Market Penetration Objective	Actual Focus Areas of HRDD
Uncertainty Competence					
Communication Competence		•			
Conflict Competence					
Motivation Competence	•				
Co-operation Competence		•			
Innovation Competence	•	•	•		
Internal Competence	•				
Market Competence		•	•		
Socio-cultural Competence					
Complexity Competence					
Functional Competence	•		•		
Process Competence	•		•		
Planning Competence	•	•	•	•	
Problem-solving Competence					
Organisation Competence					
Decision-making Competence	•	•	•	•	
Social Change Competence					
Technical Change Competence					

Table 6.6: Competences and Beiersdorf's Strategic Acquisition Management Objectives

As can be seen from table 6.6, Human Resource Due Diligence in the Beiersdorf transaction focused on aspects that are inconsistent with the future-related, individual focus taken by the Concept. According to the Concept, communication, motivation, co-operation, innovation, internal, market, functional, process, planning, and decision-making competence are vital for synergies, resource access, market development and market penetration to be achieved.[541] The above-mentioned competences were important for certain groups of both firms' employees. First, they were relevant for employees working in functions of the parties' value chains where aggregation was supposed to take place. Second, they were important for employees in functions where knowledge transfer was planned to take place, namely production, and research & development. Third, they would have been crucial for employees working in parts of the firms that were expected to contribute to the achievement of the market development and the market penetration objective. By not examining the competences in table 6.6 in HRDD, Beiersdorf overlooked competences that would have been critical to attaining the strategic objectives of the acquisition. For example, aiming for synergies and downsizing,

[541] The reasons for the substance of these competences can be derived from the argumentation in chapter 2.2.1.

without ensuring that managers were able to keep employees at lower levels motivated, could have resulted in negative effects on employee motivation, as a result of the acquisition. Seeking a knowledge and skill transfer without being aware of employees' communication competence could have resulted in failure.[542] Had all of the competences in table 6.6 been included into HRDD, M&A management could have better tailored its activities to the transaction parties' employees.

After having dealt with strategic M&A objectives in the first place, table 6.7 summarises the human resource requirements that resulted from the structural management objectives underlying the planned transaction.

Structural Objectives / Competence	Consolidation Objective	Reinvention Objective	Renewal Objective	Actual Focus Areas of HRDD
Uncertainty Competence		•		
Communication Competence	•	•		
Conflict Competence				
Motivation Competence	•	•		
Co-operation Competence	•	•		
Innovation Competence		•		
Internal Competence				
Market Competence				
Socio-cultural Competence				
Complexity Competence	•	•		
Functional Competence	•	•	•	
Process Competence	•	•	•	
Planning Competence		•	•	
Problem-solving Competence	•	•	•	
Organisation Competence		•	•	
Decision-making Competence		•	•	
Social Change Competence		•		
Technical Change Competence			•	

Table 6.7: Competences and Beiersdorf's Structural Acquisition Management Objectives

The structural M&A management objectives of the Beiersdorf transaction implied the following human resource requirements. According to the HRDD Concept, uncertainty, communication, motivation, co-operation, innovation, complexity, functional, process, planning, problem-solving, organisation, decision-making, social change, and technical change competence were critical in the planned acquisition.[543] These competences would have been relevant for employees in the following functions: distribution, human resource management, finance, and information technology. Hence, mainly support functions were affected by the structural M&A management objectives, whereas rather fewer changes would have been implied for

[542] Cf. chapter 2.2.1.

[543] The reasons for the relevance of these competences can be found in chapter 2.2.2.

marketing and research & development employees. As already mentioned, Beiersdorf concentrated on human resource aspects which were related to the past, in Human Resource Due Diligence. By not taking the competences in table 6.7 into account, Beiersdorf ignored aspects that were important to achieving the structural objectives underlying the planned merger. Undetected planning competence shortcomings could e.g. have resulted in badly timed and resource consuming changes to micro structure. A failure to analyse technical change competence could have brought about employees unexpectedly being unable to cope with new task spectra imposed upon them.[544] Evaluating the competences in HRDD would have been a precondition for Beiersdorf to produce proactive measures that would foster the achievement of its structural objectives.[545]

Besides pursuing strategic-, and structural M&A objectives, also cultural M&A management objectives were also pursued in the Beiersdorf transaction. The human resource requirements resulting from these M&A objectives are summarised in table 6.8.

Cultural Objectives / Competence	Assimilation Objective	Coexistence Objective	Commutation Objective	Actual Focus Areas of HRDD
Uncertainty Competence				
Communication Competence	•	•	•	
Conflict Competence	•		•	
Motivation Competence	•	•		
Co-operation Competence		•		
Innovation Competence				
Internal Competence				
Market Competence				
Socio-cultural Competence			•	
Complexity Competence				
Functional Competence				
Process Competence				
Planning Competence				
Problem-solving Competence				
Organisation Competence				
Decision-making Competence				
Social Change Competence	•			
Technical Change Competence				

Table 6.8: Competences and Beiersdorf's Cultural Acquisition Management Objectives

It would have been recommendable to assess communication, conflict, motivation, co-operation, socio-cultural, and social change competence in the Beiersdorf case.[546] These competences would have been relevant especially for managers, but also for employees in those

[544] Cf. chapter 2.2.2.
[545] Cf. chapter 1.3.1.
[546] The reasons for the importance of these competences are elaborated on in chapter 2.2.3.

functions that were supposed to be subject to consolidation. None of the competences in table 6.8 was evaluated in actual HRDD, which means that Beiersdorf ignored important human resource requirements to achieve its cultural acquisition objectives. For instance, undetected communication competence shortcomings could have prevented the coexistence of the transaction parties' leadership styles from being successful. Limited socio-cultural competence could have hindered the attainment of inter-firm commutation.[547] If Beiersdorf had taken the competences proposed by the Concept into account, it would have known the probability of its employees being able to fulfil the cultural objectives aimed for.

For the fourth M&A management dimension, objectives have been defined based on human resource strategy, human resource policies and practices, and human resource organisation. The human resource requirements that resulted from the objectives are presented in table 6.9.

HRM Objectives / Competence	Aggregation Objective	Amalgamation Objective	Collaboration Objective	Actual Focus Areas of HRDD
Uncertainty Competence		•	•	
Communication Competence	•	•		
Conflict Competence	•	•		
Motivation Competence	•	•	•	
Co-operation Competence	•	•		
Innovation Competence	•	•		
Internal Competence				
Market Competence		•		
Socio-cultural Competence		•		
Complexity Competence				
Functional Competence	•	•		
Process Competence	•	•		
Planning Competence		•		
Problem-solving Competence		•		
Organisation Competence		•		
Decision-making Competence		•		
Social Change Competence	•		•	
Technical Change Competence	•	•		

Table 6.9: Competences and Beiersdorf's Human Resource Management Objectives in the Acquisition

According to the HRDD Concept, uncertainty, communication, conflict, motivation, co-operation, innovation, market, socio-cultural, functional, process, planning, problem-solving, organisation, decision-making, social change, and technical change competence would have been important areas to investigate in HRDD.[548] Beiersdorf considered none of these competences in HRDD, which means that it overlooked human resource aspects that were critical for the achievement of the human resource management objectives of the planned

[547] Cf. chapter 2.2.3.
[548] The reasons for the gravity of these competences have been elaborated on in chapter 2.2.4.

acquisition. For instance, an undetected lack of technical change competence may imply that employees are assigned to positions, in which they face acquisition-induced technical changes. An unsatisfactory degree of uncertainty competence could have prevented the amalgamation of compensation and benefits policies and practices.[549] If Beiersdorf had assessed the competences shown in table 6.9 in HRDD, it would have known whether its employees' were likely to be supportive of its human resource management objectives or not.

To summarise the findings from the second case study related to the step 1 of the HRDD Concept, the following competences should have been assessed in the Beiersdorf transaction. Uncertainty, communication, conflict, motivation, co-operation, innovation, internal, market, socio-cultural, complexity, functional, process, planning, problem-solving, organisation, decision-making, social change, and technical change competence should all have been assigned high importance in Human Resource Due Diligence. The reasons for the relevance of these competences are diverse, as a result of the many underlying objectives of the planned acquisition.[550] Beiersdorf did not take the human resource requirements that followed from its acquisition objectives into account. This signifies that none of the competences, which might have been important for the achievement of the acquisition objectives, was covered in HRDD a fact which might have led to M&A management being unable to act proactively, if the transaction had come about.

Beiersdorf concentrated on past and present data in HRDD, on the individual as well as on the organisational level. Hence, the focus areas of HRDD in the Beiersdorf transaction were different from the focus areas suggested by the Concept. Nonetheless, it could have been useful to collect the organisational data prior to HRDD, since they could have supported the definition of acquisition objectives.[551] Information about the transaction parties' corporate cultures could e.g. have served as a basis for determining cultural acquisition objectives. The individual data could have complemented the results of HRDD that would have been generated when applying the Concept.[552]

6.3.3.2 Generation of Human Resource Due Diligence Information

Step 2 of the HRDD Concept concerns indicators and tools. These were selected as follows for the Beiersdorf transaction. Quantitative indicators were employed, based on present- and past-related data, which were partly input-oriented, partly behavioural and partly output-oriented. Three tools were used in the Beiersdorf case – external documents, data room information, and information from the management presentation.[553] Had the HRDD Concept been applied, future-related behavioural indicators would primarily have been employed. It would have been necessary to define several indicators for certain competences, since some of

[549] Cf. chapter 2.2.4.
[550] Cf. chapter 2.2.
[551] Cf. chapter 5.2.1.
[552] Cf. chapter 3.2.
[553] Cf. chapter 2.2.

the highly relevant competences were important due to the many acquisition objectives. It would have been possible to utilise all the tools in chapter 3.2 in the Beiersdorf case (see table 6.10). The limitations of the indicators and tools that were used for generating HRDD information should have been borne in mind when compiling this information, and when taking measures after the HRDD was completed.[554]

Competence	Underlying M&A objective	Indicators	Tools
Uncertainty Competence	Reinvention objective	• Cope with uncertainty deriving from new micro structure	Assessment centres, structured interviews, questionnaires, role plays and tests
	Amalgamation objective	• Accept uncertainty deriving from new compensation systems and performance criteria	Ditto.
	Collaboration objective	• Deal with uncertainty about where and how to proceed in the new firm	Ditto.
Communication Competence	Resource access objective	• Enable transfer of knowledge and skills	Ditto.
	Consolidation objective	• Deal with increased number of communication partners	Ditto.
	Reinvention objective	• Work with more communication partners, communicate more intensely	Ditto.
	Assimilation objective	• Establish information flows and relationships with other firm's employees	Ditto.
	Coexistence objective	• Accept new patterns of information and opinion sharing	Ditto.
	Commutation objective	• Provide comprehensible information to others and receive information in the intended way despite language barriers	Ditto.
	Aggregation objective	• Communicate more effectively	Ditto.
	Amalgamation objective	• Get used to e.g. a higher communication density	Ditto.
Conflict Competence	Assimilation objective	• Deal with different patterns of behaviour	Ditto.

[554] Cf. chapter 5.2.2.

Competence	Underlying M&A objective	Indicators	Tools
	Commutation objective	• Deal constructively with conflicts caused by different patterns of behaviour, due to differences in national cultures	Ditto.
	Aggregation objective	• Deal constructively with conflicts caused by new behavioural requirements	Ditto.
	Amalgamation objective	• Negotiate constructively in the case of conflicts due to new behavioural requirements	Ditto.
Motivation Competence	Synergy objective	• Enthuse collaborators for M&A despite downsizing	Ditto.
	Consolidation objective	• Help collaborators cope with organisational changes (new roles, states)	Ditto.
	Reinvention objective	• Compensate for missing leadership through structures and processes	Ditto.
	Assimilation objective	• Support collaborators in dealing with new patterns of behaviour	Ditto.
	Coexistence objective	• Help collaborators to acquaint themselves with new leader-subordinate relationships	
	Aggregation objective	• Help collaborators get along with new behavioural requirements	Ditto.
	Amalgamation objective	• Enhance commitment of collaborators despite changes to policies and practices	Ditto.
	Collaboration objective	• Support collaborators in dealing with unpredictable changes	Ditto.
Co-operation Competence	Resource access objective	• Enable knowledge and skill transfer in inter-firm teams	Ditto.
	Consolidation objective	• Make joint macro structure work	Ditto.
	Reinvention objective	• Enhance efficiency of new structures and processes	Ditto.
	Coexistence objective	• Adopt new patterns of behaviour	Ditto.

Competence	Underlying M&A objective	Indicators	Tools
	Aggregation objective	• Cope with new patterns of co-operation	Ditto.
	Amalgamation objective	• Change co-operation habits, e.g. introduce joint decision-making	Ditto.
Innovation Competence	Synergy objective	• Foster synergies e. g. through process innovations	Ditto.
	Resource access objective	• Make new firm stand out against competitors through product innovations	Ditto.
	Market development objective	• Find new applications for existing products	Ditto.
	Reinvention objective	• Make process innovations	Ditto.
	Aggregation objective	• Find a way of aggregating human resource strategies (process innovation)	Ditto.
	Amalgamation objective	• Show a generally higher degree of innovation	Ditto.
Internal Competence	Synergy objective	• Realise synergies in a responsible way	Ditto.
Market Competence	Resource access objective	• Ensure significance of knowledge and skills to be transferred	Ditto.
	Market development objective	• Develop new products & applications, tap new customers	Ditto.
	Amalgamation objective	• Be more market-oriented than before	Ditto.
Socio-cultural Competence	Commutation objective	• Be able to cope with people from different national cultures	Ditto.
	Amalgamation objective	• Be able to cope with people from different national cultures	Ditto.
Complexity Competence	Consolidation objective	• Create macro structure that reduces complexity, deal with every day complexity	Ditto.
	Reinvention objective	• Cope with complexity caused by new micro structure	Ditto.
Functional Competence	Synergy objective	• Work efficiently	Assessment centres, structured interviews, questionnaires and tests
	Market development objective	• Foster competitive advantage	Ditto.

Competence	Underlying M&A objective	Indicators	Tools
	Consolidation objective	• Work efficiently and foster competitive advantage	Ditto.
	Reinvention objective	• Determine suitability of new structures, work efficiently with them	Ditto.
	Renewal objective	• Perform higher ranked tasks than one's own usual tasks	Ditto.
	Aggregation objective	• Work efficiently and foster competitive advantage	Ditto.
	Amalgamation objective	• Work efficiently and foster competitive advantage	Ditto.
Process Competence	Synergy objective	• Work efficiently	Ditto.
	Market development objective	• Foster competitive advantage	Ditto.
	Consolidation objective	• Work efficiently and foster competitive advantage	Ditto.
	Reinvention objective	• Determine suitability of new processes, work efficiently with these	Ditto.
	Renewal objective	• Perform higher ranked processes than one's own usual processes	Ditto.
	Aggregation objective	• Work efficiently and foster competitive advantage	Ditto.
	Amalgamation objective	• Work efficiently and foster competitive advantage	Ditto.
Planning Competence	Synergy objective	• Plan for attainment of synergies	Ditto.
	Resource access objective	• Assess which functions to transfer knowledge and skills to	Ditto.
	Market development objective	• Define new strategy, de-termine operative mea-sures to implement it	Ditto.
	Market penetration objective	• Co-ordinate activities of new firm	Ditto.
	Reinvention objective	• Determine how, when and with what resources to make changes to micro structure	Ditto.

Competence	Underlying M&A objective	Indicators	Tools
	Renewal objective	• Plan in advance despite more sophisticated new tasks	Ditto.
	Amalgamation objective	• Plan for amalgamation to be achieved, cope with new performance criteria	Ditto.
Problem-solving Competence	Consolidation objective	• Solve problems related to new macro structure	Ditto.
	Reinvention objective	• Determine what new micro structure is supposed to be like	Ditto.
	Renewal objective	• Work towards a set goal without knowing the path towards this goals beforehand	Ditto.
	Amalgamation objective	• Find one's way towards amalgamation, cope with new performance criteria	Ditto.
Organisation Competence	Reinvention objective	• Redistribute and integrate tasks on micro level	Ditto.
	Renewal objective	• Split tasks up into subtasks and arrange for their completion	Ditto.
	Amalgamation objective	• Distribute and integrate amalgamation-related tasks, cope with new performance criteria	Ditto.
Decision-making Competence	Synergy objective	Select functions of the firms' value chains for synergy attainment	Ditto.
	Resource access objective	• Choose functions for knowledge and skill transfer from several alternatives	Ditto.
	Market development objective	• Choose strategy and operative measures from bundle	Ditto.
	Market penetration objective	• Select way of co-ordinating future activities	Ditto.
	Reinvention objective	• Decide on a new micro structure based on analysis of alternatives	Ditto.
	Renewal objective	• Consider and weigh alternative courses of action	Ditto.
	Amalgamation objective	• Select suitable ways of attaining amalgamation, cope with new performance criteria	Ditto.

Competence	Underlying M&A objective	Indicators	Tools
Social Change Competence	Reinvention objective	• Deal with new colleagues, collaborators or superiors	Assessment centres, structured interviews, questionnaires, role plays and tests
	Assimilation objective	• Adapt to new people and new patterns of behaviour (all employees)	Ditto.
	Aggregation objective	• Adopt new patterns of behaviour	Ditto.
	Collaboration objective	• Deal with new human resource managers	Ditto.
Technical Change Competence	Renewal objective	• Deal with new or modified technical requirements	Ditto.
	Aggregation objective	• Cope with new or modified technical requirements	Ditto.
	Amalgamation objective	• Get used to new or modified technical requirements	Ditto.
Uncertainty Competence	Reinvention objective	• Cope with uncertainty deriving from new micro structure	Assessment centres, structured interviews, questionnaires, role plays and tests

Table 6.10: Generation of Human Resource Due Diligence Information in the Beiersdorf Acquisition

By considering quantitative indicators, Beiersdorf has proceeded in line with the propositions of the HRDD Concept. However, inconsistently with the Concept, present and past data were used to form assumptions about employees' dispositions to act in the future.[555] The tools that were drawn on were not suitable for generating future-related information about individual employees. Nonetheless, Beiersdorf evaluated human resource aspects that are appropriate to complement the Concept for HRDD. However, it was unsuccessful in utilising future-related, behavioural indicators and tools, thereby neglecting human resource information that would have been important for further M&A management activities. Still, a vast amount of present- and past data was produced before the planned acquisition, which could have been helpful for defining acquisition objectives, if the transaction had been pursued further.

6.3.3.3 Compilation of Human Resource Due Diligence Information

The data generated in HRDD in the Beiersdorf case were neither summarised nor further processed. They might have been, according to the Beiersdorf contact person, if the acquisition had taken place. If they had applied the HRDD Concept, Beiersdorf would have

[555] Cf. chapter 3.1.

developed elementary and advanced controlling ratios based on the results of HRDD.[556] For instance, it would have been useful to determine short and middle term ratios, since some of Beiersdorf's acquisition objectives were defined for the short and others for the middle term. These ratios could have been the foundation for measures such as staffing, and human resource development following HRDD.

Person	A						B						C					
Parameter Value	**1**	**2**	**3**	**4**	**5**	**Ratio**	**1**	**2**	**3**	**4**	**5**	**Ratio**	**1**	**2**	**3**	**4**	**5**	**Ratio**
Social competence																		
Uncertainty competence	▲			•		0,250				▲•		1,000		▲		•		0,500
Communication competence	▲			•		0,250				▲•		1,000		▲		•		0,500
Conflict competence		▲		•		0,500			▲	•		0,750			▲	•		0,750
Motivation competence		▲		•		0,500				▲•		1,000		▲		•		0,500
Co-operation competence			▲	•		0,750			▲	•		0,750	▲			•		0,250
Systems competence																		
Innovation competence			▲	•		0,750			▲	•		0,750	▲			•		0,250
Internal competence		▲		•		0,500			▲	•		0,750	▲			•		0,250
Market competence			▲	•		0,750			▲	•		0,750			▲	•		0,750
Socio-cultural competence		▲		•		0,500		▲		•		0,500			▲	•		0,750
Complexity competence		▲		•		0,500		▲		•		0,500			▲	•		0,750
Specialist competence																		
Functional competence		▲		•		0,500		▲		•		0,500			▲	•		0,750
Process competence		▲		•		0,500		▲		•		0,500			▲	•		0,750
Methods competence																		
Planning competence			▲	•		0,750		▲		•		0,500			▲	•		0,750
Problem-solving competence			▲	•		0,750		▲		•		0,500			▲	•		0,750
Organisation competence			▲	•		0,750			▲	•		0,750			▲	•		0,750
Decision-making competence			▲	•		0,750			▲	•		0,750			▲	•		0,750
Change competence																		
Social change competence			▲	•		0,750	▲			•		0,250				▲•		1,000
Technical change competence			▲	•		0,750	▲			•		0,250				▲•		1,000

Actual parameter values of competencies ▲
Desired parameter values of competencies •

Figure 6.3: Compilation of the Generated Human Resource Due Diligence Information in the Beiersdorf Acquisition

6.3.4 Final Remark about the Planned Acquisition

Prior to the planned transaction with Company X, Beiersdorf carried out a detailed Human Resource Due Diligence. In this HRDD, important human resource aspects were neglected. Future-related individual aspects were left out. If Beiersdorf had applied the HRDD Concept, it would have known about the human resource requirements that followed from its M&A management objectives. As a consequence, M&A management would have been capable of taking measures to support employees in coping with these requirements. Yet, by performing

556 Cf. chapter 4.3.

HRDD the way it did, Beiersdorf succeeded in carrying out a Human Resource Due Diligence which showed a high degree of variety. Some of the human resource aspects considered by Beiersdorf could have been covered in the analyses preceding HRDD. Commenting on the further utilisation of HRDD data is difficult, since the acquisition did not take place.

6.4. Final Statement about both Case Studies

The two case studies were of a polar nature.[557] Despite this fact, they were very similar, as far as the M&A management objectives underlying them are concerned. The focus areas, indicators and tools, as well as the further utilisation of HRDD data differed significantly. The reason for this may lie in the firms' different rationales for doing HRDD, or in other characteristics of the transactions. Moreover, the ways in which it was intended to pursue M&A management objectives, differed. Beiersdorf aimed at a smooth transition, whereas DZ Bank wanted to bring about quick and effective changes. This manifests itself in, for instance, the cultural management approaches underlying both transactions. Beiersdorf aimed to enable a slow, emergent process of cultural assimilation. DZ Bank did not manage corporate culture actively, but through the staffing policies following the merger, a predefined set of values was aimed at, composed of the transaction parties' former values. Moreover, in the Beiersdorf case, the competences identified as most relevant were vital for certain employee groups. At the same time, almost all employees except those working with pure settlement tasks, were affected by the human resource requirements imposed by the merger in the DZ Bank transaction.

The differences between the Beiersdorf and the DZ Bank transaction demonstrate that the HRDD Concept can only be applied in a responsible manner if differences between transactions are respected. This could be done by distinguishing between short- and middle-term M&A objectives or by assessing which employee groups must fulfil most of the human resource requirements resulting from the M&A transaction.[558]

[557] Cf. chapter 6.1 two-tail approach.

[558] For details see introduction to chapter 2.

7 Résumé and Discussion of Research Results, and Recommendations for Future Research

This final chapter sums up the results of this thesis, and includes a critical discussion of these (chapter 7.1). Moreover, fields of further research are suggested (chapter 7.2).

7.1 Résumé and Discussion of Research Results

This chapter contains a résumé and critical discussion of the most important results of this thesis. First, chapter 1 is referred to, second chapter 2, third chapter 3, fourth chapter 5, fifth chapter 6, and sixth the research goal from chapter 1.3.2 is elaborated on individually.

(1) The starting point of this thesis was a twofold research gap.[559] Based on this research gap, the **purpose** of this thesis has been to develop a concept for Human Resource Due Diligence in the context of Mergers & Acquisitions. The purpose of this thesis has been fulfilled. An HRDD Concept has been developed that incorporates M&A specific competence requirements. The Concept can be adapted to the specific M&A context in which it is used, and it returns information that is useful for further management activities. The Concept has been developed on the basis of theoretical and empirical insights, and its application to business practice has been illustrated in two case studies. The way in which the purpose of this thesis has been addressed has been contingent on the research gap.[560] The research gap had been determined based on certain criteria for analysing previous studies. A choice of different criteria might have implied a different research gap, and accordingly, a different shape of the HRDD Concept.

This thesis has been **philosophically positioned** as systemic, following the distinction of systemic and non-systemic socio-managerial research by Ulrich. Consequently, a certain way of thinking, a certain modelling of social systems, and a certain problem-solving approach have the basis for creating the Concept. First, a holistic way of thinking has been used when creating the HRDD Concept. This holistic way of thinking can especially be seen from the fact that the Concept is based on objectives in four different management dimensions – strategy, structure, culture and human resource management. These dimensions are intertwined with each other through circular relationships, a fact which is taken into consideration in all three steps of the Concept. In step 1, interdependencies between the management objectives within and between the management dimensions are referred to.[561] In steps 2 and 3, the choice of indicators and tools, as well as of controlling

---

[559] Cf. chapter 1.1.

[560] The criteria taken into account for analysing previous studies were partly typical of a literature review – previous empirical work – and partly reflected in previous studies – e.g. the level of abstraction of the analysis. Three criteria have been defined voluntarily – the applicability of HRDD to business practice, the contingency of HRDD on the M&A context, and the usefulness of HRDD data for further management activities.

[561] Cf. chapters 2.2.1.3, 2.2.2.4, 2.2.3.4 and 2.2.4.4.

ratios, depends on the interdependencies between the M&A management objectives.[562] Second, the fact that social systems are synthetically determined according to Ulrich is taken into account when it comes to recommendations for business practice concerning the application of the Concept.[563] Professionals are recommended to carry out HRDD at several points in time before and after the completion of an M&A transaction, to account for the fact that M&A objectives and employee competences may change over time. Third, the heuristic problem-solving process of systemic studies is represented in all three steps of the concept. Despite providing focus areas for HRDD depending on the M&A objectives of a transaction, step 1 of the Concept still leaves some room for professionals to dispose of to account for the different relevance of employee competences. The Concept solely distinguishes between highly and hardly relevant competences. Professionals are, however, required to associate desired parameter values to the highly relevant competences. As far as step 2 is concerned, types of indicators and possibly useful tools for the generation of HRDD information are integral to the Concept. Still, concrete indicators and tools need to be tailored to each individual M&A transaction, in line with resource restrictions and the employees who are at the centre of attention. Related to step 3 of the Concept, types of controlling ratios are exemplified, which can be relied on for compiling the generated HRDD information. Concrete controlling ratios still need to be chosen by M&A management though, corresponding to its steering interests. Had a non-systemic perspective been taken in this study, would an analytical way of thinking have impeded considering more than one dimension of M&A management. Analytically determined input-output-relationships would have implied the search for an optimum solution to the problem addressed in this thesis. Had this thesis been written based on a different understanding of systemic studies, would the choices made in this study have been made in a way different from the way they have been.[564]

The object of analysis of this thesis has been to proactively address M&A-specific competence requirements in Human Resource Due Diligence. The perspective of analysis has been a management objective-oriented one. The choice of the problem addressed in the **object of analysis** has been contingent to the research gap detected in the review of previous studies. Had another research gap been the starting point to this thesis, the object of analysis would have been defined differently. The **perspective of analysis** of this study has one the one hand been taken, since previous studies suggested the competence requirements of M&A transaction to be dependent on M&A objectives. On the other hand, the perspective of analysis of this thesis is due to its systemic philosophical positioning. According to Ulrich, management objectives are a way for management to cope with the complexity of social systems.[565]

---

562 Cf. chapters 3 and 4.
563 Cf. chapters 2 to 6.
564 Cf. Wagner, Peter (2004), p. 15.
565 Cf. chapter 1.2.

Given the practical relevance of the problem addressed in this thesis, the **research goal** has been to develop a Concept that can be used in business practice. The research goal of this thesis has been attained: the HRDD Concept consists of normative, prescriptive insights for business practice, in line with the aim of shaping a tool for M&A management.[566] Moreover, the application of the empirically complemented HRDD Concept to business practice has been illustrated in two case studies.[567] The suitability of the HRDD Concept for business practice has also been appraised by presenting the Concept to more than 35 company representatives and consultants.

(2) The HRDD Concept has been developed based on **competence definitions** that have partly been acquired from psychological literature, and partly been developed in this study.[568] Hence, the competence definitions underlying the Concept are based on the view taken in this thesis. A review of different literature sources might have implied different competence definitions and accordingly a different shape of step 1 of the HRDD Concept.

When defining **focus areas** for the Concept, M&A literature has been relied on as the basis for generating explanations for the potential relevance of the competences in an M&A transaction. A different selection of M&A literature sources might have led to different explanations, and a different shape of step 1 of the HRDD Concept. This argumentation also applies to the M&A objectives underlying the focus areas. However, many M&A objectives used for the HRDD Concept seem to be the ones that are the most frequently pursued in M&A. This assumption, based on the literature review has been supported in the expert interviews.[569]

(3) Competences are not always manifested in **future employee behaviour**. Human beings sometimes do not behave competently, even though competence analysis has assigned certain competences to them, e.g. for psychological reasons. Moreover, a person's behaviour may be influenced by the situation in which he intends showing certain competences. Finally, competences can change over time, and even be influenced by competence analysis itself.[570] The indicators of the HRDD Concept do not consider these possibilities.

Step two of the Concept refers to **types of tools** that can be used in HRDD. The reliability and validity of these tools are referred to as decision-making criteria when selecting concrete tools for the HRDD Concept.[571] However, simply considering the reliability and validity of diagnostic tools is not sufficient to enhance their proper use. An understanding of important error sources in diagnostics is also required.[572] If error sources are not dealt

566 Cf. chapters 1.3.2.
567 Cf. chapters 6.2 and 6.3.
568 Cf. chapter 2.1.1.
569 Cf. chapter 5.2.1.4 to 5.2.1.6.
570 Cf. Erpenbeck, John/Rosenstiel, Lutz von. In: Erpenbeck, John/Rosenstiel, Lutz von (2003), p. XVIII.
571 Cf. chapter 3.2.
572 Social perception theory (Graumann), Halo effect (Thorndike), Error of central tendency (Hofstätter), Generosity error (Cronbach), Logical error (Hasemann), Contrast error (Murray), Identifying error (Guilford). Cf. Wottawa, Heinrich/Hossiep, Rüdiger (1987), p. 86. Trust can also be an error source in diagnostics.

with, the results of HRDD can be taken for granted without addressing the downsides of their underlying tools.[573] The HRDD Concept should contain a reflexive element so that management do not misuse it simply as a downsizing tool.

(4) Many of the **experts questioned about practical HRDD** in the expert survey gave extensive answers about what their firms focused on in HRDD.[574] However, the reliability of these answers has not been proven. Especially when it comes to highly confidential issues like HRDD, interviewees can tend to give over-optimistic answers that reflect the desired, but not the actual state of their practices. In the survey, this danger has been tackled by asking the experts about the actual and desired focus areas of HRDD. Besides, the purpose of the expert survey has not been to reflect social reality as well as possible, but to complement the HRDD Concept with empirical insights.

(5) Concerning the **application** of the Concept **to business practice**, two case studies have been carried out to illustrate this.[575] As a result of these case studies, it can be said that the HRDD Concept gives firms clear advice about how to shape HRDD, based on their M&A management objectives.[576] However, some of the elements of the HRDD Concept can be subject to misinterpretation. For instance, if firms have a different understanding of the term competences than that of this thesis, it can be difficult to employ the indicators, tools, and ratios suggested in the Concept. Also, if firms have a different interpretation of the competences, it can be difficult to accept the focus areas developed in this thesis.[577] As a consequence, HRDD results can be interpreted in a way different from that intended. Hence, firms willing to apply the Concept presented must be familiar with its underlying assumptions. The HRDD Concept does not take the interpretations and specifics of individual firms – e.g. own competence definitions – into consideration.[578]

(6) Upon completion of the case studies, the HRDD Concept was presented to more than 35 company representatives and consultants (who had not been involved in former empirical steps), in order to discuss its **suitability for business practice**. First, on November 26th 2004, the Concept was presented to consultants of the mmc Mollenhauer Management Consulting AG, and second, on November 29th 2004, to company representatives and consultants of the Arbeitskreis Rhein-Main of the Human-Capital-Club. According to chapter 1.3.2, the suitability of a concept for business practice can be seen from the number of steps that need to be taken by professionals when applying it for themselves,

Cf. Knebel, Heinz (2003), p. 15. The tools to be used when employing the Human Resource Due Diligence Concept are of limited reliability and validity. Hence, the controlling ratios generated based on the first two steps of the HRDD Concept are at risk. Cf. Dellmann, Klaus. In: Küpper, Hans-Ulrich/Wagenhofer, Alfred (Eds.) (2002), p. 942. Braun, Herbert (1984), p. 25. Brühwiler, Bruno (1980), p. 52.

[573] Cf. chapter 5.2.2.

[574] Cf. chapter 5.2.1.

[575] Cf. chapter 6.2 and 6.3. Still, cf. Frank, Ulrich (2003), p. 282 for a discussion of practical research goals.

[576] Cf. chapters 2 to 4.

[577] Cf. chapter 5.2.1.

[578] Still, the HRDD Concept is in line with the research results aimed at in chapter 1.3.5. Dealing with the above downsides would have required different aimed-at research results: level four in Ulrich's categorization.

and from the number of cases in which it is applicable. The discussions following the two presentations illustrated that professionals need to take three major steps for themselves when applying the Concept. First, they need to define the desired competences based on their M&A objectives, and associate them with a stage in the Likert scale.[579] Second, they need to design indicators and tools for HRDD that they have chosen based on the Concept, in such a way as to get hold of the desired information. Third, they must develop a ratio system, which allows one to arrive easily at advanced, tertiary and a totally integrated ratio. The development of such a ratio system probably requires a solid IT base to build on.[580] To be suitable for business practice, a concept must also be applicable in a large number of cases. The HRDD Concept is a concept in content for a general problem, and should be applicable to all M&A transactions, in which at least one of the M&A objectives in chapter 2.2 is pursued.

7.2 Recommendations for Future Research

This chapter serves to provide eight recommendations for further research, which are presented in line with the course of the investigation of this study.

(1) This thesis has consciously been focused on the process of HRDD.[581] Further studies might add an institutional and an instrumental perspective to the HRDD Concept. Taking an institutional perspective, the questions of who should be in charge of what when conducting Human Resource Due Diligence, and of how to cope with time and resource constraints should be considered.[582] From an instrumental perspective, the shape of concrete indicators and tools for step 2 of the Concept should be elaborated on.

(2) The HRDD Concept encompasses 3 steps: the determination of focus areas for HRDD, the generation of HRDD information, and the compilation of the generated HRDD information. Still, it remains unanswered what measures M&A management should take, based on the results of HRDD.[583] Dealing with M&A management measures in future research would useful to ensure that the problem, which is at the centre of this thesis – to proactively address the competence requirements of M&A transactions, in the future – is addressed in business practice.

---

[579] Cf. chapter 2.

[580] According to some of the professionals, who attended the 2nd presentation, the creation of an IT based ratio system is feasible rather easily.

[581] Cf. chapter 1.4.2.

[582] Especially the question of how to communicate the HRDD Concept to employees should be addressed. Cf. Daniel, Teresa A. (1999), p. 27. Howell, Robert A. (1970), p. 66. Lucks, Kai/Meckl, R. (2002), p. 495. Wall, Stephen J./Wall, Shannon Rye (2001), pp. 93ff.

[583] According to Bontis/Fitz-enz, human capital valuation is at the core of effective human capital management. Cf. Bontis, Nick/Fitz-enz, Jac (2002), p. 228. For details about measures that can be taken upon completion of HRDD cf. Lang, Karl (2000). Becker, Manfred/Schwertner, Anke (Eds.) (2002) (entire book). Hunt, John W./Downing, Stephen (1990), pp. 195f. Luoma, Mikko (2000), pp. 775ff. Fuchs, Matthias (2001) (entire book). Harrison, Joan (1999), p. 11. Kriegesmann, Bernd (2003), p. 18.

(3) The HRDD Concept does not deal with the question of how to determine M&A management objectives in a concrete transaction. Hence, it might be complemented by elaborating on how to arrive at the M&A management objectives it is based on, to facilitate the application of the Concept to business practice.

(4) The aim of the HRDD Concept has been to prescribe how HRDD should be designed in business practice, given certain M&A management objectives. Chapter 2.2 has shown that there are certain interdependencies between the management dimensions of the HRDD Concept. Given this fact, it could be interesting to assess whether certain combinations of M&A objectives are pursued in a selected number of M&A. For instance, it might be the case that 90 % of all synergetic M&A imply cultural symbiosis.[584] Knowing about the existence of the interdependencies just described may be useful to facilitate practical HRDD.[585]

(5) Insights from the expert survey have demonstrated that the Human Resource Due Diligence Concept merely covers a small extract of all human resource information that may be considered crucial in an M&A transaction. Future studies might deal with how to integrate other focus areas for HRDD, which were largely covered in previous studies[586], into the HRDD Concept.

(6) This thesis concentrates on HRDD as a tool to be made use of by M&A management. However, in a concrete M&A transaction, management may also want to make use of other tools than HRDD. These tools should be linked to HRDD in the best possible way to be useful for M&A management. Future studies might therefore deal with how to link HRDD with other tools of M&A management.

(7) In chapter 5.2, the insights from an expert survey have been used to empirically complement the Human Resource Due Diligence Concept. Given the normative research goal and the research strategy of this thesis, interdependencies between the answers to some and the answers to other questions have not been assessed. However, an analysis of such interdependencies might be interesting assuming different, more explanatory, aimed-for research results. For instance, it might be fruitful to evaluate whether there is a correlation between the actual focus areas of HRDD in certain transactions, and the suggested compilation of HRDD information.

(8) The application of the HRDD Concept to business practice has been appraised in two case studies. However, a downside of these case studies is their retrospective nature. To further assess the suitability of the Concept for business practice, action research in an on-going M&A transaction should be conducted.[587]

---

[584] Firms may want to rely on probabilities, instead of determining each M&A objective.

[585] Still, firms possibly do not always define M&A objectives that are logically in line with each other.

[586] Cf. chapter 1.1.

[587] Also, one might compare an M&A transaction in which the Concept is applied to one in which it is not applied.

Bibliography

Achleitner, Ann-Kristin: Handbuch Investment-Banking. Wiesbaden 2001.

Adelsberger, Heimo H./Stallkamp, Markus: Möglichkeiten eines zukunftsorientierten Führungsinformationssystems. In: Reichmann, Thomas (Ed.): Controlling – Jetzt aktiv steuern, nicht nur kontrollieren. Tagungsband. 18. Deutscher Controlling-Congress. Dortmund 2003, pp. 19 – 29.

Albath, Andreas: The battle for talent – Strategien für die knappe Ressource Mitarbeiter. In: HR Services, Vol. 4, Issue 2, 2002, pp. 14 – 21.

Albert, Hans: Theorie und Prognose in den Sozialwissenschaften. In: Topitsch, Ernst (Ed.): Logik der Sozialwissenschaften. 12th edition. Frankfurt am Main 1993, pp. 126 –143.

Aldering, Christopph/Hutten, Christina Freiin von: Due Diligence und Human Resources. In: Berens, Wolfgang/Brauner, Hans U./Strauch, Joachim (Eds.): Due Diligence bei Unternehmensakquisitionen. 3rd edition. Stuttgart 2002, pp. 410 – 426.

Althauser, Ulrich/Tonscheidt-Göstl, Dagmar: Kultur-Due Diligence – Erfolgsfaktor bei Fusionen und Akquisitionen. In: Personalwirtschaft, Vol. 26, Issue 8, 1999, pp. 40 – 47.

Amelang, Manfred/Bartussek, Dieter: Differentielle Psychologie und Persönlichkeitsforschung. 4th edition. Stuttgart 1997.

Angersbach, Carsten J.: Due Diligence beim Unternehmenskauf. Baden-Baden 2002.

Ansoff, Igor H.: Strategies for Diversification. In: Harvard Business Review. Vol. 35, Issue 5, 1957, pp. 113 – 124.

Argyle, Michael: Soziale Interaktion. Köln 1972.

Ashkenas, Ronald N./Francis, Suzanne C.: Integration Managers – Special Leaders for Special Times. In: Harvard Business Review, Vol. 78, Issue 6, 2000, pp. 108 – 116.

Astley, Graham W./Van de Ven, Andrew H.: Central perspectives and Debates in Organization Theory. In: Administrative Science Quarterly. Vol. 28, Issue 2, 1983, pp. 245 – 273.

Baacke, Dieter: Kommunikation und Kompetenz. München 1973.

Backhausen, Wilhelm/Thommen, Jean-Paul: Coaching – Durch systemisches Denken zu innovativer Personalentwicklung. 2nd edition. Wiesbaden 2004.

Baetge, Jörg: Bilanzanalyse. Düsseldorf 1998.

Baldridge, David C./Floyd, Steven W./Markóczy, Lívia: Are Managers from Mars and Academicians from Venus? – Toward an Understanding of the Relationship between Academic Quality and Practical Relevance. In: Strategic Management Journal. Vol. 25, Issue 11, 2004, pp. 1063 – 1074.

Bamberger, Burkhard: Der Erfolg von Unternehmensakquisitionen in Deutschland – Eine theoretische und empirische Untersuchung. Bergisch-Gladbach 1994.

Barney, James B.: Firm resources and sustained competitive advantage. In: Journal of Management, Vol. 17, Issue 1, 1991, pp. 99 – 120.

Baron, James N./Krebs, David M.: Strategic Human Resources – Frameworks for General Managers. New York et al. 1999.

Bastien, David T.: Communication, Conflict and Learning in Mergers and Acquisitions. In: Ven, Andrew H. van de/Angle, Harold L./Poole, Marshall Scott (Eds.): Research on the Management of Innovation. New York et al. 1989, pp. 367 – 396.

Baur, Matthias: M&A-Myopia und Integrationsmanagement – Mentale Barrieren bei der Umsetzung eines effektiven und effizienten Integrationsmanagements bei Mergers & Acquisitons. Wiesbaden 2004.

Beatty, Richard W./Huselid, Mark A./Schneier, Craig E.: New HR Metrics - Scoring on the Business Scorecard. In: Organizational Dynamics, Vol. 32, Issue 2, 2003, pp. 107 – 121.

Becker, Manfred/Schwertner, Anke (Eds.): Personalentwicklung als Kompetenzentwicklung. München 2002.

Becker, Robert E./Heimberg, Richard Gordon: Assessment of social skills. In: Bellack, Alan/Hersen, Michel (Eds.): Behavioral assessment. Oxford 1988, pp. 365 – 395.

Beer, Michael: Performance Appraisal. In: Lorsch, Jay W. (Ed.): Handbook of Organizational Behavior. New York 1987, pp. 286 – 300.

Behler, Steffen: Ermittlung und Entwicklung von Managementkompetenzen in wachstumsorientierten Unternehmen in der Gründungsphase. Aachen 2002.

Beiersdorf AG (Ed.): BDF Beiersdorf Geschäftsbericht 2000. Hamburg 2001.

Beiersdorf AG (Ed.): BDF Beiersdorf Geschäftsbericht 2001 – Marken und Menschen. Hamburg 2002.

Berens, Wolfgang/Strauch, Joachim: Due Diligence bei Unternehmensakquisitionen – Eine empirische Untersuchung. Frankfurt am Main et al. 2002.

Berens, Wolfgang/Strauch, Joachim: Herkunft und Inhalt des Begriffes Due Diligence. In: Berens, Wolfgang/Brauner, Hans U./Strauch, Joachim (Eds.): Due Diligence bei Unternehmensakquisitionen. 3rd edition. Stuttgart 2002, pp. 3 – 24.

Bergh, Donald D.: Executive retention and acquisition outcomes – A test of opposing views on the influence of organizational tenure. In: Journal of Management, Vol. 27, Issue 5, 2001, pp. 603 – 622.

Berghaus, Margot: Luhmann leicht gemacht – eine Einführung in die Systemtheorie. Köln et al. 2003.

Berkel, Karl: Verhandlung und Konfliktlösung. In: Sarges, Werner (Ed.): Management-Diagnostik. 3rd edition. Göttingen et al. 2000, pp. 419 – 424.

Bickford, Lawrence: Mergers and Acquisitions – How executive compensation may affect a deal. In: Compensation & Benefits Review, Vol. 29, Issue 5, 1997, pp. 53 – 59.

Biethahn, Jörg/Huch, Burkhard: Informationssysteme für das Controlling. Berlin et al. 1994.

Bing, Gordon: Due diligence techniques and analysis – Critical questions for business decisions. Westport 1996.

Birkinshaw, Julian/Bresman, Henrik/Hakanson, Lars: Managing the Post-Acquisition Integration Process – How the Human Integration and Task Integration Processes Interact to Foster Value Creation. In: Journal of Management Studies, Vol. 37, Issue 3, 2000, pp. 395 – 425.

Blake, Robert R./Mouton, Jane S.: How to achieve integration on the human side of the merger. In: Organization Dynamics, Vol. 13, Issue 3, 1985, pp. 41 – 56.

Blaschke, Dieter: Soziale Qualifikationen im Erwerbsleben. Beiträge zur Arbeitsmarkt- und Berufsforschung. Nürnberg 1987.

Blasko, Matej/Netter, Jeffrey M./Sinkey, Joseph F.: Value creation and challenges of an international transaction – The DaimlerChrysler merger. In: International Review of Financial Analysis, Vol. 9, Issue 1, 2000, pp. 77 – 102.

Böer, Frank-Michael/Stottmeister, Gerd: Personalmanagement bei Fusionen – Mitten im Merger. In: technologie & management, Vol. 51, Issue 3, 2001, w.p.

Bontis, Nick/Fitz-enz, Jac: Intellectual capital ROI – a causal map of human capital antecedents and consequents. In: Journal of Intellectual Capital, Vol. 3, Issue 3, 2002, pp. 223 – 247.

Bortz, Jürgen/Döring, Nicola: Forschungsmethoden und Evaluation – für Human- und Sozialwissenschaftler. 3rd edition. Berlin et al. 2002.

Boudreau, John W.: Strategic Human Resource Management Measures – Key Linkages and the PeopleVantage Model. Center for Advanced Human Resource Studies. Working Paper 98 – 28. CAHRS Cornell University 1998.

Bramson, Ruth N.: HR's Role in Mergers and Acquisitions. In: Training & Development, Vol. 54, Issue 10, 2000, pp. 59 – 66.

Braun, Herbert: Risikomanagement – Eine spezifische Controllingaufgabe. Stuttgart 1984.

Breitstein, Joanna: The Human Cost. In: Pharmaceutical Executive, January 2001, Backpage.

Brockbank, Wayne/Ulrich, David: The New HR Agenda – 2002 Human Resource Competency Study. Executive Summary. University of Michigan Business School 2003.

Brockhoff, Klaus: Leistungen der Betriebswirtschaftslehre für Wirtschaft und Gesellschaft. In: Egger, Anton/Grün, Oskar/Moser, Reinhard (Eds.): Managementinstrumente und –konzepte – Entstehung, Verbreitung und Bedeutung für die Betriebswirtschaftslehre. Stuttgart 1999, pp. 27 – 62.

Brown, Mark G.: Kennzahlen – Harte und weiche Faktoren erkennen, messen und bewerten. München, Wien 1997.

Brühwiler, Bruno: Risk Management – eine Aufgabe der Unternehmungsführung. Bern, Stuttgart 1980.

Bühner, Rolf: Mitarbeiter mit Kennzahlen führen – der Quantensprung zu mehr Leistung. 4th edition. Landsberg 2000.

Bundesverband der Deutschen Volksbanken und Raiffeisenbanken (BVR) (Ed.): Bündelung der Kräfte – Ein Verbund, eine Strategie. Bonn 1999.

Bungard, Walter: Team- und Kooperationsfähigkeit. In: Sarges, Werner (Ed.): Management-Diagnostik. 3rd edition. Göttingen et al. 2000, pp. 405 – 414.

Buono, Anthony F./Bowditch, James L./Lewis, John W.: When Cultures Collide – The Anatomy of a Merger. In: Human Relations, Vol. 38, Issue 5, 1985, pp. 477 – 500.

Buono, Anthony F./Bowditch, James L.: The Human Side of Mergers & Acquisitions – Managing Collisions Between People, Cultures and Organizations. San Francisco, London 1989.

Burke, Joe: Due Diligence in Mergers & Acquisitions. In: Internal Auditor, Vol. 57, Issue 5, 2000, pp. 36 – 40.

Burrell, Gibson/Morgan, Gareth: Sociological Paradigms and Organisational Analysis. London 1979.

Burrows, Donald M.: How People Problems can Sap Value From a Deal. In: Mergers & Acquisitions – The Dealmaker's Journal, Vol. 35, Issue 9, 2000, pp. 36 – 40.

Canepa, Anchillo: Die Due Diligence im M&A-Prozess. Bern 1998.

Carrier, Martin: Wissenschaftstheorie. In: Mittelstraß, Jürgen (Ed.): Enzyklopädie Philosophie und Wissenschaftstheorie. Band 4. Stuttgart, Weimar 1996, pp. 738 – 745.

Cartwright, Sue/Cooper, Cary L.: Managing mergers, acquisitions and strategic alliances – Integrating people and cultures. 2nd edition. Oxford 1996.

Cascio, Wayne F./Sweet, Donald H.: Human Resource Planning, Employment & Placement. 2nd edition. Washington 1988.

Casse, Pierre: People Are Not Resources. In: Journal of European Industrial Training, Vol. 18, Issue 5, 1994, pp. 23 – 26.

Chalmers, Alan F.: Wege der Wissenschaft – Einführung in die Wissenschaftstheorie. 5th edition. Berlin et al. 2001.

Chandler, Alfred Dupont: Strategy and Structure – Chapters in the History of the Industrial Enterprise. Massachusetts 1962.

Chatterjee, Sayan/Lubatkin, Michael H./Schweiger, David M./Weber, Yaakov: Cultural differences and shareholder value in related mergers – Linking equity and human capital. In: Strategic Management Journal, Vol. 13, Issue 13, 1992, pp. 319 – 334.

Chmielewicz, Klaus: Forschungskonzeptionen der Wirtschaftswissenschaft. 3rd edition. Stuttgart 1994.

Claßen, Martin: Rollen des Personalmanagers. In: Personalwirtschaft, Vol. 30, Issue 7, 2003, pp. 51 – 54.

Clemente, Mark N./Greenspan, David S.: Empowering Human Resources in the Merger & Acquisition Process – Guidance for HR Professionals in the Key Areas of M&A Planning & Integration. New York 1999.

Clever, Holger: Post-Merger-Management. Stuttgart el al. 1993.

Cohen, Michael D./March, James G./Olsen, Johan P.: A Garbage Can Model of Organizational Choice. In: Administrative Science Quarterly, Vol. 17, Issue 1, 1972, pp. 1 – 25.

Copeland, Thomas E./Weston, Fred J.: Financial Theory and Corporate Policy. 3rd edition. Reading et al. 1992.

Cornelli, Gerhard/Rosenstiel, Lutz von: Führung durch Motivation – Mitarbeiter für Organisationsziele gewinnen. 2nd edition. München 2001.

Corporate Leadership Council: The Role of HR in Mergers and Acquisitions – Executive Enquiry. March 1999.

Cummings, Larry L.: Compensation, Culture and Motivation – A Systems Perspective. In: Organizational Dynamics, Vol. 12, Issue 3, 1984, pp. 33 – 44.

Cyert, Richard M./March, James G.: Eine verhaltenswissenschaftliche Theorie der Unternehmung. 2nd edition. Stuttgart 1995.

Daniel, Teresa A.: Between Trapezes – The Human Side of Making Mergers and Acquisitions Work. In: Compensation & Benefits Management. Winter 1999, pp. 19 – 37.

Datta, Deepak K./Grant, John H.: Relationship between type of acquisition, the autonomy given to the acquired firm, and acquisition success – An empirical analysis. In: Journal of Management, Vol. 16, Issue 1, 1990, pp. 29 – 44.

Datta, Deepak K.: Organizational Fit and Acquisition Performance – Effects of Post-Acquisition Integration. In: Strategic Management Journal, Vol. 12, Issue 4, 1991, pp. 281 – 297.

Daum, Jürgen H.: Intangible Assets oder die Kunst, Mehrwert zu schaffen. Bonn 2002.

De Voge, Sylvia/Shiraki, Jeffrey: People Factors – The Missing Link in Merger Success. In: Compensation & Benefits Management, Vol. 16, Issue 1, 2000, pp. 26 – 32.

De Voge, Sylvia/Spreier, Scott: The Soft Realities of Mergers. In: Across the Board, Vol. 36, Issue 10, 1999, pp. 27 – 32.

Deal, Terrence E./Kennedy, Allen A.: Corporate Cultures – The Rites and Rituals of Corporate Life. Reading 1999.

Deering, Anne/Dilts, Robert/Russell, Julian: Alpha Leadership. Chichester 2002.

Deiser, Roland: Post-Acquisition Management – A Process of Strategic and Organisational Learning. In: Krogh, Georg von/Sinatra, Alessandro/Singh, Harbir (Eds.): The Management of Corporate Acquisitions. London et al. 1994, pp. 359 – 390.

Dellmann, Klaus: Kennzahlen und Kennzahlensysteme. In: Küpper, Hans-Ulrich/Wagenhofer, Alfred (Eds.): Handwörterbuch Unternehmensrechnung und Controlling. 4th edition. Stuttgart 2002, pp. 939 – 950.

Deutscher Manager-Verband e.V.: Handbuch soft skills – Band 3: Methodenkompetenz. Zürich, Singen 2003.

Deyhle, Albrecht: Entwicklungstendenzen im Controlling. In: Risak, Johann/Deyhle, Albrecht (Eds.): Controlling – state of the art und Entwicklungstendenzen. Rolf Eschenbach zum 60. Geburtstag. 2nd edition. Wiesbaden 1992, pp. 359 – 385.

DG Bank Deutsche Genossenschaftsbank AG (Ed.): Geschäftsbericht 2000. Frankfurt am Main 2001.

Dickmann, Michael: Aufgaben des HR-Managements bei Mergers & Acquisitions. In: Personalführung, Vol. 35, Issue 5, 2002, pp. 60 – 69.

Dielmann, Klaus: Unternehmenskauf und Human Ressourcen – Due Diligence Prüfung, in: Personal, Vol. 49, Issue 9, 1997, S. 470 – 473.

Donahue, Kristen B.: How to Ruin a Merger – Five People-Management Pitfalls to Avoid. In: Harvard Management Update, Vol. 6, No. 9, 2001, pp. 1 – 4.

Dooley, Kevin J./Zimmermann, Brenda J.: Merger as Marriage – Communication Issues in Post-Merger Integration. Arizona State University. Working Paper. w.Y.

Dr. Wieselhuber und Partner Unternehmensberatung: Veränderungsmanagement – aus der Praxis der Veränderung von Unternehmen. München 2003.

DZ Bank Deutsche Zentral-Genossenschaftsbank AG (Ed.): Geschäftsbericht 2002. Frankfurt am Main 2003.

Eberle, Walter: Die wertneutrale Persönlichkeitseinschätzung – Eine Voraussetzung für die systematische Personalentwicklung. In: Personalführung, Vol. 29, Issue 3, 1996, pp. 220 – 223.

Ebert, Günter: Kennzahlen – Struktur-/Prozesskennzahlen und Bereichskennzahlen auf einen Blick (inkl. Formeln). Landsberg 1999.

Eccles, Robert G./Lanes, Kersten L./Wilson, Thomas C.: Akquisitionen – Häufig viel zu teuer bezahlt. In: Harvard Business Manager, Vol. 22, Issue 2, 2000, pp. 80 – 90.

Eckert, Angelika: Unerkannte Potenziale. In: Personalwirtschaft, Vol. 29, Issue 12, 2002, pp. 23 – 26.

Edvinsson, Leif/Brünig, Gisela: Aktivposten Wissenskapital. Wiesbaden 2000.

Eichhorn, Wolfgang: Die Begriffe Modell und Theorie in der Wirtschaftswissenschaft. In: Raffée/Abel, Bodo (Eds.): Wissenschaftstheoretische Grundfragen der Wirtschaftswissenschaften. München 1979, pp. 60 – 104.

Erpenbeck, John/Rosenstiel, Lutz von: Einführung. In: Erpenbeck, John/Rosenstiel, Lutz von (Eds.): Handbuch Kompetenzmessung – Erkennen, verstehen und bewerten von Kompetenzen in der betrieblichen, pädagogischen und psychologischen Praxis. Stuttgart 2003, pp. IX – XL.

Faix, Werner G./Laier, Angelika: Soziale Kompetenz – Wettbewerbsfaktor der Zukunft. 2nd edition. Wiesbaden 1994.

Fatzer, Gerhard: Unternehmens- oder Organisationskultur als grundlegendes Konzept von Beratung und Veränderungsprozessen. In: profile, Vol. 2, Issue 4, 2002, pp. 49 – 57.

Felder, Rupert: Mergers & Acquisitions – eine Aufgabe für den Personalbereich. In: Personal, Vol. 53, Issue 3, 2001, pp. 156 – 161.

Femppel, Kurt: Das Personalwesen in der deutschen Wirtschaft – eine empirische Untersuchung. München 2000.

Feyerabend, Paul: Wider den Methodenzwang. Frankfurt am Main 2003.

Fisch, Jan Hendrik: Innere Kündigung als Folge einer sich selbsterfüllenden Prophezeiung – Wenn Stewards mit Agents verwechselt werden. In: Zeitschrift für Personalforschung, Vol. 17, Issue 2, 2003, pp. 215 – 223.

Fischer, Heinz/Steffens-Duch, Silvia: Unternehmenskultur bei Akquisitionen und Fusionen. In: Personal, Vol. 53, Issue 1, 2001, pp. 49 – 53.

Fischer, Thomas M./Vielmeyer, Uwe/Wenzel, Julia: Relevanz von mitarbeiterbezogenen Angaben in der Unternehmenspublizität – Empirische Ergebnisse von deutschen börsennotierten Unternehmen. In: Dürndorfer, Martina/Friederichs, Peter (Eds.): Human Capital Leadership – Strategien und Instrumente zur Wertsteigerung der wichtigsten Ressource von Unternehmen. Hamburg 2004, pp. 271 - 286.

Fittkau, Bruno: Kommunikation. In: Sarges, Werner (Ed.): Management-Diagnostik. 3rd edition. Göttingen et al. 2000, pp. 382 – 394.

Flamholtz, Eric G.: Human Resource Accounting. Boston 2001.

Flor, Jan Riis: Georg Edward Moore – Der Verfechter des Common sense. In: Hügli, Anton/Lübcke, Paul (Eds.): Philosophie im 20. Jahrhundert. Band 2 – Wissenschaftstheorie und Analytische Philosophie. Hamburg 1993, pp. 63 – 81.

Frank, Ulrich: Einige Gründe für eine Wiederbelebung der Wissenschaftstheorie. In: Die Betriebswirtschaft, Vol. 63, Issue 3, 2003, pp. 278 – 292.

Frey, Bruno S./Osterloh, Margit: Managing motivation – wie Sie die neue Motivationsforschung für Ihr Unternehmen nutzen können. 2nd edition. Wiesbaden 2002.

Friederichs, Peter: Personal als Change Agent bei Fusionen. In: Personal, Vol. 51, Issue 7, 1999, pp. 336 – 339.

Friedman, Brian S./Hatch, James A./Walker, David M.: Mehr-Wert durch Mitarbeiter – Wie sich Human Capital gewinnen, steigern und halten lässt. Neuwied 1999.

Fuchs, Matthias: Coaching als Instrument zur Integration der Humanressourcen bei Mergers & Acquisitions. Wiesbaden 2001.

Gabriel, Roland/Beier, Dirk: Informationsmanagement in Organisationen. Stuttgart 2003.

Galpin, Timothy J./Herndon, Mark: The Complete Guide to Mergers and Acquisitions – Process Tools to Support M&A Integration at Every Level. New York 2000.

Gaughan, Patrick A.: Mergers, Acquisitions, and Corporate Restructurings. 3rd edition. New York 2002.

Gebauer, Michael: Information systems on human capital in service sector organizations. In: New Library World, Volume 104, Issue 1184/1185, 2003, pp. 33 – 41.

Gebert, Diether: Organisationsstruktur. In: Sarges, Werner (Ed.): Management-Diagnostik. 3rd edition. Göttingen et al. 2000, pp. 156 – 161.

Geiß, Wilfried: Betriebswirtschaftliche Kennzahlen – theoretische Grundlagen einer problemorientierten Kennzahlenanwendung. Frankfurt am Main et al. 1986.

Gerig, Valentin: Kriterien zur Beurteilung unternehmerischen Handelns von Mitarbeitern und Führungskräften. München 1998.

Gerpott, Torsten J.: Abschied von der Spitze. In: Zeitschrift für betriebswirtschaftliche Forschung, Vol. 46, Issue 1, 1994, pp. 4 – 31.

Gerpott, Torsten J.: Integrationsgestaltung und Erfolg von Unternehmensakquisitionen. Stuttgart 1993.

Gethmann, Carl F.: Entdeckungszusammenhang/Begründungszusammenhang. In: Mittelstraß, Jürgen (Ed.): Enzyklopädie Philosophie und Wissenschaftstheorie. Band 1. Stuttgart, Weimar 1996, pp. 549 – 550.

Girod, Bernd/Rabenstein, Rudolf/Stenger, Alexander: Einführung in die Systemtheorie – Signale und Systeme in der Elektrotechnik und Informationstechnik. 2nd edition. Stuttgart et al. 2003.

Glasl, Friedrich: Konfliktmanagement – Ein Handbuch für Führungskräfte und Berater. 6th edition. Bern, Stuttgart 1999.

Gleich, Ronald: Balanced Scorecard. In: Die Betriebswirtschaft, Vol. 57, Issue 3, 1997, pp. 432 – 435.

Gleich, Ronald: Das System des Performance Measurement – Theoretisches Grundkonzept, Entwicklungs- und Anwendungsstand. München 2001.

Gleich, Ronald: Performance Measurement als Controllingaufgabe. In: Gleich, Ronald/Möller, Klaus/Seidenschwarz, Werner/Stoi, Roman: Controllingfortschritte – Prof. Dr. Péter Horváth zum 65. Geburtstag. München 2002, pp. 50 – 75.

Gleich, Ronald: Performance Measurement im Controlling. In: Gleich, Ronald/Seidenschwarz, Werner (Eds.): Die Kunst des Controlling – Prof. Dr. Péter Horváth zum 60. Geburtstag. München 1997, pp. 343 – 366.

Gleich, Ronald: Performance Measurement. In: Die Betriebswirtschaft, Vol. 57, Issue 1, 1997, pp. 114 – 117.

Gmür, Markus/Thommen, Jean-Paul: Human Resource Management. Zürich 2005 (forthcoming).

Godefried, Christoph: ...Kontrolle ist besser – Möglichkeiten und Grenzen der Due Diligence beim Unternehmenskauf. In: Finanzierung, Leasing, Factoring, Vol. 47, Issue 2, 2000, pp. 46 – 51.

Goldberg, Andrew J.: Mergers & Acquisitions Due Diligence – Buyer Beware. In: Corporate Board, Vol. 20, Issue 116, 1999, pp. 18 – 22.

Gomez, Peter/Probst, Gilbert: Die Praxis des ganzheitlichen Problemlösens – Vernetzt denken, Unternehmerisch handeln, Persönlich überzeugen. 2nd edition. Bern et al. 1997.

Graf, Jürgen: Kompetenzentwicklung – Kompetenz geht vor. In: managerSeminare, Vol. 13, Issue 52, 2002, pp. 108 – 114.

Grant, Robert M.: The Resource-Based Theory of Competitive Advantage – Implications for Strategy Formulation. In: California Management Review, Vol. 33, Issue 3, 1991, pp. 114 – 135.

Greengard, Samuel: Due Diligence – The Devil in the Details. In: Workforce, Vol. 78, Issue 10, 1999, pp. 68 – 73.

Große-Oetringhaus, Wigand F.: Sozialkompetenz – ein neues Anspruchsniveau für die Personalpolitik. In: Zeitschrift für betriebswirtschaftliche Forschung, Vol. 45, Issue 3, 1993, pp. 270 – 295.

Gutknecht, John E./Keys, J. Bernard: Mergers, acquisitions and takeovers – maintaining morale of suvivors and protecting employees. In: Academy of Management Executive, Vol. 7, Issue 3, 1993, pp. 26 – 36.

Gut-Villa, Cornelia: Human Resource Management bei Mergers & Acquisitions. Bern 1997.

Gwynne, Peter: Keeping the Right People. In: Sloan Management Review, Vol. 43, Issue 2, 2002, p. 19.

GZ Bank Genossenschafts-Zentralbank AG (Ed.): Geschäftsbericht 2000. Frankfurt am Main/ Stuttgart 2001.

Haleblian, Jerayr/Finkelstein, Sydney: The Influence of Organizational Acquisition Experience on Acquisition Performance – A Behavioral Learning Perspective. In: Administrative Science Quarterly, Vol. 44, Issue 1, 1999, pp. 29 – 56.

Hamel, Gary/Prahalad, C.K.: The Core Competence of the Corporation. Boston 1990.

Hanson, Norwood R.: Patterns of Discovery – An Enquiry into the Conceptual Foundations of Science. Cambridge 1958.

Harrison, Joan: Stay Bonuses – M&As Golden Carrot. In: Mergers & Acqusitions, Vol. 34, Issue 1, 1999, pp. 10 – 12.

Haspeslagh, Philippe C./Jemison, David B.: Akquisitionsmanagement – Wertschöpfung durch strategische Neuausrichtung des Unternehmens. Frankfurt am Main, New York 1992.

Haspeslagh, Philippe C./Jemison, David B.: Managing Acquisitions – Creating Value through Corporate Renewal. New York 1991.

Henkel, Martin: Führungspotential – Typologie der Führungskräfte. In: Personalwirtschaft, Vol. 21, Issue 11, 1994, pp. 28 – 34.

Hentze, Joachim/Kammel, Andreas: Personalwirtschaftslehre 1 – Grundlagen, Personalbedarfsermittlung, -beschaffung, -entwicklung und -einsatz. 7th edition. Bern et al. 2001.

Hilb, Martin: Integriertes Personal-Management – Ziele – Strategien – Instrumente. 10th edition. Neuwied 2002.

Hill, Hermann: Vom Administrator zum Wertschöpfer. In: Personalwirtschaft, Vol. 30, Issue 5, 2003, pp. 16 – 21.

Hitt, Michael A./Bierman, Leonard/Shimizu, Katsuhiko/Kochhar, Rahul: Direct and Moderating Effects of Human Capital on Strategy and Performance in Professional Service Firms – A Resource-Based Perspective. In: Academy of Management Journal, Vol. 44, Issue 1, 2001, pp. 13 – 28.

Hofstede, Gerd: The cultural relativity of organizational practices and theories. In: Journal of International Business Studies, Fall 1983, pp. 75 – 89.

Hogrebe, Wolfram: Eindeutigkeit und indiskrete Ontologie. In: Sukale, Michael (Ed.): Sprache, Theorie und Wirklichkeit. Frankfurt am Main et al. 1990, pp. 151 – 171.

Höher, Friederike/Koall, Iris: Vielfalt als Leitkultur – Kulturentwicklung durch Managing Diversity. In: profile, Vol. 2, Issue 4, 2002, pp. 68 – 78.

Holmes, Len: HRM and the irresistible rise of the discourse of competence. In: Personnel Review, Vol. 24, Issue 4, 1995, pp. 34 – 49.

Homburg, Christian: Kotau vor den Analysten – Fusionen und Akquisitionen zerstören wertvolle Kundenbeziehungen und niemand merkt es. In: managermagazin, Vol. 30, Issue 1, 2000, pp. 80 – 82.

Horváth, Péter/Gleich, Ronald/Voggenreiter, Dietmar: Controlling umsetzen – Fallstudien, Lösungen und Basiswissen. 3rd edition. Stuttgart 2001.

Horváth, Péter/Gleich, Ronald: Controlling als Teil des Risikomanagements. In: Dörner, Dietrich/Horváth, Péter/Kagermann, Henning (Eds.): Praxis des Risikomanagements – Grundlagen, Kategorien, branchenspezifische und strukturelle Aspekte. Stuttgart 2004b, pp. 99 – 126.

Horváth, Péter/Möller, Klaus (Eds.): Intangibles in der Unternehmenssteuerung – Strategien und Instrumente zur Wertsteigerung des immateriellen Kapitals. München 2004a.

Horváth, Péter/Reichmann, Thomas: Vahlens Großes Controlling Lexikon. 2nd edition. München 2003.

Hossiep, Rüdiger: Konsequenzen aus neueren Erkenntnissen zur Potentialbeurteilung. In: Rosenstiel, Lutz von/Lang-von Wins, Thomas (Eds.): Perspektiven der Potentialbeurteilung. Göttingen et al. 2000, pp. 75 – 105.

Howell, Robert A.: Plan to Integrate Your Acquisitions. In: Harvard Business Review, Vol. 48, Issue 6, 1970, pp. 66 – 76.

Huang, Tung-Chun: The effects of linkage between business and human resource management strategies. In: Personnel Review, Vol. 30, Issue 2, 2001, pp. 132 – 151.

Hubner, Ulrich: Die Qualifizierung zum Führen von Mitarbeitern als betriebspädagogisches Problem. München 1985.

Huczynski, Andrzej/Buchanan, David A.: Organizational Behaviour – An Introductory Text. 4th edition. Harlow 2001.

Huffcutt, Allen I./Arthur, Winfried: Hunter and Hunter (1984) Revised – Interview Validity for Entry-Level Jobs. In: Journal of Applied Psychology, Vol. 79, No. 2, 1994, pp. 184 – 190.

Hunt, John W./Downing, Stephen: Mergers, acquisitions and human resource management, In: International Journal of Human Resource Management, Vol. 1, Issue 2, 1990, pp. 195 – 209.

Hunt, John W./Lees, Stan/Grumbar, John J./Vivian, Philip D.: Acquisitions – The Human Factor. London 1987.

Ioannis, Tsaousis/Ioannis, Nikolaou, E.: The Stability of the Five-Factor Model of Pesonality in Personnel Selection and Assessment in Greece. In: International Journal of Selection and Assessment, Vol. 9, No. 4, 2001, pp. 290 – 301.

Itami, Hiroyuki: Mobilizing Invisible Assets. Boston 1987.

Ivancevich, John M./Schweiger, David M./Power, Frank R.: Strategies for Managing Human Resources During Mergers and Acquisitions. In: Human Resource Planning, Vol. 10, Issue 1, 1987, pp. 19 – 35.

Ivancevich, John M./Stewart, Kim A.: Appraising management talent in acquired organizations – A four-tiered recommendation. In: Human Resource Planning, Vol. 12, Issue 2, 1989, pp. 141 – 154.

Jaeger, Michael: Personalmanagement bei Mergers & Acquisitions: Strategien – Instrumente – Erfolgsfaktoren. Neuwied 2001.

Jaensch, Günter: Unternehmensbewertung bei Akquisitionen in den USA. In: Colbe, Walther Busse von/Coenenberg, Alfred G. (Eds.): Unternehmensakquisitionen und Unternehmensbewertung – Grundlagen und Fallstudien. Stuttgart 1992.

Jansen, Stephan A./Pohlmann, Niko: Anforderungen und Zumutungen – Das HR Management bei Fusionen. In: Personalführung, Vol. 33, Issue 2, 2000, pp. 30 – 39.

Jansen, Stephan A.: Die 7 K's des Merger-Managements. In: Zeitschrift für Führung und Organisation, Vol. 71, Issue 1, 2002, pp. 6 – 13.

Jansen, Stephan A.: Mergers & Acquisitions – Unternehmensakquisitionen und -kooperationen – Eine strategische, organisatorische und kapitalmarkttheoretische Einführung. 4th edition. Wiesbaden 2001.

Jemison, David B./Sitkin, Sim B.: Corporate acquisitions – A process perspective. In: Academy of Management Review, Vol. 11, Issue 1, 1986, pp. 145 – 163.

Jetter, Wolfgang: Effiziente Personalauswahl. Stuttgart 1996.

Jochmann, Walter: Schlüsselgröße für Unternehmenserfolg. In: Unternehmer-Magazin, Vol. 48, Issue 4, 1999, pp. 18 – 21.

Johanson, Ulf: Why the concept of human resource costing and accounting does not work – A lesson from seven Swedish cases. In: Personnel Review, Vol. 28, Issue 1/2, 1999, pp. 91 – 107.

Jungermann, Helmut: Entscheiden. In: Sarges, Werner (Ed.): Management-Diagnostik. 3rd edition. Göttingen et al. 2000, pp. 247 – 253.

Kaiser, Arnim: Grundlagen der Weiterbildung – Schlüsselqualifikationen in der Arbeitnehmer-Weiterbildung. Neuwied 1992.

Kaiser, Stephan: Entwicklung von Humanressourcen – Eine ressourcen- und lernorientierte Perspektive. Wiesbaden 2001.

Kalpaka, Annita: Interkulturelle Kompetenz – Kompetentes sozialpädagogisches Handeln in der Einwanderungsgesellschaft. In: Zeitschrift für Migration und Soziale Arbeit, 1998, pp. 589 – 614.

Kalra, Satish Kumar: Human potential management – time to move beyond the concept of human resource management? In: Journal of European Industrial Training, Vol. 21, Issue 5, 1997, pp. 176 – 180.

Kane, Bob/Crawford, John/Grant, David: Barriers to effective HRM. In: International Journal of Manpower, Vol. 20, Issue 8, 1999, pp. 494 – 515.

Kanning, Uwe Peter/Walter, Manuela: Systematisches Training sozialer Kompetenzen, in: Personalführung, 4/2003, pp. 38 – 42.

Kanning, Uwe Peter: Grundlagen psychologischer Diagnostik. In: Kanning, Uwe Peter/ Holling, Heinz (Eds.): Handbuch personaldiagnostischer Instrumente. Göttingen et al. 2002, pp. 47 – 92.

Kanning, Uwe Peter: Soziale Kompetenz – Definition, Strukturen und Prozesse. In: Kanning, Uwe Peter (Ed.): Themenheft Soziale Kompetenz. In: Zeitschrift für Psychologie – mit Zeitschrift für angewandte Psychologie, Vol. 113, Issue 4, 2002, pp. 154 – 163.

Kanning, Uwe Peter: Soziale Kompetenz. In: Wenninger, Gerd (Ed.): Lexikon der Psychologie – Band 4. Heidelberg 2001, p. 197.

Kaplan, Robert S./Norton, David P.: Balanced Scorecard – Strategien erfolgreich umsetzen. Stuttgart 1997.

Kaplan, Robert S./Norton, David P.: Die strategiefokussierte Organisation – Führen mit der Balanced Scoredcard. Stuttgart 2001.

Karlins, Marvin: The Human Use of Human Resources. Columbus 1981.

Kast, Rudolf/Wucknitz, Uwe D.: Konzeption und Einsatz einer HR Due-Diligence. In: Personalführung, Vol. 35, Issue 9, 2002, pp. 48 – 53.

Katz, David M.: HR Managers Can Help Cut Merger Losses. In: National Underwriter, Property & Casualty/Risk & Benefits, Vol. 104, Issue 32, 2000, pp. 3 – 5.

Katz, Robert L.: Skills of an Effective Administrator. In: Harvard Business Review, Vol. 52, Issue 10, 1974, pp. 90 – 102.

Kauffeld, Simon/Grote, Sven/Frieling, Ekkehart: Das Kassler-Kompetenz-Raster. In: Erpenbeck, John/von Rosenstiel, Lutz (Eds.): Handbuch Kompetenzmessung – Erkennen, verstehen und bewerten von Kompetenzen in der betrieblichen, pädagogischen und psychologischen Praxis. Stuttgart 2003, pp. 261 – 282.

Kay, Ira T./Shelton, Mike: The people problem in mergers. In: The McKinsey Quarterly, Vol. 37, Issue 4, 2000, pp. 27 – 37.

Kempf, Wilhelm: Soziales Lernen. In: Frey, Dieter/Greif, Siegfried (Eds.): Sozialpsychologie – Ein Handbuch in Schlüsselbegriffen. Weinheim 1987, pp. 326 – 329.

Kerr, Christine: Human resourcing following a merger. In: The International Journal of Career Management, Vol. 7, Issue 2, 1995, pp. 7 – 9.

Kerr, Jeffrey L./Slocum, John W.: Managing Corporate Culture Through Reward Systems. In: Academy of Management Executive, Vol. 1, Issue, 2, 1987, pp. 99 – 108.

Kirsch, Werner: Wegweiser zur Konstruktion einer evolutionären Theorie der strategischen Führung – Kapitel eines Theorieprojektes. 2nd edition. München 1997.

Kittner, Michael: "Human Resources" in der Unternehmensbewertung. In: Der Betrieb, Vol. 50, Issue 46, 1997, pp. 2285 – 2290.

Kleinmann, Martin: Assessment-Center – Stand der Forschung, Konsequenzen für die Praxis. Göttingen 1997.

Klimecki, Rüdiger G./Gmür, Markus: Personalmanagement – Strategien, Erfolgsbeiträge, Entwicklungsperspektiven. 2nd edition. Stuttgart 2001.

Klingebiel, Norbert: Integriertes Performance Measurement. Wiesbaden 2000.

Klingebiel, Norbert: Performance measurement – Grundlagen, Ansätze, Fallstudien. Wiesbaden 1999.

Knebel, Heinz: Der Engpassfaktor „Mensch“ – Erfahrungen mit Personalbeurteilungen in der Praxis. In: Personal, Vol. 55, Issue 9, 2003, pp. 12 – 15.

Kobi, Jean-Marcel/Eversberg, Horst: Personalrisikomanagement – eine neue Dimension im Human Resource Management – Strategien zur Steigerung des People Value. Wiesbaden 1999.

Kobi, Jean-Marcel: Human Resources im kulturellen und strategischen Kontext. Bern 1990.

Koch, Tomas: Koordination von Integrationen. In: M&A Review, Vol. 12, Issue 2, 2001, pp. 163 – 173.

Köhler-Braun, Katharina: Unternehmenskultur und Human Resource Management. In: Personal, Vol. 52, Issue 1, 2000, pp. 28 – 33.

Krause, Detlef: Luhmann-Lexikon – Eine Einführung in das Gesamtwerk von Niklas Luhmann. 3rd edition. Stuttgart 2001.

Krieger, David J.: Einführung in die allgemeine Systemtheorie. München 1996.

Kriegesmann, Bernd: Lernen in Organisationen – oder lernende Organisatoren? – Individuelle Kompetenz zur Innovation setzt organisationale Lernprozesse und komplexe Systemtransformationen voraus. In: Personalführung, Vol. 36, Issue 4, 2003, pp. 18 – 27.

Kriz, Willy Christian: Lernziel Systemkompetenz – Planspiele als Trainingsmethode. Göttingen 2000.

Kromrey, Helmut: Empirische Sozialforschung – Modelle und Methoden der Datenerhebung und Datenauswertung. 8th edition. Opladen 1998.

Krüger, Wilfried: Das 3W-Modell – Bezugsrahmen für das Wandlungsmanagement. In: Krüger, Wilfried (Ed.): Excellence in Change – Wege zur strategischen Erneuerung. Wiesbaden 2000, pp. 15 – 30.

Kuhn, Thomas S.: Die Struktur wissenschaftlicher Revolutionen. Frankfurt am Main 2003.

Lajoux, Alexandra Reed/Elson, Charles M.: The Art of M&A Due Diligence – Navigating Critical Steps and Uncovering Crucial Data. New York 2000.

Lajoux, Alexandra Reed: The Art of M&A Integration – A Guide to Merging Resources, Processes and Responsibilities. New York 1998.

Lamnek, Siegfried: Qualitative Sozialforschung. Band 2 – Methoden und Techniken. Weinheim 1995.

Lang, Karl: Bildungs-Controlling – Personalentwicklung effizient planen, steuern und kontrollieren. Wien 2000.

Lang, Rudolf W.: Schlüsselqualifikationen – Handlungs- und Methodenkompetenz, Personal und Soziale Kompetenz. München 2000.

Larsson, Rikard/Finkelstein, Sydney: Integrating strategic, organizational, and human resource perspectives on mergers and acquisitions – A case survey of synergy realisation. In: Organization Science, Vol. 10, Issue 1, 1999, pp. 1 – 26.

Lawrence, Paul R.: How to Deal with Resistance to Change. In: Harvard Business Review, Vol. 32, Issue 3, 1954, pp. 49 – 57.

Leibold, Marius/Probst, Gilbert J. B./Gibbert, Michael: Strategic Management in the Knowledge Economy – New Approaches and Business Applications. Erlangen 2002.

Lev, Baruch/Daum, Jürgen H.: Intangible Assets – Neue Ansätze für Unternehmenssteuerung und Berichtswesen. In: Horváth, Péter/Gleich, Ronald (Eds.): Neugestaltung der Unternehmensplanung – Innovative Konzepte und erfolgreiche Praxislösungen. Stuttgart 2003, pp. 33 – 50.

Lichtsteiner, René A.: Meßgrößen zur strategischen Führung im Personalmanagement. In: Klimecki, Rüdiger G./Remer, Andreas (Eds.): Personal als Strategie – mit flexiblen und lernbereiten Human-Ressourcen Kernkompetenzen aufbauen. Neuwied et al. 1997.

Lickert, Stephan: Unternehmenszusammenschlüsse – Konsequenzen für das Humankapital. Bern et al. 2000.

Liepmann, Detlev/König, Ferdinand/Stübig, Jacob: Innovation und Innovationsmanagement als kreative Konzepte. In: Marggraf, Claudia (Ed.): Soziale Kompetenz und Innovation. Frankfurt am Main et al. 1995, pp. 137 – 163.

Lubatkin, Michael/Schweiger, David M./Weber, Yaakov: Top Management Turnover in Related M&A's – An Additional Test of the Theory of Relative Standing. In: Journal of Management, Vol. 25, Issue 1, 1999, pp. 55 – 73.

Lucks, Kai/Meckl, Reinhard: Strukturierung von M&A Projekten – Der prozessorientierte Ansatz. In: M&A Review, Vol. 13, Issue 10, 2002, pp. 494 – 499.

Lüdi, Markus/Eicken, Sabine: Anforderungen und Rahmenbedingungen des Personalmanagements im Rahmen der Post-Merger Integration (I). In: M&A Review, Vol. 11, Issue 1, 2000a, pp. 11 – 15.

Lüdi, Markus/Eicken, Sabine: Strategien und Massnahmen der UBS-Personalfunktion im Rahmen der Post-Merger Integration (II). In: M&A Review, Vol. 11, Issue 2, 2000b, pp. 55 – 61.

Luhmann, Niklas: Soziale Systeme – Grundriß einer allgemeinen Theorie. Frankfurt am Main 1984.

Luoma, Mikko: Investigating the link between strategy and HRD. In: Personnel Review, Vol. 29, Issue 6, 2000, pp. 769 – 790.

Mace, Myles L./Montgomery, George G.: Management Problems of Corporate Acquisitions. Boston 1962.

Manteufel, Andreas/Schiepek, Günter: Systemspiele und Systemkompetenz – Ein Beitrag zu systemtheoretisch begründeter Praxis. In: Systhema, Vol. 7, Issue 3, 1993, pp. 19 – 27.

Marggraf, Claudia: Teamkompetenz – Ein Qualifikationsziel der Berufsausbildung. In: Marggraf, Claudia (Ed.): Soziale Kompetenz und Innovation. Frankfurt am Main et al. 1995, pp. 11 – 103.

Marks, Mitchell Lee/Mirvin, Philip H.: Rebuilding After the Merger – Dealing with „Survivor Sickness". In: Organizational Dynamics, Vol. 21, Issue 2, 1992, pp. 18 – 32.

Marks, Mitchell Lee/Mirvis, Philip H.: Merger Syndrome: Stress and Uncertainty – Part I. In: Mergers and Acquistions, Vol. 20, Issue 2, 1985, pp. 50 – 55.

Marten, Kai-Uwe/Köhler, Annette G.: Due Diligence in Deutschland – Eine empirische Untersuchung. In: Finanz Betrieb, Vol. 1, Issue 11, 1999, pp. 337 – 348.

Mary, Michael/Nordholt, Henny: Change – Lust auf Veränderung. Bergisch Gladbach 2004.

Mayerhofer, Helene: Personal als Deal-Breaker? – Aufgaben des Personalmanagements im M&A Prozess: Due Diligence Review für Human Ressourcen. In: Zeitschrift für Führung und Organisation, Vol. 71, Issue 2, 2002, pp. 68 – 74.

Mayring, Philipp: Qualitative Inhaltsanalyse. In: Jüttemann, G. (Ed.): Qualitative Forschung in der Psychologie. Heidelberg 1989, pp. 187 – 211.

Mayrshofer, Daniela/Kröger, Hubertus A.: Prozeßkompetenz in der Projektarbeit – ein Handbuch für Projektleiter, Prozeßbegleiter und Berater. 2nd edition. Hamburg 2001.

Mc Leod, Douglas: HR Managers can be crucial for successful mergers. In: Business Insurance, Vol. 35, Issue 28, 2001, pp. 6 – 7.

McKay, Jim/Qureshi, Imran: Getting a head start on the deal's people issues. In: Mergers & Acquisitions – The Dealmaker's Journal. Vol. 36, Issue 7, pp. 33 – 38.

Meinefeld, Werner: Realität und Konstruktion. Erkenntnistheoretische Grundlagen einer Methodologie der empirischen Sozialforschung. Opladen 1995.

Meyer, Claus: Betriebswirtschaftliche Kennzahlen und Kennzahlen-Systeme. 2nd edition. Stuttgart 1994.

Meyer, Roswitha: Entscheidungstheorie – ein Lehr- und Arbeitsbuch. 2nd edition. Wiesbaden 2000.

Milgrom, Paul/Roberts, John: The Economics of Organisation and Management. Englewood Cliffs 1992.

Milling, Peter: Kybernetische Überlegungen beim Entscheiden in komplexen Systemen. In: Milling, Peter (Ed.): Entscheiden in komplexen Systemen. Wissenschaftliche Jahrestagung der Gesellschaft für Wirtschafts- und Sozialkybernetik vom 29. und 30. September 2000 in Mannheim – Band 20: Wirtschaftskybernetik und Systemanalyse. Berlin 2002, pp. 11 – 26.

Mirvis, Philip H.: Negotiations after the sale – The roots and ramifications of conflict in an acquisition. In: Journal of Occupational Behaviour, Vol. 6, Issue 1, 1985, pp. 65 – 84.

Mittelstraß, Jürgen: Das Maß des Fortschritts – Mensch und Wissenschaft in der Leonardo-Welt. In: Frankfurter Allgemeine Zeitung. No. 26, 31 January 2002, w.p.

Müller, Burkhard: Vermittlung von Methodenkompetenz für kaufmännisch-administrative Tätigkeiten – kognitives Training mit Hilfe heuristischer Regeln. München 1995.

Müller, Werner R.: Welche Welten sollen gelten? – oder: Was ist der Mitarbeiter wert? In: Bruhn, Manfred (Ed.): Wertorientierte Unternehmensführung – Perspektiven und Handlungsfelder für die Wertsteigerung von Unternehmen. Wiesbaden 1998, pp. 231 –249.

Müller-Böling, Detlef/Klandt, Heinz: Methoden empirischer Wirtschafts- und Sozialforschung – eine Einführung mit wirtschaftswissenschaftlichem Schwerpunkt. 3rd edition. Köln, Dortmund 1996.

Müller-Stewens, Günter/Frankenberger, Sebastian: Nicht ohne die Mitarbeiter. In: Personal, Vol. 56, Issue 4, 2004, pp. 34 – 38.

Müller-Stewens, Günter/Lechner, Christoph: Strategisches Management – wie strategische Initiativen zum Wandel führen. 2nd edition. Stuttgart 2003.

Müller-Stewens, Günter/Spickers, Jürgen: Akquisitionsmanagement. In: Die Betriebswirtschaft, Vol. 54, Issue 5, 1994, pp. 663 – 678.

Müller-Stewens, Günther: Personalwirtschaftliche und organisationstheoretische Problemfelder bei Mergers & Acquisitions. In: Ackermann, Karl-Friedrich/Scholz, Hartmut (Eds.): Personalmanagement für die 90er Jahre. Stuttgart 1991, pp. 157 – 171.

Nahavandi, Afsaneh/Malekzadeh, Ali R.: Acculturation in Mergers and Acquisitions. In: Academy of Management Review, Vol. 13, Issue 1, 1988, pp. 79 – 90.

Nahavandi, Afsaneh/Malekzadeh, Ali R.: Successful Mergers through Acculturation. In: Krogh, Georg von/Sinatra, Alessandro/Singh, Harbir (Eds.): The Management of Corporate Acquisitions. London et al. 1994, pp. 293 – 306.

Napier, Nancy K.: Mergers & Acquisitions, Human Resource Issues and Outcomes – A Review and Suggested Typology. In: Journal of Management Studies, Vol. 26, Issue 3, 1989, pp. 271 – 289.

Neuberger, Oswald: Führen und führen lassen – Ansätze, Ergebnisse und Kritik der Führungsforschung. 6th edition. Stuttgart 2002.

Neuberger, Oswald: Unternehmenskultur. In: Sarges, Werner (Ed.): Management-Diagnostik. 3rd edition. Göttingen et al. 1995, pp. 162 – 165.

Neumann, Petra/Rumpf, Bernd-Michael: Kritische Erfolgsfaktoren von Post-Merger-Integrationen. In: M&A Review, Vol. 9, Issue 2, 1998, pp. 57 – 62.

Nonaka, Ikujiro/Toyann, Ryoko/Nagata, Akiya: A Firm as a Knowledge-Creating Entity – A New Perspective on the Theory of the Firm. In: Industrial and Corporate Change, Vol. 9, Issue 1, 2000, pp. 1 – 20.

Olbrich, Michael: Unternehmenskultur und Unternehmenswert. Wiesbaden 1999.

Ortwig, Harald: Grundlagen betrieblicher Sozialkompetenz – für Berufseinsteiger, Fachkräfte und Führungsnachwuchs. Aachen 2002.

Osterloh, Margit/Frost, Jetta: Prozessmanagement als Kernkompetenz – Wie Sie Business Reengineering strategisch nutzen können. 4th edition. Wiesbaden 2003.

Overton, Bruce B.: Mergers and Other Restructurings – The Compensation and Benefits Issues. In: Compensation & Benefits Review, Vol. 23, Issue 4, 1991, pp. 39 – 45.

Pablo, Amy: Determinants of Acquisition Integration Level – A Decision-Making Perspective, In: Academy of Management Journal, Vol. 37, Issue 4, 1994, pp. 803 – 836.

Pack, Heinrich: Due Diligence. In: Picot, Gerhard (Ed.): Handbuch Mergers & Acquisitions – Planung, Durchführung, Integration. 2nd edition. Stuttgart 2002, pp. 221 – 253.

Papmehl, André: Personal-Controlling – Human-Ressourcen effektiv entwickeln. 2nd edition. Heidelberg 1990.

Persch, Peter-Roman: Die Bewertung von Humankapital – eine kritische Analyse. München, Mering 2003.

Pfahler, Thomas: Humankapital und Effizienz. Bern 2000.

Pfeffer, Jeffrey: Competitive advantage through people. Boston 1994.

Pfützner, Robert: Kooperativ führen – eine Führungslehre für Vorgesetzte. 6th edition. Köln 1994.

Pichler, Martin: Wen fördern, wen nicht? In: wirtschaft & weiterbildung, Vol. 13, Issue 5, 2001, pp. 16 – 21.

Picot, Gerhard: Wirtschaftliche und wirtschaftsrechtliche Parameter bei der Planung von Mergers & Acquisitions. In: Picot, Gerhard (Ed.): Handbuch Mergers & Acquisitions – Planung, Durchführung, Integration. 2nd edition. Stuttgart 2002, pp. 3 – 32.

Pöck, Thomas: Organisatorische Voraussetzungen erfolgreicher Wertschöpfungspartnerschaften – Dargestellt am Beispiel der Automobilindustrie. Wiesbaden 2002.

Pollack, Walter/Pirk, Dieter: Personalentwicklung in lernenden Organisationen – Konzepte, Beispiele, Übungen. Wiesbaden 2001.

Prim, Rolf/Tilmann, Heribert: Grundlagen einer kritisch-rationalen Sozialwissenschaft. Studienbuch zur Wissenschaftstheorie Karl Poppers. 8th edition. Wiebelsheim 2000.

Pritchett, Price: After the Merger – Managing the Shockwaves. Dallas 1985, pp. 13 – 15.

Probst, Gilbert J.B./Deussen, Arne/Eppler, Martin J./Raub, Steffen P.: Kompetenz-Management – Wie Individuen und Organisationen Kompetenz entwickeln. Wiesbaden 2000.

Pümpin, Cuno: Unternehmenskultur, Unternehmensstrategie und Unternehmenserfolg. In: Allgemeine Treuhand AG (Ed.): Die Bedeutung der Unternehmenskultur für den künftigen Erfolg ihres Unternehmens. Zürich 1984, pp. 11 – 26.

Putz-Osterloh, Wiebke: Problemlösen. In: Sarges, Werner (Ed.): Management-Diagnostik. 3rd edition. Göttingen et al. 2000, pp. 240 – 246.

Raffée, Hans: Grundprobleme der Betriebswirtschaftslehre. 9th edition. Göttingen 1995.

Ranft, Annette L./Lord, Michael D.: Acquiring New Knowledge – The Role of Retaining Human Capital in Acquisitions of High-Tech Firms. In: The Journal of High Technology Management Research, Vol. 11, Issue 2, 2000, pp. 295 – 319.

Redman, Tom/Mathews, Brian P.: Service quality and human resource management – A review and research agenda. In: Personnel Review, Vol. 27, Issue 1, 1998, pp. 57 – 77.

Reetz, Lothar: Zur Bedeutung der Schlüsselqualifikationen in der Berufsausbildung, in: Reetz, Lothar/Reitmann, Thomas (Eds.): Schlüsselqualifikationen – Fachwissen in der Krise? Hamburg 1990, pp. 16 – 35.

Reichenbach, Hans: Experience and Prediction – An Analysis of the Foundations and the Structure of Knowledge. Chicago, London 1938, 1966, § 1.

Reichmann, Thomas/Lachnit, Laurenz: Planung, Steuerung und Kontrolle mit Hilfe von Kennzahlen. In: Zeitschrift für betriebswirtschaftliche Forschung, Vol. 28, Issue 5, 1976, pp. 705 – 723.

Reichmann, Thomas: Controlling mit Kennzahlen und Managementberichten. In: Freidank, Carl-Christian/Mayer, Elmar (Eds.): Controlling-Konzepte – Neue Strategien und Werkzeuge für die Unternehmenspraxis. 6th edition. Wiesbaden 2003, pp. 5 – 30.

Reilly, Richard R./Chao, Georgia T.: Validity and Fairness of Some Alternative Employee Selection Procedures. In: Personnel Psychology, Vol. 35, Issue 1, 1982, pp. 1 – 64.

Reither, Frank: Komplexitätsmanagement – Denken und Handeln in komplexen Situationen. München 1997.

Remer, Andreas: Personal und Management im Wandel der Strategien. In: Klimecki, Rüdiger G./Remer, Andreas (Eds.): Personal als Strategie – Mit flexiblen und lernbereiten Human-Ressourcen Kernkompetenzen aufbauen. Neuwied 1997, pp. 399 – 417.

Ridder, Hans-Gerd: Personalwirtschaftslehre. Stuttgart et al. 1999.

Riedl, Joachim: Strategie und Personal – Ansätze zur Personalorientierung der strategischen Unternehmensführung. Wiesbaden 1995.

Risberg, Anette: Employee Experiences of Acquisition Processes. In: Journal of World Business, Vol. 36, Issue 1, 2001, pp. 58 – 84.

Robbins, Stephen: Organizational Behavior. 10th edition. New Jersey 2003.

Rockholtz, Carsten: Marktwertorientiertes Akquisitionsmanagement – Due Diligence-Konzeption zur Identifikation, Beurteilung und Realisation akquisitionsbedingter Synergiepotentiale. Frankfurt 1998.

Rohleder, Claus D.: Vision & Leadership – Ein Beispiel für ein Cultural Change-Programm. In: Kienbaum, Jochen (Ed.): Visionäres Personalmanagement. 3rd edition. Stuttgart 2001, pp. 105 – 114.

Rosenstiel, Lutz von: Grundlagen der Organisationspsychologie – Basiswissen und Anwendungshinweise. 5th edition. Stuttgart 2003.

Rosenstiel, Lutz von: Motivation im Betrieb – mit Fallstudien aus der Praxis. 10th edition. Leonberg 2001.

Rüegg-Stürm, Johannes: Das neue St. Galler Management-Modell – Grundkategorien einer integrierten Managementlehre. 2nd edition. Bern, Stuttgart, Wien 2003.

Rühli, Edwin: Unternehmungsführung und Unternehmungspolitik. Band 1. 3rd edition. Bern, Stuttgart, Wien 1996.

Rummler, Geary A./Brache, Alan P.: Improving Performance – How to Manage the White Space on the Organization Chart. 2nd edition. San Francisco 1995.

Sachs, Sybille/Hauser, Andrea: Das ABC der betriebswirtschaftlichen Forschung – Anleitung zum wissenschaftlichen Arbeiten. Zürich 2002.

Sackmann, Sonja A.: Unternehmenskultur – Analysieren, Entwickeln, Verändern. Neuwied 2002.

Salecker, Jürgen: Der Kommunikationsauftrag von Unternehmen bei Mergers & Acquisitions – Problemdimensionen und Gestaltungsoptionen der Kommunikation bei Unternehmensübernahmen. Bern 1995.

Sales, Amy/Mirvis, Philip H.: When cultures collide – Issues in acquisition. In: Kimberly, John/Quinn, Robert E. (Eds.): New Futures – The Challenge of Managing Corporate Transitions. Homewood 1984, pp. 107 – 133.

Sandler, Guido G.: Synergie – Konzept, Messung und Realisation. Verdeutlicht am Beispiel der horizontalen Diversifikation durch Akquisitionen. St. Gallen 1991.

Sandt, Joachim/Schäffer, Utz/Weber, Jürgen: Balanced Performance Measurement Systems and Manager Satisfaction – Empirical Evidence from a German Study. Vallendar 2001.

Sarges, Werner/Wottowa, Heinrich: Testverfahren im HR-Management – Einführung. In: Sarges, Werner/Wottowa, Heinrich (Eds.): Handbuch wirtschaftspsychologischer Testverfahren. Lengerich et al. 2001, pp. VII – XII.

Sarges, Werner: Diagnose von Managementpotential für eine sich immer schneller und unvorhersehbarer ändernde Wirtschaftswelt. In: Rosenstiel, Lutz von/Lang-von Wins, Thomas: Perspektiven der Potentialbeurteilung. Göttingen et al. 2000, pp. 107 – 128.

Sarges, Werner: Eignungsdiagnostische Überlegungen für den Managementbereich. In: Sarges, Werner (Ed.): Management-Diagnostik. 3rd edition. Göttingen et al. 2000, pp. 1 – 21.

Sattelberger, Thomas (Ed.): Humankapital schafft Shareholder Value – Personalpolitik in wissensbasierten Unternehmen. Köln 1999.

Sauermann, Sabine: Organisatorische Gestaltungsalternativen eines unternehmensinternen M&A Managements, Wiesbaden 2000.

Schäfer, Anita: Bewertung intellektuellen Kapitals. Osnabrück 2001.

Schäffer, Utz/Weber, Jürgen: Erfolg durch Kontrolle. Vallendar 2002.

Schäffer, Utz: Kontrolle als Lernprozess. Wiesbaden 2001.

Schäffer, Utz: Strategische Steuerung mit der Balanced Scorecard. In: Freidank, Carl-Christian/Mayer, Elmar (Eds.): Controlling-Konzepte – Neue Strategien und Werkzeuge für die Unternehmenspraxis. 6th edition. Wiesbaden 2003, pp. 487 – 516.

Schein, Edgar H.: Coming to a New Awareness of Organizational Culture. In: Sloan Management Review, Vol. 25, Issue 2, 1984, pp. 3 – 16.

Schein, Edgar H.: Organizational Culture and Leadership. San Francisco, London 1986.

Schein, Edgar H.: The Art of managing human resources. Oxford et al. 1987.

Schein, Edgar H.: Unternehmenskultur. Frankfurt am Main 1995.

Scherer, Andreas Georg: Kritik der Organisation oder Organisation der Kritik? – Wissenschaftstheoretische Bemerkungen zum kritischen Umgang mit Organisationstheorien. Kieser, Alfred (Ed.): Organisationstheorien. 5th edition. Stuttgart et al. 2002, pp. 1 – 37.

Schiepek, Günter: Ausbildungsziel Systemkompetenz. In: Reiter, Ludwig (Ed.): Von der Familientherapie zur systemischen Perspektive. 2nd edition. Berlin 1997, pp. 181 – 215.

Schlieper-Damrich, Rolf: Integration verlangt Führung – Thesen zu "Merger-Fähigkeit". In: Personalführung, Vol. 33, Issue 2, 2000, pp. 40 – 42.

Schmeisser, Wilhelm: Due Diligence-Prüfung im Personal-Controlling. In: Personalwirtschaft, Vol. 26, Issue 6, 1999, pp. 50 – 56.

Schmidt, Frank L./Hunter, John E.: Meßbare Personmerkmale – Stabilität, Variabilität und Validität zur Vorhersage zukünftiger Berufsleistung und berufsbezogenen Lernens. In: Kleinmann, Martin/Strauß, Bernd (Eds.): Potentialfeststellung und Personalentwicklung. 2nd edition. Göttingen et al. 2000, pp. 15 – 43.

Schmidt, Frank L./Hunter, John E.: The Validity and Utility of Selection Methods in Personnel Psychology – Practical and Theoretical Implications of 85 Years of Research Findings. In: Psychological Bulletin, Vol. 124, Issue. 2, 1998, pp. 262 – 274.

Schmidt, Herbert: Humanvermögensrechnung – Instrumentarium zur Ergänzung der unternehmerischen Rechnungslegung – Konzepte und Erfahrungen. Berlin 1982.

Schmidt, Sascha L./Schettler, Marc A.: Ziele von Unternehmenszusammenschlüssen. In: Zeitschrift für Führung und Organisation, Vol. 68, Issue 6, 1999, pp. 312 – 317.

Schmitz, Winfried F.: Due Diligence for Corporate Acquisitions. London 1996.

Schneider, Helmut: Das aktuelle Stichwort – Kompetenzen. In: Personalwirtschaft, Vol. 19, Issue 9, 1992, p. 51.

Schnell, Rainer/Hill, Paul B./Esser, Elke: Methoden der empirischen Sozialforschung. 6th edition. München, Wien 1999.

Scholz, Christian (Ed.): Innovative Personalorganisation – Center-Modelle für Wertschöpfung, Strategie, Intelligenz und Virtualisierung. Neuwied 1999.

Scholz, Christian/Stein, Volker/Bechtel, Roman: Human Capital Management – Wege aus der Unverbindlichkeit. München 2004.

Scholz, Christian: Personalmanagement – informationsorientierte und verhaltenstheoretische Grundlagen. 5th edition. München 2000.

Schomann, Marc: Wissensorientiertes Performance Measurement. Wiesbaden 2001.

Schreier, Claus: Kulturelle Integration grenzüberschreitender Akquisitionen. Osnabrück 2001.

Schreyögg, Georg: Organisation – Grundlagen moderner Organisationsgestaltung. 4th edition. Wiesbaden 2003.

Schuler, Heinz/Barthelme, Dorothea: Soziale Kompetenz als berufliche Anforderung. In: Seyfried, Brigitte (Ed.): Stolperstein Sozialkompetenz – Was macht es so schwierig sie zu erfassen, zu fördern und zu beurteilen? Berichte zur beruflichen Bildung – Band 179. Bielefeld 1995, pp. 77 – 116.

Schuler, Heinz/Funke, Uwe (Eds.): Eignungsdiagnostik in Forschung und Praxis – psychologische Information für Auswahl, Beratung und Förderung von Mitarbeitern. Stuttgart 1991.

Schuler, Heinz: Das Rätsel der Merkmals-Methoden-Effekte – Was ist „Potential" und wie lässt es sich messen? In: Rosenstiel, Lutz von/Lang-von Wins, Thomas (Eds.): Perspektiven der Potentialbeurteilung. Göttingen et al. 2000, pp. 53 – 71.

Schuler, Heinz: Organisationspsychologie – Grundlagen und Personalpsychologie. Göttingen et al. 2004.

Schuler, Randall S./Jackson, Susan E.: HR Issues and Activities in Mergers and Acquisitions. In: European Management Journal, Vol. 19, Issue 3, 2001, pp. 239 – 253.

Schulte, Christof: Personal-Controlling mit Kennzahlen. 2nd edition. München 2002.

Schulte, Karl Werner: Investition und Besteuerung. Institut für Finanzmanagement an der EUROPEAN BUSINESS SCHOOL. Oestrich-Winkel w.y.

Schweiger, David M./De Nisi, Angelo S.: Communication with employees following a merger – A longitudinal field experiment. In: Academy of Management Journal, Vol. 34, Issue 1, 1991, pp. 110 – 135.

Schweiger, David M./Ivancevich, John M./Power, Frank R.: Executive Actions For Managing Human Resources Before and After Acquisition. In: Academy of Management Executive, Vol. 1, Issue 2, 1987, pp. 127 – 138.

Schweiger, David M./Ivancevich, John M.: Human Resources – The Forgotten Factor in Mergers and Acquisitions. In: Personnel Administrator, Vol. 30, Issue 11, 1985, pp. 47 – 61.

Schweiger, David M./Walsh, James P.: Mergers and acquisitions – An interdisciplinary view. In: Rowland, Kendrith M./Ferris, Gerard R. (Eds.): Research in Personnel and Human Resources Management. Vol. 8. Greenwich 1990, pp. 41 – 107.

Schweiger, David M./Weber, Yaakov: Strategies for managing human ressources during mergers and acquisitions – An empirical investigation. In: Human Resource Planning, Vol. 2, 1989, pp. 69 – 86.

Scott, Cornelia: Due diligence in der Praxis – Risiken minimieren bei Unternehmenstransaktionen. Wiesbaden 2001.

Selzer, Helmut M.: Methoden steuern Lernprozesse. In: Schweizer, Gerd/Selzer, Helmut M. (Eds.): Methodenkompetenz lehren und lernen – Beiträge zur Methodendidaktik in Arbeitslehre, Wirtschaftslehre, Wirtschaftsgeographie. Dettelbach 2001, pp. 9 – 30.

Shelton, Lois M.: Strategic business fits and corporate acquisitions – An empirical evidence. In: Strategic Management Journal, Vol. 9, Issue 3, 1988, pp. 279 – 287.

Shields, Karen: What HR Needs to Review During Due Diligence. In: HR Focus, Vol. 77, Issue 10, 2000, pp. S2 – S3.

Shrivastava, Paul: Postmerger integration. In: Journal of Business Strategy, Vol. 7, Issue 1, 1986, pp. 65 – 76.

Siegert, Theo: Humankapital – Erfolgsmessung und Partizipation. In: Bühler, Wolfgang/ Siegert, Theo (Eds.): Unternehmenssteuerung und Anreizsysteme. Kongress-Dokumentation – 52. Deutscher Betriebswirtschaftler-Tag 1998. Stuttgart 1999, pp. 17 – 46.

Siehl, Caren/Ledford, Gerald/Silverman, Richard/Fay, Peter: Postmerger Integration – Preventing Culture Clashes from Botching a Merger. In: Mergers and Acquisitions, Vol. 22, Issue 4, 1988, pp. 51 – 57.

Siehl, Caren/Smith, Dayle/Kissinger Omura, Ann: After the Merger – should executives stay or go? In: Academy of Management Executive, Vol. 4, Issue 1, 1990, pp. 50 – 60.

Simon, Hermann: Kollision der Kulturen. In: managermagazin, Vol. 29, Issue 6, 1999, pp. 96 – 98.

Simons, Robert: Control in the Age of Empowerment. In: Harvard Business Review, Vol. 73, Issue 2, 1995, pp. 80 – 88.

Sinclair, John: Collins Cobuild English Dictionary – Helping learners with real English. London 1995.

Spremann, Klaus: Asymmetrische Information. In: Zeitschrift für Betriebswirtschaft, Vol. 60, Issue 5/6, 1990, pp. 561 – 586.

Staehle, Wolfgang H.: Management – eine verhaltenswissenschaftliche Perspektive. 8th edition. München 1999.

Stahl, Günter K./Voigt, Andreas: Meta-Analyses of the Performance Implications of Cultural Differences in Mergers and Acquisitions. Academy of Management Best Conference Paper 2004, IM, pp. I1 – I5.

Stahl, Günter K.: Management der sozio-kulturellen Integration bei Unternehmenszusammenschlüssen und -übernahmen. In: Die Betriebswirtschaft, Vol. 61, Issue 1, 2001, pp. 61 – 80.

Staudt, Erich/Groeters, Ulrich/Hafkesbrink, Joachim/Treichel, Heinz-Reiner: Kennzahlen und Kennzahlensysteme – Grundlagen zur Entwicklung und Anwendung. Berlin 1985.

Staudt, Erich/Rehbein, Monika: Innovation durch Qualifikation – Personalentwicklung und neue Technik. Frankfurt am Main 1988.

Steffen, Jonathan: Cultural Due Diligence – A specialist communication service for M&A transactions. In: Strategic Communication Management, Vol. 5, Issue 1, 2000, pp. 18 – 22.

Steinmann, Horst/Schreyögg, Georg: Management – Grundlagen der Unternehmensführung. 5th edition. Wiesbaden 2000.

Steinöcker, Reinhard: Mergers and Acquisitions – strategische Planung von Firmenübernahmen – Konzeption, Transaktion, Controlling. Düsseldorf, Regensburg 1998.

Stewart, Thomas A.: Intellectual Capital – The New Wealth of Organizations. New York 1997.

Strack, Rainer/Villis, Ulrich/Klose, Frank: Wertsteigerung durch Mitarbeiter. In: Personalwirtschaft, Vol. 30, Issue 12, 2003, pp. 23 – 27.

Strasser, Brigitte: Informationsasymmetrien bei Unternehmensakquisitionen. Frankfurt am Main et al. 2000.

Süverkrüp, Christian: Ziele und Erfolg internationalen technologischen Wissenstransfers durch Unternehmensakquisitionen – Eine empirische Untersuchung am Beispiel deutsch-amerikanischer und amerikanisch-deutscher Akquisitionen. Frankfurt et al. 1991.

Taubert, Rolf/Piorr, Rüdiger: Feedbackorientierte Potentialerhebung – Anhaltspunkte für Leistungsprognosen. In: Personalführung, Vol. 32, Issue 4, 1999, pp. 46 – 53.

Teall, John L.: Mergers Activity and Managerial Compensation. In: Review of Financial Economics, Vol. 2, Issue 1, 1992, pp. 55 – 68.

Teece, David J./Pisano, Gary/Shuen, Amy: Dynamic capabilities and strategic management. In: Strategic Management Journal, Vol. 18, Issue 7, 1997, pp. 509 – 533.

Thommen, Jean-Paul: Betriebswirtschaftslehre. In: Gabler Wirtschaftslexikon. 16th edition. Wiesbaden 2004a, pp. 440 – 445.

Thommen, Jean-Paul: Lexikon der Betriebswirtschaftslehre – Managementkompetenz von A bis Z. Zürich 2004b.

Thommen, Jean-Paul: Betriebswirtschaftslehre. 5th edition. Zürich 2002.

Thommen, Jean-Paul: Management-Kompetenz durch Weiterbildung. In: Thommen, Jean-Paul (Ed.): Management-Kompetenz – die Gestaltungsansätze des Executive MBA der Hochschule St. Gallen. Wiesbaden 1995, pp. 11 – 29.

Thommen, Jean-Paul: Die Lehre der Unternehmensführung – Eine wissenschaftshistorische Betrachtung im deutschsprachigen Raum. Bern 1983.

Tichy, Noel M./Fombrun, Charles J./Devanna, Mary Anne: Strategic Human Resource Management. In: Sloan Management Review, Vol. 23, Issue 2, 1982, pp. 47 – 61.

Tobin, Daniel R.: The knowledge-enabled-organization – moving from „training" to „learning" to meet business goals. New York 1998.

Töpfer, Armin: Mergers & Acquisitions – Anforderungen und Stolpersteine. In: Zeitschrift für Führung und Organisation, Vol. 69, Issue 1, 2000, pp. 10 – 17.

Träm, Michael: Führung braucht Zeit – Der Mythos der ersten 100 Tage. München 2002.

Uder, Helmuth L./Kramarsch, Michael H.: Buying is Fun, Merging is Hell – Mergers & Acquisitions managen durch erfolgreiche Integration der Human Resources. In: M&A Review, Vol. 11, Issue 7, 2001, pp. 324 – 331.

Ueckert, Hans: Planung, Organisation und Kontrolle. In: Sarges, Werner (Ed.): Management-Diagnostik. 3rd edition. Göttingen et al. 2000, pp. 254 – 262.

Ulrich, Dave: Intellectual Capital = Comp x Comm. In: Sloan Management Review, Vol. 39, Issue 2, 1998, pp. 15 – 27.

Ulrich, Hans/Krieg, Walter/Malik, Fredmund: Zum Praxisbezug der systemorientierten Betriebswirtschaftslehre. In: Ulrich, Hans (Ed.): Zum Praxisbezug der Betriebswirtschaftslehre – in wissenschaftstheoretischer Sicht. Bern, Stuttgart 1976, pp. 135 – 151.

Ulrich, Hans: Systemorientiertes Management – Werk von Hans Ulrich. Studienausgabe. St. Gallen et al. 2001.

Ulrich, Peter/Hill, Wilhelm: Wissenschaftstheoretische Grundlagen der Betriebswirtschaftslehre. In: Wirtschaftswissenschaftliches Studium, Vol. 5, Issue 5, 1976, pp. 304 – 309 and pp. 345 – 350.

Unterköfler, Herbert: Human Resource Due Diligence. In: Kranebitter, Gottwald (Ed.): Due Diligence – Risikoanalyse im Zuge von Unternehmenstransaktionen. München 2002, pp. 127 – 134.

Vahs, Dietmar/Wuth, Steffen: Kritischer Erfolgsfaktor – Personalmanagement. In: Personal, Vol. 53, Issue 12, 2001, pp. 668 – 672.

Vahs, Dietmar: Change Management in schwierigen Zeiten – Erfolgsfaktoren und Handlungsempfehlungen für die Gestaltung von Veränderungsprozessen. Wiesbaden 2003.

Van Fleet, Lisa A.: Employee Benefits in Mergers and Acquisitions. In: Banking Law Journal, Vol. 113, Issue 9, 1996, pp. 881 – 901.

Vogel, Dieter H.: M&A – Ideal und Wirklichkeit. Wiesbaden 2002.

Volkart, Rudolf: Unternehmensbewertung und Akquisitionen. Zürich 1999.

Vorbrugg, Georg: Risks and Liabilities. In: Droste (Ed.): Mergers & Acquisitions in Germany. Illinois et al. 1995, pp. 115 – 151.

Wagner, Peter: Komplexe Theorien im Praxiseinsatz. In: Personalmagazin, Vol. 6, Issue 1, 2004, p. 15.

Wall, Stephen J./Wall, Shannon Rye: Post-Merger Management – Die optimale Integrationsstrategie. Landsberg 2001.

Weber, Manfred/Sandt, Joachim: Erfolg durch Kennzahlen – neue empirische Erkenntnisse. Vallendar 2001.

Weber, Manfred: Kennzahlen – Unternehmen mit Erfolg führen. 3rd edition. Freiburg im Breisgau 2002.

Weibler, Jürgen: Personalführung. München 2001.

Weidemann, Anja/Paschen, Michael: Dauerbrenner Potenzial. In: management & training, Vol. 3, Issue 3, 2002, pp. 22 – 25.

Weinert, Ansfried B.: Persönlichkeitstests. In: Sarges, Werner (Ed.): Management-Diagnostik. 3rd edition. Göttingen et al. 2000, pp. 419 – 424.

Weismüller, Albert: Akquisitionscontrolling bei Mannesmann. In: Zeitschrift für betriebswirtschaftliche Forschung, Vol. 49, Issue 10, 1997, pp. 892 – 911.

Wellhöfer, Peter R.: Schlüsselqualifikation Sozialkompetenz – Theorie und Trainingsbeispiele. Stuttgart 2004.

Werner, Markus: Post-Merger-Integration – Problemfelder und Lösungsansätze. In: Zeitschrift für Führung und Organisation, Vol. 68, Issue 6, 1999, pp. 332 – 337.

Whalley, Michael/Semler, Franz-Jörg: International Business Acquisitions – Major Legal Issues and Due Diligence. The Hague et al. 1996.

Williamson, Oliver E.: Die Institutionen des Kapitalismus – Unternehmungen, Märkte, Kooperationen. Tübingen 1990.

Willke, Helmut: Systemtheorie I – Grundlagen. Eine Einführung in die Grundprobleme der Theorie sozialer Systeme. 6th edition. Stuttgart 2000.

Willke, Helmut: Systemtheorie III – Steuerungstheorie. 3rd edition. Stuttgart 2001.

Wilson, Rowan: Organizational Culture Analysis. In: Strategic Communication Management, Vol. 4, Issue 6, 2000, pp. 16 – 21.

Wiltz, Stefan: Steuerung von Gehaltsstrukturen bei Firmenzusammenschlüssen. In: Personal, Vol. 51, Issue 1, 1999, pp. 14 – 20.

Wirtgen, Jörg: Human Resource Management bei Unternehmenszusammenschlüssen. In: Personal, Vol. 51, Issue 1, 1999, pp. 6 – 8.

Wirtz, Bernd W.: Mergers & Acquisitions Management – Strategie und Organisation von Unternehmenszusammenschlüssen. Wiesbaden 2003.

Witt, Frank H.: Theorietraditionen der betriebswirtschaftlichen Forschung – Deutschsprachige Betriebswirtschaftslehre und angloamerikanische Management- und Organisationsforschung. Wiesbaden 1995.

Witte, Eberhard: Phasen-Theorem und Organisation komplexer Entscheidungsverläufe. In: Zeitschrift für betriebswirtschaftliche Forschung, Vol. 20, Issue 10, 1968, pp. 625 – 647.

Wöhe, Günter: Einführung in die Allgemeine Betriebswirtschaftslehre. 21st edition. München 2002.

Wood, Judy: Structuring Compensation Plans for Mergers & Acquisitions. In: Compensation & Benefits Review, Vol. 24, Issue 5, 1992, pp. 47 – 56.

Worrach, Cornelia: Der Mensch – das Mass aller Dinge. In: Personalwirtschaft, Vol. 28, Issue 1, 2001, pp. 66 – 69.

Wottawa, Heinrich/Hossiep, Rüdiger: Grundlagen psychologischer Diagnostik – eine Einführung. Göttingen et al. 1987.

Wottawa, Heinrich: Perspektiven der Potentialbeurteilung – Themen und Trends. In: Rosenstiel, Lutz von/Lang-von Wins, Thomas: Perspektiven der Potentialbeurteilung. Göttingen et al. 2000, pp. 27 – 51.

Wright, Patrick M./Rowland, Kendrith M./Ferris, Gerald R.: Perspectives on Human Resources Management. In: Zeitschrift für Personalforschung, Vol. 8, Issue 3, 1994, pp. 336 – 352.

Wucknitz, Uwe D.: Bewertung von Personal in der Due Diligence. In: Personal, Vol. 53, Issue 12, 2001, pp. 674 – 678.

Wucknitz, Uwe D.: Handbuch Personalbewertung – Messgrößen, Anwendungsfelder, Fallstudien. Stuttgart 2002a.

Wucknitz, Uwe D.: HR Due Diligence – Die Analyse personeller Wert- und Risikofaktoren bei der Unternehmensbewertung. In: IM – Die Zeitschrift für Information Management Consulting, Vol. 17, Issue 1, 2002b, pp. 36 – 43.

Wunderer, Rolf/Arx, Sabina von: Personalmanagement als Wertschöpfungscenter – integriertes Organisations- und Personalentwicklungskonzept. Wiesbaden 1998.

Wunderer, Rolf/Bruch, Heike: Umsetzungskompetenz – Diagnose und Förderung in Theorie und Unternehmenspraxis. München 2000.

Wunderer, Rolf/Jaritz, André: Unternehmerisches Personalcontrolling – Evaluation der Wertschöpfung im Personalmanagement. Neuwied 1999.

Wunderer, Rolf/Schlagenhaufer, Peter: Personal-Controlling – Funktionen, Instrumente, Praxisbeispiele. Stuttgart 1994.

Wunderer, Rolf: Führung und Zusammenarbeit – Eine unternehmerische Führungslehre. 5th edition. Wiesbaden 2003.

Yin, Robert K.: Case Study Research – Design and Methods. 3rd edition. Thousand Oaks et al. 2003.

Zhang, Charles: The Art of Coordination. In: Internal Auditor, Vol. 55, Issue 2, 1998, pp. 5 – 7.

Zingheim, Patricia K./Schuster, Jay R.: Using Pay Systems as Rallying Point for Merged Workforces. In: Mergers & Acquisitions, Vol. 36, Issue 5, 2001, pp. 37 – 42.

Zingheim, Patricia K.: Retaining Top Talent. In: Executive Excellence, Vol. 18, Issue 3, 2001, p. 20.

Zwahlen, Beat: Motive und Gefahrenpotentiale bei einer Unternehmensakquisition – Eine erfolgreiche Akquisitions- und Integrationsstrategie einer multinationalen Unternehmung am Fallbeispiel „Nestlé-Rowntree“. Zürich 1994.

MIX
Papier aus verantwortungsvollen Quellen
Paper from responsible sources
FSC® C105338

If you have any concerns about our products,
you can contact us on
ProductSafety@springernature.com

In case Publisher is established outside the EU,
the EU authorized representative is:
Springer Nature Customer Service Center GmbH
Europaplatz 3, 69115 Heidelberg, Germany

Printed by Libri Plureos GmbH
in Hamburg, Germany